LASTING VALUE

OPEN SPACE PLANNING AND PRESERVATION SUCCESSES

Rick Pruetz, FAICP

Routledge
Taylor & Francis Group
LONDON AND NEW YORK

To Adrian, Jay, Erica, Gena, Jeromy, Josh, Jean,
and the memory of my father, Eric.

First published 2012 by the American Planning Association

Published 2017 by Routledge
2 Park Square, Milton Park, Abingdon, Oxon OX14 4RN
711 Third Avenue, New York, NY 10017, USA

Routledge is an imprint of the Taylor & Francis Group, an informa business

ISBN: 9781611900033 (pbk)

Library of Congress Control Number 2011939325

CONTENTS

LIST OF ILLUSTRATIONS

Unless otherwise noted, all photographs are by the author.

ACKNOWLEDGMENTS

I thank the many people who helped me write this book, particularly Philip Caton, Tom Daniels, Jennifer DeLong, Lawrence Durr, Rose Farmer, Pete Fogg, Nicole Fyffe, Darren Greve, Larry Liggett, Susan Payne, James Raives, Marc Roberts, John Snook, Ron Stewart, John Theilacker, Tara Tracy, John Zawitoski, and Dan Zimmerman. I especially thank APA Planners Press editor Timothy Mennel for his support and encouragement.

1

INTRODUCTION: PLANNING PRESERVATION

More than one million acres of forests, farms, and other rural lands are converted to development every year. As a result, we reduce the reliability of our water supply, increase the cost of infrastructure, eliminate the habitat of our fellow species, heighten our exposure to wildfires, decrease our ability to grow food locally, and threaten the balance of town and countryside that we once considered an American ideal. Many people accept this wastefulness as an inevitable by-product of progress. This book recognizes those who do not.

Lasting Value celebrates selected cities, towns, and counties that excel at preserving natural areas, farmland, and other types of open space. These communities understand the multiple benefits of protecting their surrounding countryside, including watershed protection, local food security, outdoor recreation, and growth management. They plan the protection of their rural areas with as much care as they plan the development of their urban areas. They use permanent conservation tools to address the uncertainty that accelerates rural decline and sprawl. They achieve their preservation goals by partnering with private conservancies as well as public agencies and by using multiple implementation strategies, often of their own invention. They take sustainability seriously, preserving nature-friendly places so that future generations can enjoy some of the bounty given to us. In short, they are creating communities of lasting value.

The title of this book comes from a core mission of the American Planning Association (APA) to "help create communities of lasting value" (APA 2011). In its policy guide on sustainability, APA suggests numerous paths to securing a

1

"promising and sustainable future for all children," including open space acquisition and the preservation of wildlife habitat (APA 2000). APA's policy on agricultural land preservation also supports the incorporation of farmland preservation into smart growth planning at the state and local levels (APA 1999). Similarly, other organizations promoting sustainability and smart growth include preservation as a key strategy component. For example, "preservation of open space, farmland, natural beauty and critical environmental areas" is one of the 10 Smart Growth Principles advocated by the Smart Growth Network, a partnership of 43 organizations, including APA, the American Farmland Trust, Congress for the New Urbanism, the Local Government Commission, the Natural Resources Defense Council, the U.S. Environmental Protection Agency, and the Urban Land Institute (Smart Growth Network 2011).

Excellence in open space preservation requires farsightedness, commitment, and persistence from planning professionals, elected officials, and of course, the general public. In other words, it's no walk in the park. But fortunately, the planning process is ideally suited to nurturing the components needed for success. Consequently, before presenting profiles of individual communities, in the remainder of this introduction I explore the planning process as a catalyst for preservation, a forum for developing goals and strategies, and a laboratory for creating implementation tools that fit the community.

Planning as Catalyst

The planning process invites people to understand their communities by joining citizen advisory groups, attending meetings, visiting websites, or perhaps just reading their local newspapers. A planning study can be a revelation to the uninitiated and a wake-up call for those who assume they know the score. Many communities featured in *Lasting Value* skillfully use the information-gathering and dissemination phases of the planning process to highlight the significance of rural resources, warn of threats to their natural heritage, and encourage action while open space is still available and affordable.

Highlighting Significance

Why should urban residents care what happens in the countryside? People pay closer attention to that question when it is answered as part of a planning process affecting the future of their communities. The cities and counties in the following chapters take full advantage of the planning process to underscore the diverse ways in which cities and suburbs rely on rural land for economic vitality, water management, recreation, habitat preservation, locally grown food, and a sense of place.

The plans for many of the counties in this book stress the contributions of agriculture to community character and tourism as well as jobs and economic development. The Lancaster County, Pennsylvania, comprehensive plan emphasizes that agriculture accounts for more than $3 billion in economic output, while tourism, which largely relies on the charm of Lancaster County's idyllic working landscape, generates even more income and supports more than 20,000 jobs (Lancaster County 2005; Lancaster County 2006). In building this case for the significance of agriculture, the Lancaster County comprehensive plan creates a strong foundation for goals and implementation measures that have produced the most successful local farmland preservation program in the nation (*Farmland Preservation Report* 2010).

Similarly, the introduction to the Lexington–Fayette County, Kentucky, 1999 Rural Service Area Plan includes a section directly addressing the issue of significance, entitled "The Importance of the Rural Service Area to the Community." In this section, the plan itemizes the benefits of a strong agricultural economy and the interconnection of rural character and cultural heritage with a thriving tourism industry that supports more than 14,000 jobs throughout the Bluegrass region. By highlighting these benefits, Lexington–Fayette County succeeded in adopting a model rural area plan. In turn, that plan laid the groundwork for implementing one of the most closely watched purchase of development rights (PDR) programs in the United States (Lexington–Fayette County 1999).

Evaluating Threats

Public support for preservation can be galvanized when planning studies document the pace of rural change. In 1980, the Functional Master Plan for the Preservation of Agriculture and Rural Open Space of Montgomery County, Maryland, warned that development was rapidly eliminating farmland, resulting in a loss of more than 26,000 acres in the 1970s alone. Following this and other alarming facts, the functional plan proceeded to establish arguably the most successful countryside preservation program in the country (Maryland–National Capital Park and Planning Commission 1980).

In 1971, the threat to rural Marin County, California, was bluntly summarized in the title of its open space preservation plan: *Will the Last Place Last?* The citizens responded to this question the following year by approving the formation of the Marin County Regional Park and Open Space District. In partnership with numerous open space agencies, Marin County has now permanently preserved roughly one-half of its total land area despite being one bridge away from the City of San Francisco (Marin County 2008).

In its 1996 Agricultural and Farmland Protection Plan, Suffolk County, New York—at the end of Long Island and 50 miles east of New York City—estimated farmland losses at 18,000 acres over the previous 28 years and warned of ongo-ing development pressure (Suffolk County 1996). Ten years later, in *Long Island's Last Stand*, a coalition of public agencies and private organizations expressed even greater alarm, adopting an end-game mentality and predicting that any remaining vacant land in Suffolk County that was not permanently preserved would be lost to development within a decade. Despite the fact that more than $1 billion had already been spent there on open space preservation, the voters of Suffolk County once again reached into their pockets in 2007, approving another $600 million for the preservation of coastal wetlands and other environmental resources (Suffolk County 2007; Nature Conservancy 2007).

The 1998 strategic plan of Burlington County, New Jersey, emphasized that the county was losing twice as much farmland as it was preserving. Using that sta-tistic for support, the plan established a goal of preserving the greatest amount of farmland in the shortest amount of time. Burlington County implemented that goal with an array of innovative approaches that now constitute one of the 10 most successful local farmland preservation programs in the nation (Burlington County 2008; *Farmland Preservation Report* 2010).

In 2002, Chester County, Pennsylvania, used its open space plan, Linking Landscapes, to warn residents that the county was losing 5,000 acres of rural land to development *every year*. Perhaps because this statistic was so shocking, the plan was also able to establish an ambitious target of permanently preserv-ing 5,000 acres of open space per year through the combined efforts of its home owners associations, private land trusts, and land acquisition programs at the federal, state, county, and municipal levels (Chester County 2002).

Some plans sound their alarms in an almost poetic way. After quadrupling in size between 1950 and 1970, the City of Phoenix, Arizona, adopted An Open Space Plan for the Phoenix Mountains, which was ultimately recognized with a National Planning Landmark Award from APA. This plan begins with the following straightforward assessment of the city's attitude toward its surroundings prior to the plan's adoption in 1972:

> We have been busily dividing, reshaping, and exploiting our vast resource at an unprecedented rate and with little awareness of its intrinsic value. The anguish of a few at bulldozer progress has gone largely unheeded by a local population and gov-ernment exuberant in the intense activity of rapid growth. Arizona is so rich in scenery and land that we have given little thought to what our communities will be like when our major open spaces have disappeared. (Phoenix 1972, 1)

Identifying Opportunities

The planning process also offers an ideal venue for repeating the truism that land isn't getting any cheaper. In promoting his plans for the Minneapolis parks

system, Horace Cleveland argued for rapid implementation before land speculation made real estate prices prohibitively expensive. That was in 1883. The citizens agreed, approving the creation of a parks board and the start of that city's
famous Grand Rounds, now the heart of one of the most highly regarded park
systems in the country (Roise 2000).

In 1934, a plan by Ansel Hall and the Olmsted Brothers urged citizens in
Alameda County, California, to pay for an ambitious new park system at the lowest point of the Great Depression. Despite the dismal state of the economy, the
Hall-Olmsted plan argued that the timing couldn't be better, because the local
water utility had just declared 10,000 acres of foothills and canyons as surplus
land. In other words, the land would never again be this affordable. The voters
overwhelmingly agreed, approving a new tax and creating the East Bay Regional
Park District, now the largest regional park agency in the United States (Ahrens
2006; McCreery 2010).

Developing Goals and Strategies

With open space preservation, reaching your destination is easier when you know
where you are going. The planning process is ideally suited to helping communities develop appropriate goals as well as strategies that make those goals achievable. Many of the communities in this book demonstrate the role that planning
plays in determining what to save and how to save it.

What Should Be Saved?

Planning is indispensible to the difficult process of deciding what land to target for
permanent preservation. Focused plans may concentrate on individual resources,
such as prime farmland or the habitat of endangered species. But comprehensive
plans are ideal for studying alternatives and developing strategies that achieve
multiple community goals: efficient provision of infrastructure and public services,
protection of water supply and quality, growth management, maximization of recreational opportunities, and security of locally grown food, as well as preservation
of farmland and environmental resources. Many of the communities discussed in
the following chapters plan for the preservation of multiple resources, while some
of these communities plan for the preservation of the countryside as a whole.

In 1994, Santa Cruz, California, adopted a greenbelt master plan in which
open space largely surrounds the city, strengthening the urban limit line while
preserving agricultural land, coastal resources, parkland, and habitat (Press
2002). The Open Land and Trails Plan for Santa Fe County, New Mexico, aims
to achieve multiple objectives by preserving sites with archaeological and historic as well as environmental significance, in keeping with its goal of protecting

cultural landscapes shaped by the interaction of people and nature over time (Santa Fe County 2000). Instead of preparing only a multispecies conservation plan, Pima County, Arizona, created the more holistic and award-winning Sonoran Desert Conservation Plan, which coordinates the conservation of cultural landmarks, riparian corridors, mountain parks, and ranchlands, as well as wildlife habitat (Pima County 1998). The comprehensive plan of Dane County, Wisconsin, looks to open space preservation as a means of connecting recreational nodes, separating communities, and guiding urban growth—goals that the county and its many partners are implementing through a combination of open space acquisition tools and a network of hiking, bicycling, and water trails (Dane County 2007).

The life expectancy of a preservation program can sometimes be extended by expanding the list of resources to be preserved. During its first 10 years of existence, the Agricultural Preservation and Open Space District of Sonoma County, California, concentrated on farmland preservation to such an extent that some feared the voters might not reauthorize the special sales tax that funds the program. With that in mind, the county board approved a new acquisition plan that ensures balanced funding of greenbelts, natural resources, and recreational land, as well as farmland (Wells 2000). Following that readjustment, the voters extended the tax through 2031, and the district has proceeded to preserve 83,000 acres, earning Sonoma County a County Leadership in Conservation Award from the Trust for Public Land and the National Association of Counties (Trust for Public Land 2007).

In developing rural plans, some communities rediscover that rural resources are interconnected. Or as John Muir said, "When we try to pick out anything by itself, we find it hitched to everything else in the universe" (Muir 1911). In working on its Rural Service Area Land Management Plan: Our Rural Heritage in the Next Century, which was adopted on April 8, 1999, Lexington–Fayette County, Kentucky, rediscovered the difficulty of trying to save some aspects of the countryside without saving them all. The county long understood the need to protect its famous horse farms, the cornerstone of the community's image as well as its agricultural and tourism economies. But through environmental analysis performed for this plan, the county also learned that 30 percent of the rural area consists of environmentally sensitive areas that are hard to protect in isolation because they generally follow streams that cross the entire landscape. Further studies documented the fragility of the rural area's historic settlements and the tremendous expense required to sensitively widen numerous scenic roads lined with stately trees and iconic stone fences. When all of this information had been assembled and digested, the Rural Service Area Land Management Plan concluded that the countryside should be protected as a whole. To implement that plan, Lexington–Fayette County downzoned almost all of the rural area to a maximum density of one dwelling per 40 acres and adopted a PDR program that is already more than halfway to its goal of permanently preserving 50,000 acres, more than one-quarter of Lexington–Fayette County's total land area (Lexington–Fayette County 1999; Lexington–Fayette County 2011).

A similar conclusion was reached in Albuquerque/Bernalillo County, New Mexico, through a planning process in which an open space task force was formed from several citizen organizations, including the Bosque del Rio Grande Nature Preserve Society, Save the Volcanoes, Save the Sandias, and Save the Arroyos. Their work helped produce the 1975 Albuquerque/Bernalillo County Comprehensive Plan, which called for the preservation of a 50,000-acre open space network, including all aspects of open space from the Rio Grande flood-plains and extinct volcanoes to the foothills of the Sandia Mountains and basalt escarpments covered with ancient rock art (Albuquerque 2010).

Planning studies can also provide input for the making of critical choices between development and preservation options. In 1969, the City of Palo Alto, in Santa Clara County, California, concluded that buying the foothills above the city would be more cost effective than allowing them to be developed. This conclusion helped convince the voters to dedicate $20 million per year of property tax to the Midpeninsula Regional Open Space District (MROSD), which has since acquired 26 preserves protecting more than 58,000 acres (MROSD 2010; Press 2002).

How Should Open Space Be Saved?

The planning process can help communities weigh the benefits of permanent preservation (through land purchase and easement acquisition), versus impermanent protection (through zoning and environmental regulations adopted by elected officials). Most communities combine impermanent and permanent protection techniques, such as traditional zoning plus parkland acquisition. However, the communities profiled in this book are best known for their achievements in permanent preservation, and their plans often describe the benefits of permanent preservation.

As one obvious benefit, the owners of permanently preserved properties receive compensation by selling their conservation easements, development rights, or the land itself. This opportunity for compensation can allow a level of land protection that might not otherwise be possible in communities where political opposition would preclude strict land-use controls that do not offer compensation.

The communities discussed in *Lasting Value* also recognize the limitations of impermanent tools, such as zoning, if the goal is actually permanent preservation. For example, Linking Landscapes: A Plan for the Protected Open Space Network in Chester County, Pennsylvania, which sets a target of permanently preserving 5,000 acres of open space annually, explains that zoning alone is not sufficient, because it is subject to variances and amendments (Chester County 2002).

In addition, some of the plans in this book go further and explain the negative effects of uncertainty. The Montgomery County, Maryland, 1980 Functional Master Plan for the Preservation of Agriculture and Rural Open Space used a diagnosis of "impermanence syndrome" to describe a condition in which farmers are never certain whether or not their neighbors will be rezoned for a residential subdivision or some other development that will render farming difficult if not impossible. Impermanence syndrome convinces farmers that land conversion is inevitable and that farming and rural life in general are doomed in their area. This conviction causes landowners to defer stewardship and forego agricultural investments. As production decreases, agricultural businesses disappear, and profitability becomes increasingly difficult to attain. The resulting rural blight makes it easier for local governments to ultimately justify rezoning the land for urban uses, since these places have already lost their rural vitality. In turn, each change from rural to urban zoning only increases the sense of futility, prompting more cycles of neglect and rezoning (Maryland–National Capital Park and Planning Commission 1980).

To fight impermanence syndrome, Montgomery County's 1980 functional plan called for the designation of 93,000 contiguous acres as an agricultural reserve and a downzoning of this area to a maximum density of one dwelling unit per 25 acres. Because the goal for the Agricultural Reserve is permanent preservation, the plan also instituted a transfer of development rights (TDR) program, which is now one of five mechanisms that owners of land in the Agricultural Reserve can use to receive compensation for permanently preserving their land using conservation easements. Today more than 70,000 acres of the Agricultural Reserve is under permanent easement, giving Montgomery County the distinction of ranking second among the nation's most successful farmland preservation programs (*Farmland Preservation Report* 2010). More importantly, the program is successfully combating impermanence syndrome, as demonstrated by the fact that not a single acre in the Agricultural Reserve has been rezoned since 1980 (Zawitoski 2011).

Permanent preservation reverses the progression of impermanence syndrome. Reports from program managers and expert observers in Lancaster County, Pennsylvania; Montgomery County, Maryland; and Berks County, Pennsylvania, indicate that farmers become more optimistic about the future of local agriculture when their neighbors permanently preserve their land (Daniels 2011; DeLong 2010; Zawitoski 2011). As a result, agriculture thrives, and more land is placed under permanent easement. Maps document that farms are preserved in clusters, as nearby farmers gain confidence from one another, confirming one program manager's observation that "preservation is contagious" (Zawitoski 2011).

Creating Effective Implementation

Plans are more effective when implementation is not an afterthought. The communities profiled in *Lasting Value* use the planning process to create innovative solutions, develop multifaceted preservation programs, and form partnerships that combine private-sector organizations and public agencies from every level of government.

Creative Solutions

Success in open space preservation sometimes means having to invent new implementation techniques. The East Bay Regional Park District, in California's Alameda and Contra Costa counties, now the largest regional park district in the nation, was the first regional special park district in the country (East Bay Regional Park District 2010). In 1967, the citizens of Boulder, Colorado, became the first voters to approve a sales tax devoted exclusively to open space preservation (Boulder 2009). In 1979, the voters of King County, Washington, approved a $50 million Farmlands Preservation Bond, making this the first jurisdiction in the nation in which the citizens agreed to tax themselves to preserve farmland (Buckland 1987).

In 1958, Lexington–Fayette County, Kentucky, created the first urban growth boundary in the nation, an innovation that was recognized with a National Planning Landmark Award from APA. Several other communities in this book have followed Lexington–Fayette County's lead. In 1973, Santa Clara County, California, adopted a plan confining growth to urban service areas that cannot be changed without approval from the Local Agency Formation Commission (Santa Clara County 1994). The Santa Cruz County, California, 1980 general plan created rural service lines as well as urban service lines around its communities (Santa Cruz County 1994). The 1990 general plan of Contra Costa County, California, established an urban limit line designating 35 percent of the county's land area for urban development and 65 percent for rural preservation (Greenbelt Alliance 2003).

Preservation goals routinely exceed the funding available from taxes, fees, grants, and other traditional sources. Not surprisingly, many of the communities included in the following chapters turn to nontraditional tools, such as TDR, which is ultimately powered by profits from private development rather than public funds. Some TDR programs operate without any public-sector funding assistance.

The most famous example is the TDR program in Montgomery County, Maryland, which has preserved more than 52,000 acres to date using a completely private market.

Other communities have achieved significant success by using other funding sources to initially buy TDRs, which are then deposited in a TDR bank for resale to developers. As discussed in the chapter on Burlington County, New Jersey, the New Jersey Pinelands TDR program has to date preserved almost 59,000 acres with the assistance of a state-financed TDR bank. King County, Washington, has used TDR to preserve 142,000 acres, making theirs the most successful TDR program in the nation. Like many counties in the state of Washington, King County dedicates a portion of its property tax revenue to open space preservation. But in addition to buying land and easements with its Conservation Futures Fund, King County also buys and banks TDRs. When the King County TDR bank sells these TDRs, it can use the proceeds to buy additional TDRs, thereby creating an ongoing, revolving fund for preservation (Pruetz 2010).

Palm Beach County, Florida, maximizes the buying power of an open space bond by joining it with a highly innovative TDR mechanism. The county used the bond to buy 35,000 acres of environmentally sensitive land. But Palm Beach County did not simply retire the development potential from these acquired parcels, which is what most communities do when they buy land. Instead, the county severed 9,000 TDRs from these properties, deposited them in its TDR bank, and began selling them to developers who want additional residential density using the county's TDR program. In fiscal year 2004–2005 alone, TDR sales generated more than $10 million in revenue that the county would not have received otherwise. The county applies the revenue from the sale of these TDRs to expansion and maintenance of its Natural Area System (Palm Beach County 2005).

In 1999, Collier County, Florida, solved a seemingly intractable land-use conflict by inventing a new tool called rural land stewardship. This mechanism grants transferable credits based on the quality of the land being preserved and the degree of conservation that the landowner chooses to impose on it. Developers purchased these credits in order to build the smart-growth new town of Ave Maria, located in the center of the planning area. Since 2002, this program has placed more than 54,000 acres under easement, making it one of the most successful TDR programs in the United States (Pruetz 2010).

Sometimes communities transact complex deals to implement their open space plans. In Albuquerque, New Mexico, by 1982 most of the land in the Sandia Mountains within the Cibola National Forest was preserved, with the exception of the 8,000-acre Elena Gallegos grant. When development threatened this foothill property, the Albuquerque City Council bought it using a temporary sales tax, retained 640 acres as a park, and transferred the rest to the U.S. Forest Service in return for 18,000 acres of surplus federal land. The city deposits proceeds from the sale of these surplus federal lands in an open space trust fund used for ongoing open space management (Albuquerque 2010).

Well-Stocked Toolbox

Using the planning process, communities often realize that their preservation goals cannot be reached without a combination of tools. A background report for the growth management element of Lancaster County, Pennsylvania, observed that 200 farms were on the waiting list for its PDR program. In addition to calling for expanded funding for the PDR program, the report recommended the creation of multijurisdictional TDR programs throughout the county and even the establishment of a countywide TDR program (Blue Ribbon Commission 2005).

Parks and Open Space of Boulder County, Colorado, uses no fewer than 10 preservation methods, including TDR and land and easement acquisitions funded by a combination of property tax and a voter-approved 0.45 percent open space sales/use tax, which generates $17 million for preservation purposes annually (Boulder County 2008). Armed with these financial resources, Boulder County has created a 94,000-acre open space and trail system. When joined with federal and state lands, the permanently preserved open space totals more than two-thirds of Boulder County's entire land area.

Suffolk County, New York, began implementing its 1964 report, *Planning for Open Space in Suffolk County*, by adopting the first farmland preservation program in the nation to use PDR. Today, it uses a set of 10 implementation programs and has spent more than $1 billion on open space and farmland protection, reportedly more than any other community in the nation (American Farmland Trust 2009). In addition, the individual municipalities within Suffolk County supplement the county's work with their own open space preservation tools, which include intra-jurisdictional TDR ordinances, programs funded by real estate transfer taxes, and participation in mechanisms that implement the Central Pine Barrens Regional Plan.

Many municipalities profiled in this book manage local programs that supplement the preservation tools at work at the county and higher levels. Even though the East Bay Regional Park District is the largest regional park agency in the nation, the City of Livermore, in Alameda County, California, adopted a TDR program designed to preserve farmland north of the city, under county jurisdiction. Livermore also adopted a specific plan in which development within the city's urban growth boundary pays for preservation of vineyards south of the city. This specific plan won APA's National Outstanding Planning Award for Implementation and has preserved more than 4,000 acres to date (Roberts 2010).

Making Connections

Using the planning process, communities can formulate ways of achieving their open space preservation goals through partnerships with foundations, land trusts, and private environmental organizations, as well as agencies from local, regional, state, and federal governments.

Private land trusts have been particularly successful at preserving open space in many of the communities in this book. For example, the Brandywine Conservancy alone holds easements on 43,000 acres of open space in Chester County, Pennsylvania, and two adjacent counties (Brandywine Conservancy 2010). In Linking Landscapes: A Plan for the Protected Open Space Network in Chester County, Chester County not only sets a target of preserving 5,000 acres of open space per year but relies on private land trusts to accomplish 30 percent of that goal, or 1,500 acres per year. To assist in that effort, Chester County created the Preservation Partnership Program, which provides funding to nonprofit conservation organizations for projects that preserve significant natural, historic, cultural, and agricultural resources (Chester County 2002; Chester County 2008).

Due to efforts at the federal, state, and local levels, more than one million acres in Collier County, Florida, are in permanently protected open space, roughly 80 percent of the county's total land area (Collier County 2010). In one particularly innovative example of cooperation, the Arizona-Florida Land Exchange Act was used to swap property in Arizona for 108,000 acres of land in Collier County. Some of the land acquired in Collier County became Ten Thousand Islands National Wildlife Refuge, which now preserves part of the largest remaining mangrove forest in North America (U.S. Fish and Wildlife Service 2010). Another portion of the exchange expanded Big Cypress National Preserve, and the remainder was used to enlarge the Florida Panther National Wildlife Refuge (U.S. Fish and Wildlife Service 2005).

Plans can also coordinate the open space holdings of several different public agencies and private nonprofit organizations. The Greenway, Park and Recreation Plan for Berks County, Pennsylvania, establishes a hierarchy of greenway corridors connecting ecological hubs with one another and with smaller nodes containing environmental, recreational, or historic features. Berks County supplies one of the nodes: Tulpehocken Creek Valley Park, featuring restorations of 19th-century locks, mills, and stone structures built along the now abandoned Union Canal. But the four largest hubs are owned by agencies other than the county, specifically a raptor sanctuary, a private nonprofit conservancy, the Commonwealth of Pennsylvania, and the federal government (Berks County 2007).

Similarly, Palm Beach County, Florida, sponsored a plan that coordinates the management and use of more than 165,000 acres of publicly owned conservation lands in northern Palm Beach County and southern Martin County. The area, known as the Northeast Everglades Natural Area (NENA), includes more than 300 miles of trails, 25 natural areas, 14 miles of Atlantic Ocean shoreline, four wildlife refuges, two state parks, and a National Wild and Scenic River. The NENA plan calls for a coordinated acquisition strategy and an extensive trail system linking the various components, with the goal of creating a world-class destination comparable to a national park (Palm Beach County 2010).

Preservation Success Stories

The following profiles further explore the planning process as a way to motivate, strategize, and implement effective preservation programs. These success stories also demonstrate the importance of dedicated professionals, farsighted elected officials, and responsible citizens who are willing to save rural land while it is still affordable and available. These cities, towns, and counties are working toward a future in which urban development is balanced by a stable, preserved countryside capable of providing locally grown food, safe drinking water, and other green infrastructure while protecting wildlife habitat and open space for those seeking refuge from the pace of modern life. In short, they are creating sustainable places—communities of lasting value.

2

ALAMEDA COUNTY, CALIFORNIA

In 1928, open space advocates from Oakland, Berkeley, and surrounding communities in California saw a golden opportunity to create a regional park system across the bay from the City of San Francisco. The voters agreed to a proposed Olmsted Brothers plan, approving the nation's first regional park special district by 71 percent during the lowest point in the Great Depression. Since then, the East Bay Regional Park District has grown to serve all of Alameda and Contra Costa counties and protect more than 100,000 acres of open space, making it the largest regional park agency in the United States. In recognition of that accomplishment, the district was honored with a National Planning Landmark Award by the American Planning Association (APA).

The origins of this planning achievement began more than a century ago, when competing private water companies acquired land for future reservoirs in the Berkeley Hills. The East Bay Municipal Utility District (EBMUD) subsequently acquired the private water companies and built a new system that imported water from the Mokelumne River basin, in the Sierra Nevada mountain range. With that system in place, EBMUD found itself with 10,000 acres of surplus watershed lands within easy reach of Oakland, Berkeley, and other cities spreading along the eastern shores of San Francisco Bay (Kent 2009).

Robert Sibley, an engineering professor at the University of California, envisioned the preservation of EBMUD's excess holdings as parklands stretching for 22 miles from Wildcat Canyon, east of Richmond, to Lake Chabot, east of San Leandro. Sibley appointed himself as "Temporary Chairman, East Bay Metropolitan

15

Park Association" and asked Ansel Hall, an employee of the National Park Service, to prepare a preliminary report, which confirmed that the surplus property was ideal for open space preservation. For additional credibility, the team hired Olmsted Brothers, the prestigious landscape architectural firm, to take Hall's report to the next level. The Olmsted-Hall plan was handsomely illustrated and carefully documented the need for a regional park system. Importantly, the plan emphasized the wisdom of protecting this land while it was still in public ownership. "The lands now publicly owned, if sold, would necessarily bring prices *far below any possible replacement value* . . . Their possible value to the public for park purposes cannot be accurately estimated because no cash value can be set upon matters of health, pleasure and recreation" (Olmsted and Hall 1930, 25).

The Olmsted-Hall plan was so powerful that the open space advocates printed and distributed several thousand copies. More than 13,000 citizens demonstrated their enthusiastic support for the plan by signing a petition to implement its recommendations. However, EBMUD was not on board with the key assumption that the public utility would expand its responsibilities and get into the open space business. Nor was EBMUD willing to simply donate this land to another public agency. As a creative solution, park advocates convinced the California legislature to allow the formation of the nation's first regional park "special

Figure 2-1.　Unusual landforms dot the East Bay Regional Park District's 6,859-acre Sunol Regional Wilderness.

district" if the electorate approved and if funding could be found to buy the land from EBMUD. By a margin greater than two to one, the voters of seven cities in Alameda County approved the formation of the East Bay Regional Park District and agreed to tax themselves to pay for it at the rate of five cents for every $100 of property value. This occurred in 1934, when the United States was still at the bottom of the Great Depression (Ahrens 2006; McCreery 2010).

In the 1930s, the district acquired four parks and built a golf course, a botanical preserve, a lake, and a trail system with the help of the Works Progress Administration. Following World War II and its aftermath, the district began another golden era in 1962, when the position of general manager was filled by William Penn Mott Jr., who later directed the California Department of Parks and Recreation and the National Park Service. With Mott in charge, the district doubled its tax rates, acquired seven additional parks, and expanded into Contra Costa County. Under Richard Trudeau, who served as general manager from 1968 to 1985, the district continued to save thousands of acres of irreplaceable open space despite political unrest, economic turmoil, and a taxpayer revolt. With Pat O'Brien at the helm from 1988 to 2010, the district added another 17 parks with a total of 38,000 acres (McCreery 2010).

In addition to showing strong leadership, the district has used sound planning to creatively adapt to California's volatile funding environment. The district's 1973 plan, prepared with the help of Stewart Udall, former U.S. secretary of the interior, proposed a robust acquisition schedule based on an increased tax rate. Then California voters threw a curveball in 1978 with adoption of Proposition 13, a tax-limitation measure that cut the district's revenues in half. In an era of skyrocketing land prices, the district had to save rapidly disappearing open space with less money. The 1980 master plan consequently confined park improvements to a maximum of 10 percent of the district's property, with the remaining 90 percent dedicated to preservation of open space in its natural state (McCreery 2010).

To offset the funding gap created by Proposition 13, the district supplemented its tax revenues with a share of the money generated by a succession of statewide park bonds approved by California voters. In 1986 alone, the voters approved a $100 million statewide parkland bond, with more than $2 million earmarked for the East Bay Regional Park District. But the district's 1989 master plan proposed acquisition of an additional 27,500 acres of open space. The price tag for that plan far exceeded the funding generated by these two mechanisms. Consequently, the district board decided to ask the voters to approve a regional park bond. This was a risky approach, because such measures were required to pass by a two-thirds majority. However, the district counted on a positive voter response to a park plan that clearly articulated the benefits of an expanded regional system. The bet paid off. The voters delivered the required super majority, approving Measure AA, a $225 million parks bond with a funding split of 75 percent for the district and 25 percent for city park systems within the region. Measure AA ended up preserving more than 34,000 acres and adding more than 100 miles to the district's trail system (East Bay Regional Park District 2010b; McCreery 2010).

In 1992, the district boundaries expanded for the sixth time, encompassing the Livermore area, at the far eastern end of Alameda County. After 60 years, the district finally served all parts of both Contra Costa and Alameda counties. The 1997 master plan established a blueprint for serving the entire region, calling for the addition of one regional park, seven preserves, two recreation areas, six shorelines, and 39 new trails (East Bay Regional Park District 1997).

By 2004, the district could see that its primary source of acquisition funding, Measure AA, would soon run dry. Rather than retrench, in its 2007 master plan, the district doubled down, identifying no less than 67 new preservation projects (East Bay Regional Park District 2010b). The district counted on implementing this plan by repeating its 1988 hit, Measure AA. The 2008 model, Measure WW, asked voters to extend the tax at the rate approved by Measure AA: $10 per $100,000 of assessed property value. This rate was projected to generate $500 million of revenue, of which 75 percent would be used by the district and 25 percent would be distributed to localities. Drawn to the polls for the election of President Barack Obama, the voters approved Measure WW by 71 percent, well in excess of the necessary two-thirds majority (East Bay Regional Park District 2010b; McCreery 2010). Measure WW is said to be the largest local park bond measure to pass in the United States (Kent 2009).

In addition to the East Bay Regional Park District, other public agencies have preserved key environmental lands in Alameda County. Along the shores of San Francisco Bay, the federal government protects 30,000 acres in the Don Edwards San Francisco Bay National Wildlife Refuge (U.S. Fish and Wildlife Service 2010). The San Francisco Water District preserves another 38,000 acres of open space in Alameda County for watershed protection with limited public access. The state of California contributes three recreation areas, two marine reserves, a state sea-shore, and a state beach to the open space inventory of Alameda County, including the Robert Crown Memorial State Beach, which preserves Crab Cove, California's first estuarine marine reserve (California State Parks 2010; East Bay Regional Park District 2010a).

Many municipalities in Alameda County are also deeply committed to open space preservation. For example, the voters of Oakland have approved three bond measures since 1990, raising a total of more than $80 million in conservation funding. Oakland is particularly proud of its open space jewel, Lake Merritt, which the city declared as a national wildlife refuge in 1869, making it the first in the United States (Oakland 2010).

The City of Livermore, in eastern Alameda County, uses transfer of development credits to preserve its northern greenbelt. Livermore also adopted a

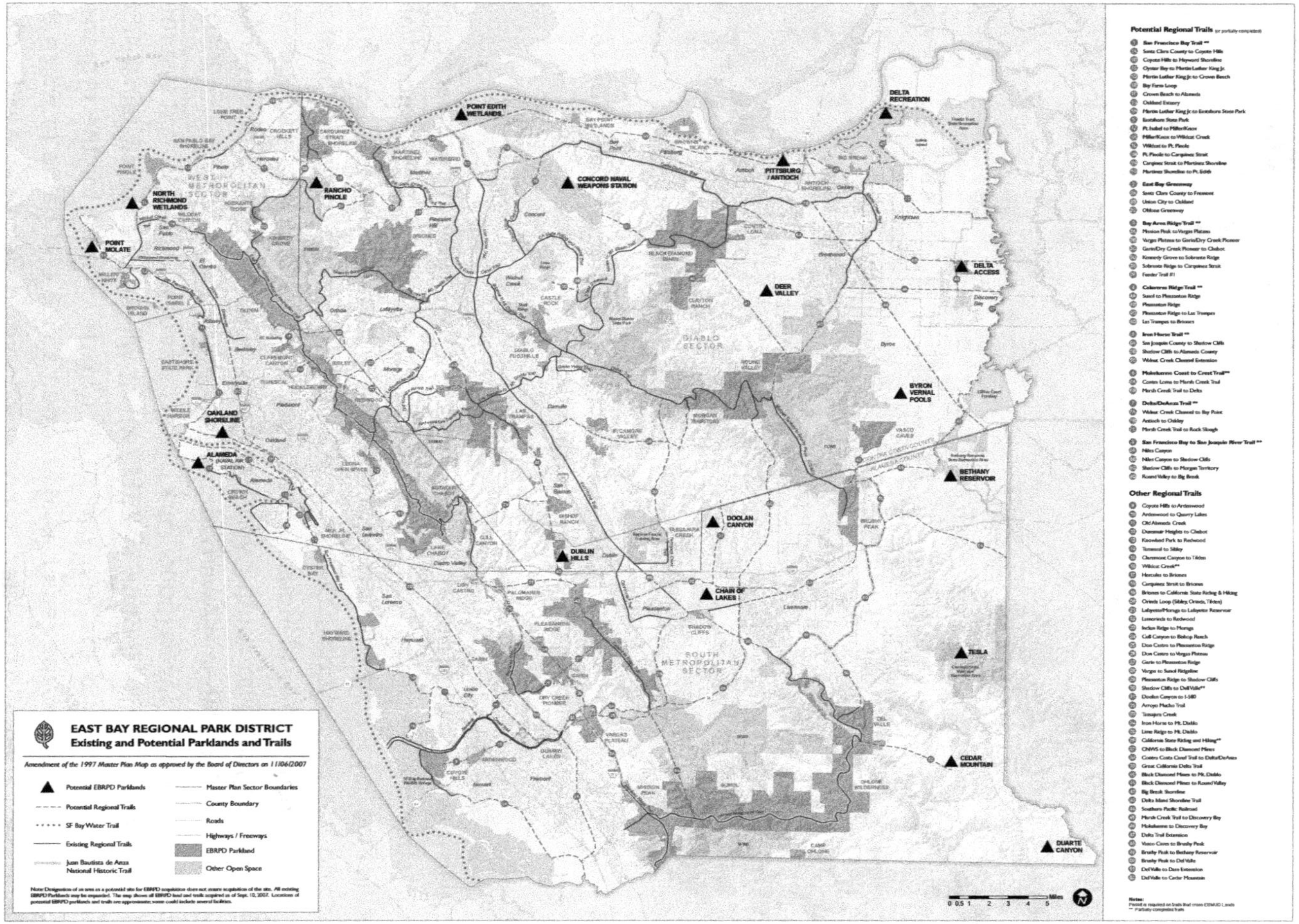

Figure 2-2.   The East Bay Regional Park District's 2007 plan was instrumental in gaining voter approval for Measure WW, the largest local park bond measure to pass in the United States. [Source: East Bay Regional Park District]

Figure 2-3. The City of Livermore uses development requirements and TDR to preserve its vineyards and its wine-region heritage.

specific plan in which development within the city's urban growth boundary pays for preservation of vineyards south of the city. To date, the South Livermore Valley Specific Plan has reached its target of facilitating the creation of 38 new small wineries and has preserved 4,000 acres of vineyards. These accomplishments support agritourism as a local industry and help Livermore build its reputation as a premier wine region. The South Livermore Valley Specific Plan also won APA's National Outstanding Planning Award for Implementation in 2006 (Roberts 2010).

As of 2010, the East Bay Regional Park District was at work on its next system-wide plan, scheduled for adoption in 2011, which will emphasize sustainability, environmental justice, and the implications of climate change for the regional parks. Some believe that the region is in an open space end game in which all land will be permanently committed to preservation or development within the next two or three decades (McCreery 2010). Regardless of the accuracy of that prediction, the East Bay Regional Park District is already recognized as the largest regional park system in the nation, with more than 100,000 acres of parkland in 65 parks and 1,100 miles of trails (East Bay Regional Park District 2010c).

3

ALBUQUERQUE AND BERNALILLO COUNTY, NEW MEXICO

The City of Albuquerque and surrounding Bernalillo County, New Mexico, offer a wealth of geologic, environmental, and cultural treasures. The Sandia Mountains and two other ranges rise a mile above the city, creating a dramatic backdrop to the east. Volcanic cinder cones top the mesa west of the city, fronted by a lava-flow escarpment decorated with ancient rock carvings. The Rio Grande river and its cottonwood forest meander through the valley floor in between. Despite a current population of more than 630,000, much of this inheritance has been preserved, thanks in part to an inclusive planning process and creative implementation strategies.

Between 1950 and 1970, Bernalillo County's population more than doubled, due partly to outdoor recreational opportunities as well as an agreeable climate and the growth of governmental agencies, particularly those related to national defense (Albuquerque/Bernalillo County 2003). Farsighted individuals succeeded in preserving 8,500 acres of open space by 1968. But environmental protection shifted to a higher gear in 1969, when the City Goals Committee officially sanctioned the preservation of open space and its individual components. Citizen organizations formed to advocate for the preservation of various natural features, including the Bosque del Rio Grande Nature Preserve Society, Save the Volcanoes, Save the Sandias, and Save the Arroyos. These groups worked together as the Open Space Task Force to help prepare the 1975 Albuquerque/Bernalillo County Comprehensive Plan, which included the Plan for Major Open Space as one of its three volumes (Albuquerque 2010a; Bernalillo County 2010).

The 1975 plan called for the preservation of almost 50,000 acres of natural features in an open space network within the city and county. The city-county comprehensive plan currently in effect largely retains these original open space goals. In 2003 and 2004, the voters rejected the formal consolidation of Albuquerque and Bernalillo County. Nevertheless, the city and county often partner on open space preservation efforts and are co-owners of some of the preserves described below (Albuquerque/Bernalillo County 2003).

Upon adoption of the 1975 plan, the city formally established the Albuquerque Major Public Open Space Program (Bernalillo County 2003). Early successes were scored in the West Mesa Open Space, where 14,929 acres are now preserved in six properties, including almost 4,000 acres protecting five volcanic cones that were active more than 100,000 years ago. Four of these preserves are now units of the Petroglyph National Monument, protecting 17 miles of basalt rock escarpment containing almost 20,000 images of animals, symbols, and supernatural beings carved into the rock by Native Americans and early Spanish settlers (Albuquerque 2010b).

Portions of this escarpment were initially protected by the creation of Indian Petroglyph State Park, at Boca Negra, and Albuquerque's Volcano City Park. In 1986, the entire escarpment was listed in the National Register of Historic Places as Las Imagenes National Archeological District. At the urging of the Friends of the Albuquerque Petroglyphs and others, the U.S. Congress formally established

Figure 3-1.   Volcanic cinder cones preserved by Albuquerque are just a few minutes' drive from downtown.

7,300 acres there as a national monument in 1990, becoming the only unit of the National Park System created primarily to preserve and study rock art (Lamb 1993).

In 1980, open space advocates focused on the foothills of the Sandia Mountains, which dominate the eastern skyline of Albuquerque. Most of the land in the Sandia Mountains was previously preserved as part of the Cibola National Forest. However, threats of development hovered over a prominent 8,000-acre foothill property known as the Elena Gallegos grant. In response to petitions signed by 15,000 people, the Albuquerque City Council adopted a quarter-cent sales tax for three years and bought the Elena Gallegos grant in 1982. The city retained 640 acres as Elena Gallegos Picnic Area and Albert G. Simms Park and transferred the rest to the U.S. Forest Service in return for 18,000 acres of surplus federal land. The city deposits proceeds from the sale of these surplus federal lands in an open space trust fund used for ongoing open space management (Albuquerque 2010a). The U.S. Forest Service added most of the remaining acreage to the Sandia Mountain Wilderness area, which now contains 37,877 acres of rugged terrain with 117 miles of trails accessible from Albuquerque (Wilderness.net 2010).

In 1983, New Mexico established Rio Grande Valley State Park, which is managed by Albuquerque using money generated by the city's Open Space Trust Fund (Albuquerque 2010a). This 4,300-acre park preserves 20 miles of the Rio Grande floodplain forest, or *bosque*, as it bisects Albuquerque from the Sandia Pueblo on the north to the Isleta Pueblo on the south. From the park's nature center, hikers and bicyclists can access a 16-mile trail, Paseo del Bosque, as well as the Aldo Leopold Forest Trail, named for the father of modern ecology, who once lived and worked in Albuquerque (Albuquerque 2010b).

In 1997, the voters again approved a quarter-cent sales tax for three years, which raised roughly $36 million, a portion of which was used to buy four farms. Albuquerque partnered with the State of New Mexico, the Village of Los Ranchos de Albuquerque, and Bernalillo County to buy Los Poblanos Fields. This 138-acre farm is leased to a dairy and Rio Grande Community Farms, a nonprofit organic farm supporting local food networks. One-quarter of the fields is reserved for feeding wildlife, including flocks of geese and sandhill cranes that feast in the cornfields here from November to February. In all, Albuquerque owns five farms with a combined area of 366 acres. A grand total of 28,786 acres of open space was preserved as of 2008 by the Open Space Program, or almost 24 percent of the city's total land area (Albuquerque 2010b; Albuquerque 2010c).

Bernalillo County has also been implementing the open space acquisition goals of the city-county comprehensive plan, beginning with a grassroots campaign to save the Gutierrez-Hubbell House. This adobe hacienda was built in the 1840s and once housed a stagecoach stop and trading post on El Camino Real. The restored building now serves as a living history museum and demonstration farm providing training in sustainable agriculture (Bernalillo County 2010).

Figure 3-2.   Petroglyph National Monument protects 20,000 pieces of ancient rock art.

The land preserved by Albuquerque and Bernalillo County is only a portion of the 110,656 acres of publicly owned open space within the county boundaries. In addition to the 96,192 acres managed by the U.S. Forest Service, the federal Bureau of Land Management controls 5,376 acres. The New Mexico State Park system owns another 6,976 acres, including Manzano Mountains State Park as well as the Rio Grande Nature Center State Park in Albuquerque (Albuquerque/ Bernalillo County 2003).

In addition to preserving open space, Albuquerque maintains an ongoing effort to help people understand and appreciate their natural areas. In 1978, the city and Albuquerque Public Schools collaborated with the University of New Mexico, nonprofit organizations, and individual volunteers to publish *Albuquerque's Environmental Story*. The book is now supplemented by a website, which illustrates the need for sustainability and the preservation of natural areas and cultural resources that are essential to community character and well-being. For more than 30 years, *Albuquerque's Environmental Story* has supported the curriculum used in elementary, middle, and high schools (Friends of Albuquerque's Environmental Story 2010). This consistent educational effort contributes greatly to citizen support for open space preservation and, in turn, helps explain how Albuquerque and Bernalillo County have largely achieved the goals of their Plan for Major Open Space.

DEVELOPMENT AREAS

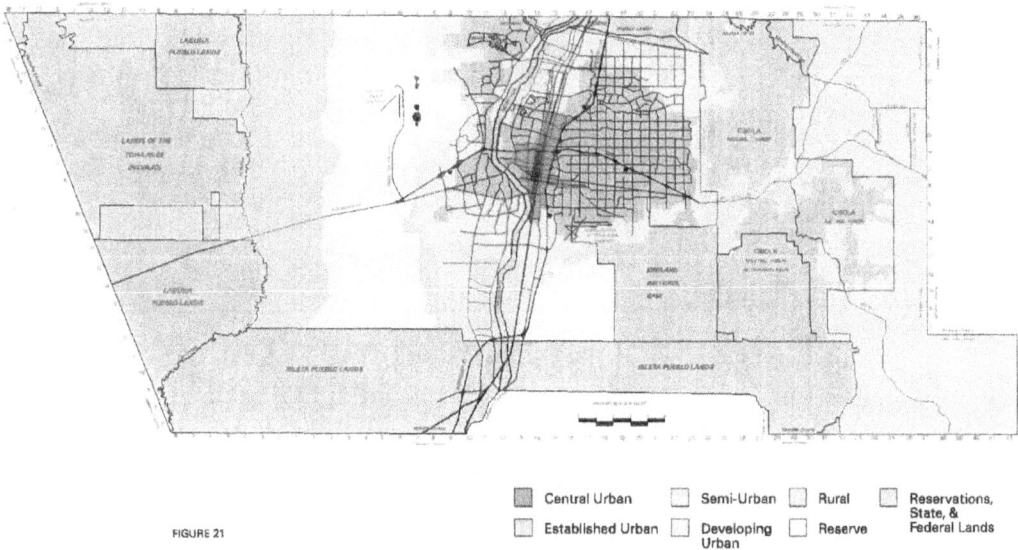

FIGURE 21

| Central Urban | Semi-Urban | Rural | Reservations, State, & |
| Established Urban | Developing Urban | Reserve | Federal Lands |

Figure 3-3.   Almost half of Bernalillo County is in reservations, state properties, and federal lands, as well as open space preserved by Albuquerque and Bernalillo County. *[Source: Albuquerque/Bernalillo County]*

4

BERKS COUNTY, PENNSYLVANIA

Berks County, Pennsylvania, farmers are bullish on the future of farming. They have already permanently preserved more than 67,000 acres of farmland, an accomplishment that both reflects and generates confidence in the long-term viability of agriculture there. In addition, almost as much open space has been permanently protected in parks, preserves, and greenways. Preserved farmland and open space represent more than 23 percent of the county's land area, a remarkable achievement for a community that lies within an hour's drive of downtown Philadelphia.

Berks County surrounds its largest city, Reading, 56 miles northwest of Philadelphia. Despite a population of 374,000, Berks County maintains a relatively intact rural landscape consisting largely of farmland and wooded slopes, including two ridges of the Appalachian Mountains, which form much of the northern and southern borders of the county. Hex signs are just some of the many indications that Berks County is part of Pennsylvania Dutch Country, named for its original, predominantly German-speaking settlers (Berks County 2008a).

Berks County farms generated sales of $368 million in 2007, the third-highest of any county in Pennsylvania (USDA 2007). Despite the significance of agriculture to the local economy, development pressure has taken its toll on farmland here. Between 1964 and 1992, Berks County farmland dropped in area from 307,644 to 221,981 acres, a loss of almost 30 percent (Berks County 2003).

In the 1980s, the county formed a farmland preservation committee to prepare a farmland preservation strategy, which was ultimately incorporated in the county's 1991 comprehensive plan (Bowers 2003). The 2003 comprehensive plan, Berks

Figure 4-1.   Preservation plans support the agriculture and tourism industries in Pennsylvania Dutch Country.

Vision 2020, maintains this focus on agricultural land preservation, calling for the permanent protection of at least 200,000 acres of agricultural land through easement acquisition or effective agricultural preservation zoning (Berks County 2003).

Since land use in Pennsylvania is controlled by municipalities, Berks County implements its plans partly by offering incentive programs designed to motivate its boroughs and townships to adopt county policies and regulations. One program offers funding and staff support to two or more municipalities that complete a joint comprehensive plan. These joint comprehensive plans are designed to foster regional cooperation and achieve consistency with the county's comprehensive plan. To date, the program has produced 19 joint comprehensive plans involving 62 municipalities. The Joint Comprehensive Planning Program has won awards from the Commonwealth of Pennsylvania, the Pennsylvania chapter of the American Planning Association, and the U.S. Department of Housing and Urban Development (Berks County 2009).

In a second incentive program, Berks County pays the entire expense when two or more municipalities prepare a joint zoning ordinance consistent with their joint comprehensive plan and form a joint zoning board to administer it. In a third incentive program, Berks County provides limited reimbursement when municipalities prepare and adopt effective agricultural zoning. In Berks County, effective

Figure 4-2.   Berks County has preserved more than 67,000 acres of farmland
to date.

agricultural zoning typically caps residential development at densities ranging
from one dwelling per 20 acres to one unit per 50 acres. As of 2003, seven townships used this incentive program, resulting in the adoption of agricultural zoning
on 57,000 acres of farmland (Berks County 2003).

In addition to encouraging municipalities to adopt effective plans and regulations, Berks County permanently preserves agricultural land through its Agricultural Conservation Easement (ACE) program. The ACE program, established in
1989, is a purchase of development rights tool that combines state and county
money to buy agricultural easements from willing sellers. By 2008, the ACE program for Pennsylvania as a whole involved 57 counties and had preserved more
than 400,000 acres of farmland. The Pennsylvania share of the funding comes primarily from cigarette taxes. Although Pennsylvania initially provided the bulk of
the funding for the statewide ACE program, in 2008, the 57 participating counties spent more on ACE than the state (Pennsylvania 2008).

The success of the Berks County ACE program is partly due to strong financial
support from the county. Berks County exceeds Pennsylvania's minimum match
fund contribution (Pennsylvania 2008). As of 2008, Pennsylvania had spent $62.7
million, and Berks County had spent $56.4 million to purchase 530 easements in
Berks County, a total funding amount greater than that of any county in Pennsylvania with the exception of Lancaster County (Berks County 2008b).

Berks County also makes each funding dollar accomplish more preservation. The county's ACE program has purchased easements at an average cost of $2,047 per acre, which is considerably lower than the average per-acre cost incurred as of 2008 in some other southeastern Pennsylvania counties, such as the $5,367 paid by Chester County and the $10,492 paid by Montgomery County (Berks County 2008b).

The Berks County Agricultural Land Preservation Board capped ACE easement purchases at $2,000 per acre until 2006 and then raised the maximum payment to its current level of $2,500 per acre (Hildebrand 2006). In comparison, Chester County sets a limit of $12,000 per acre, and Montgomery County has no maximum purchase price (Pennsylvania 2008). Since the average appraised value of easements often exceeds the $2,500 ceiling, many Berks County farmers donate a portion of the value of these development rights in order to participate in the program. In fact, as of 2008, participants in Berks County had donated more than $26 million worth of acreage in these bargain sales (Berks County Agricultural Land Preservation Board 2008).

Fundamentally, the Berks County ACE program is a success because many Berks County farmers are willing to sell their easements, even at bargain sale prices. One member of the ACE program staff noted that farmers often apply for the program after a neighbor or family member has participated, indicating the power of interpersonal influence (DeLong 2010). Clusters of preserved Berks County farmland also suggest that confidence in the future viability of farmland may grow with each nearby farm that is preserved. More than three-quarters of the 530 easements recorded in Berks County by 2008 were concentrated in 12 of Berks County's 44 townships (Berks County 2008b).

In December 2005, the Berks County Board of Commissioners reinvigorated the ACE program by approving a $36 million line of credit to fund the local share of the ACE program (Hildebrand 2006). By 2008, Berks County had become the number one ACE program in Pennsylvania (Berks County 2008b). The Berks County Conservancy, a nonprofit conservation organization, also acquires farmland easements (Berks County Conservancy 2010). When the 5,518 acres preserved by the conservancy are added to the 61,780 acres protected by the ACE program, preserved Berks County farmland totals 67,298 acres, making the Berks County farmland preservation program the third-most successful locally operated farmland preservation program in the nation (*Farmland Preservation Report* 2010).

In addition to garnering an impressive record in agricultural land preservation, Berks County is also building a reputation for other preservation successes. In its 1991 comprehensive plan, Berks County identified environmentally sensitive areas and conducted a Natural Areas Inventory, which identified habitat in

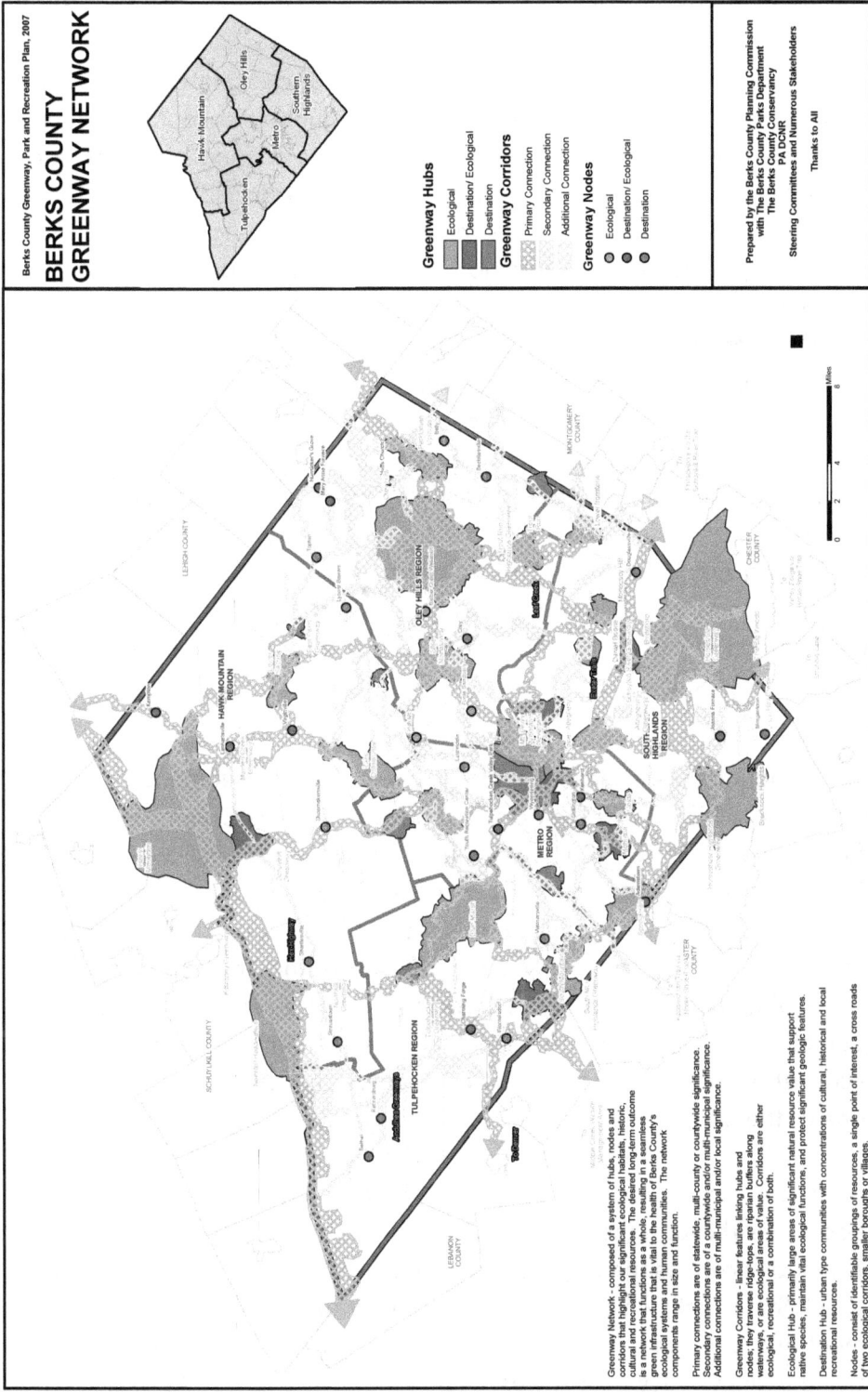

Figure 4-3.   The Berks County Greenway, Park and Recreation Plan aims to preserve, expand, and link three critical open space elements: green infrastructure or ecology, heritage resources, and parks. [Source: Berks County]

need of protection. Three years later, the county's 1994 Open Space and Recreation Plan proposed a coordinated approach to open space preservation using greenways that link stream corridors, historic sites, and natural areas throughout the county.

The 2003 comprehensive plan, Berks Vision 2020, designated rural conservation and environmental hazard areas and subsequently encouraged municipalities to implement the necessary land-use protections using its Conservation Zoning Incentive Program (CZIP) (Berks County 2007). In CZIP, Berks County reimburses up to $10,000 of the costs incurred when boroughs and townships develop and adopt effective conservation zoning or cluster development (Berks County 2008c).

The 2007 Greenway, Park and Recreation Plan aims to preserve, expand, and link three critical open space elements: green infrastructure or ecology, heritage resources, and parks. Through a hierarchy of greenway corridors, the 2007 plan aims to protect significant environmental and historic assets while increasing recreational opportunities and expanding access for residents and visitors (Berks County 2007).

In developing the 2007 plan, Berks County used the Natural Lands Trust's SmartConservation Model to identify ecological greenway hubs for the proposed Greenway Network. Four of the largest hubs are already preserved or partly preserved:

- Hawk Mountain, the largest ecological hub, is a key segment of Blue Mountain, which forms the northern border of Berks County. Every fall, an average of 20,000 hawks, eagles, and falcons soar over Blue Mountain during their southerly migration. It was once a popular spot for shooting birds of prey for sport, but key portions of this hub are now preserved for bird watching as part of the privately owned Hawk Mountain Sanctuary, the world's first raptor refuge. In addition to the 2,600 acres in the sanctuary, more than 13,000 additional acres of public and private land there are permanently protected in one of the largest contiguous tracts of protected forestland in southeastern Pennsylvania (Hawk Mountain Sanctuary 2007). One of the more spectacular segments of the world-famous Appalachian Trail also winds through the rugged ridges of this hub.
- The hub known as the Big Woods incorporates the 6,000-acre French Creek State Park, which contains 35 miles of trails, including a segment of the Horse-shoe Trail, a 130-mile-long hiking and equestrian trail that links Valley Forge, west of Philadelphia, with the Appalachian

Trail. This hub is also home to Hopewell Furnace National Historic Site, a restored "iron plantation" that produced cannons and shot for the Continental Army during the Revolutionary War.

- Blue Marsh Lake, a recreational area surrounding a reservoir created by the U.S. Army Corps of Engineers, serves as another hub. This complex incorporates a living history museum with a 19th-century farm and an 18th-century farm in the National Register of Historic Places. Schoolchildren come here to learn about rural life in the 1700s and to try their hand at traditional farming tasks.

- The 500-acre Neversink Mountain Preserve, owned by the Berks County Conservancy, anchors another hub, between the city of Reading and the Schuylkill River, offering a nine-mile trail system near the urbanized heart of Berks County (Berks County Conservancy 2010).

The 2007 plan is summarized in a Greenway Network map, which depicts these hubs and identifies other sites as additional hubs or nodes because they contain recreational, cultural, or historic resources instead of, or in addition to, ecological features. Again, many of these sites have already been preserved or are in the process of being preserved. For example, the county has continued to resurrect segments of the Union Canal, which was primarily used to barge coal from the Susquehanna River to the city of Reading between 1828 and 1881. In Tulpehocken Creek Valley Park, the county has restored many historic structures from the Union Canal era, including locks, mills, and a covered bridge, as well as other buildings and ruins from the 19th century. These attractions have been linked by the Union Canal Walking and Bicycle Trail, which lets bicyclists and walkers meander beside Tulpehocken Creek, getting a lesson in natural as well as industrial history as they exercise.

Since interconnectivity is the overriding goal, all of the 2007 plan's greenways connect to the backbone of the Greenway Network: the Schuylkill River Trail, a bicycling and hiking path. When completed, the Schuylkill River Trail will travel 42 miles through Berks County, connecting 17 separate communities. The Schuylkill River Trail lies within the Schuylkill River National and State Heritage Area, designated by Pennsylvania in 1995 and by the U.S. Congress in 2000. National heritage areas are designed to revitalize regions using natural and cultural resource preservation, education, recreation, and heritage tourism. The Schuylkill River heritage area aims to ultimately extend the Schuylkill River Trail between Pottsville and Philadelphia, allowing a 140-mile journey through five counties (Berks County 2007).

The 2007 plan reports that public parks and open space in Berks County already total 54,294 acres, with another 5,649 acres in private facilities such as

Hawk Mountain Sanctuary and Neversink Mountain Preserve (Berks County 2007). When this open space total is added to the 67,298 acres of preserved farmland, Berks County has permanently preserved a total of 127,241 acres, or more than 23 percent of the total land area in the county.

Berks County confirms the old saying that nothing succeeds like success. At last count, more than 200 farmers were waiting to participate in the county's ACE program (Oberholtzer and Esseks 2008). Perhaps as owners see thousands of acres of farmland and open space being preserved, they grow increasingly confident that farming and rural living still have a future there.

5

BOULDER AND BOULDER COUNTY, COLORADO

Like many plans by Frederick Law Olmsted Jr., the 1908 plan for the City of Boulder, Colorado, emphasized open space preservation, in this case calling for the preservation of a "City Forest" in the surrounding foothills, mountains, and valleys. Now, a century later, the City of Boulder's Open Space and Mountain Parks protect most of this land and provide a 130-mile trail system for its exploration. The city has also partnered with Boulder County to jointly preserve much of Boulder Valley as a permanent greenbelt, giving Boulder the feel of a city tucked within a national park. In addition, Boulder County has created a 94,000-acre countywide open space and trail network using a wide array of preservation techniques. When these lands are joined with other public lands, including Roosevelt National Forest and Rocky Mountain National Park, preserved open space represents more than two-thirds of the county's total land area. In short, this collaborative effort has, amazingly, brought much of Olmsted's original vision to life.

Boulder lies at the base of the Front Range of the Rocky Mountains at an elevation of 5,430 feet, only 25 miles northwest of downtown Denver. In 1908, Frederick Law Olmsted Jr. visited Boulder, and his plan, *The Improvement of Boulder, Colorado*, was published two years later. Olmsted was overwhelmed by the beauty of Boulder's natural setting, as shown in his proposal to create a city forest:

In the great tract of unspoiled foothill scenery lying above and beyond the Chautauqua grounds Boulder has a priceless possession. [I]t will become possible for anyone to traverse in the course of two hours' leisurely walking or driving, as beautiful, wild and refreshing scenery as any that thousands upon thousands of busy, hardworking

Americans spend largely of their money and time to enjoy by traveling thousands of miles from home. We have little specific advice to offer beyond the caution not to spoil what a bountiful nature has provided. (Olmsted 1910, 97)

For the first half of the 20th century, Boulder grew at a moderate pace, and the city made limited but critical open space acquisitions. In 1910, a proposal was floated to build an amusement park at the top of Flagstaff Mountain, a prominent landmark overlooking downtown Boulder (Cushman and Cushman 2006). In keeping with the Olmsted plan, the citizens of Boulder preserved 1,200 acres on Flagstaff Mountain and effectively launched what was to become one of the most successful open space programs in the United States. Today, the trail up Flagstaff Mountain rewards hikers with outstanding views of the city, surrounded by thousands of acres of permanently preserved open space (Boulder 2009).

Between 1950 and 1970, the population of Boulder more than tripled, fueled partly by growing enrollment at the University of Colorado–Boulder. Environmental activists were particularly alarmed by proposals to build houses on the hillsides

Figure 5-1.   Chautauqua Meadow at dawn creates a fitting setting for the Flatirons, the red sandstone cliffs that form a backdrop for Boulder.

that the Olmsted plan had identified for open space. These citizens, who ulti-mately formed the group PLAN–Boulder County, gathered enough signatures for a voter initiative to amend the city charter, preventing the pumping of city water to land higher than a prescribed elevation called the Blue Line. In 1959, the vot-ers approved the initiative by 76 percent, putting a sizeable speed bump in the path of hillside development (Plantico 2008).

The next battle was fought over a scenic property above the Blue Line known as Enchanted Mesa. The owners wanted to develop it, and PLAN–Boulder County thought it should be preserved as open space. In 1962, Boulder residents again voiced their support for preservation by approving a bond measure to buy the land. In 1964, a subsequent campaign raised additional donations from the gen-eral public when a condemnation trial determined that another $10,000 would be needed to fully compensate the owners of Enchanted Mesa (Plantico 2008).

From the vantage point of Flagstaff Mountain, staff from the Boulder Parks and Recreation Department envisioned the broad outlines of the city's first open space plan, which was subsequently refined and approved by the parks board and the city council. This plan documented and illustrated preservation goals that the electorate was asked to adopt in November 1967 along with a 0.4-cent sales tax to be used exclusively for open space acquisition (Hudson 1990). PLAN–Boulder County campaigned for the measure using reprints of the original 1910 Olmsted plan to emphasize the long history of the greenbelt concept for Boul-der. That measure passed by 57 percent, making Boulder the first U.S. city in which the voters adopted a sales tax dedicated to open space preservation. In 1989, the voters approved an additional sales tax increment of 0.3 cents for 15 years to keep pace with land acquisition needs (Boulder 2009).

In 1978, the city and county adopted the joint Boulder Valley Comprehensive Plan, which used open space as its foundation. In the plan, open space defines urban boundaries while providing green-infrastructure benefits, including the protection of water resources, wildlife habitat, agriculture, scenic views, outdoor recreation, and overall quality of life (Boulder 2009). The city and county use multiple approaches to implement this plan, such as an interjurisdictional trans-fer of development rights (TDR) program, which encourages the redirection of growth away from areas planned for open space. These transfers are guided by an inter-government agreement in which the city accepts a specified amount of development potential from Boulder Valley land under county jurisdiction, and the county preserves the rural character of lands under its jurisdiction within the planned greenbelt (Pruetz 2003).

Boulder County in its own right is nationally recognized for open space pres-ervation. In 1968, the county began developing an open space preservation plan with an extensive public-involvement component. In 1975, the county created the Parks and Open Space Department, which promptly acquired its first holdings,

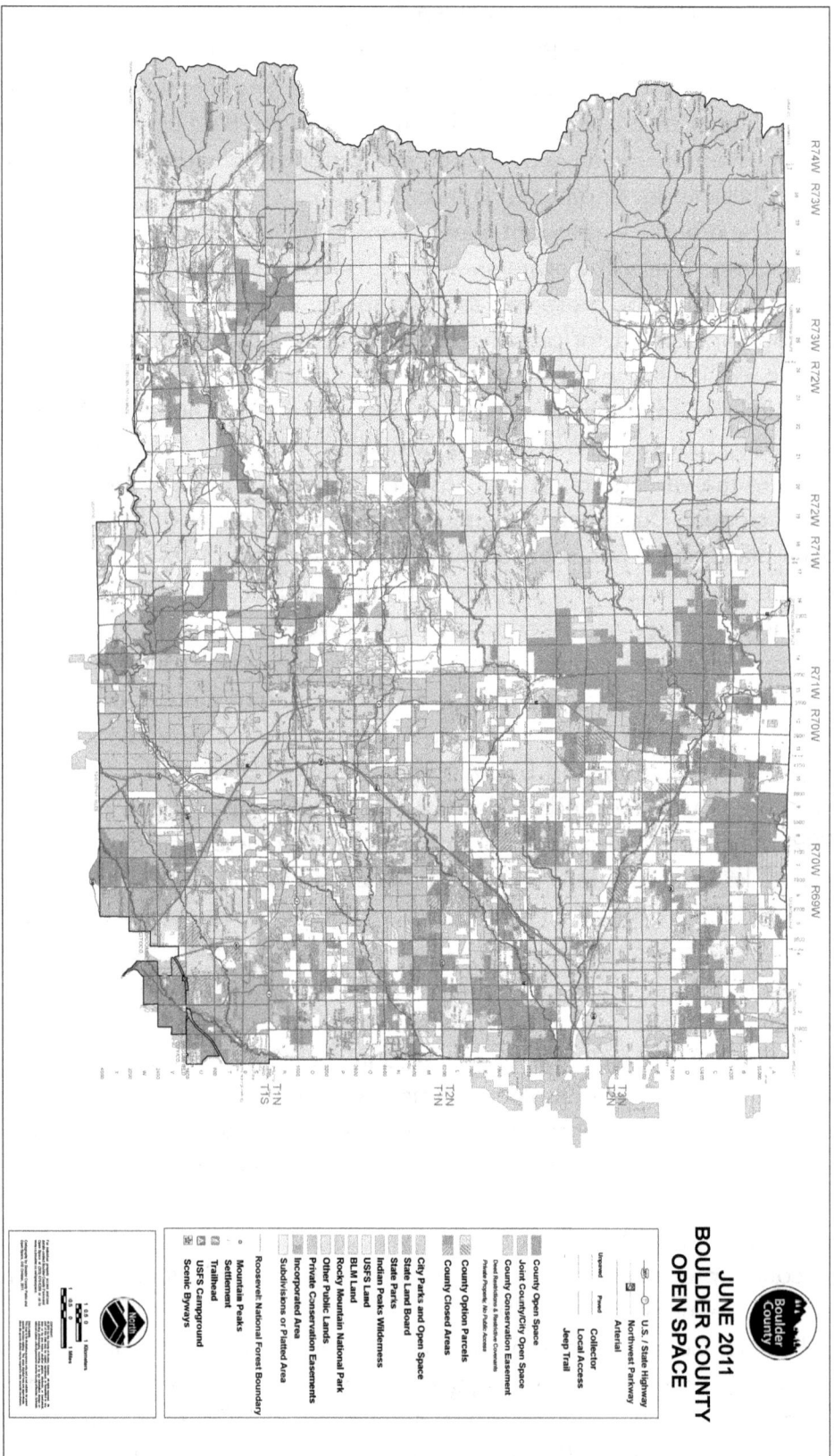

Figure 5-2. More than two-thirds of Boulder County's total land area is preserved in open space. [Source: Boulder County]

JUNE 2011
BOULDER COUNTY
OPEN SPACE

U.S. / State Highway
Northwest Parkway
Arterial
Collector
Local Access
Jeep Trail

Unpaved   Paved

County Open Space
Joint County/City Open Space
County Conservation Easement
City Parks and Open Space
County Option Parcels
County Closed Areas
State Parks
State Land Board
Indian Peaks Wilderness
USFS Land
BLM Land
Rocky Mountain National Park
Other Public Lands
Private Conservation Easements
Incorporated Area
Subdivisions or Platted Area

Roosevelt National Forest Boundary
Mountain Peaks
Settlement
Trailhead
USFS Campground
Scenic Byways

R74W R73W R72W R71W R70W R69W

T3N
T2N
T2N
T1N
T1N
T1S

the Betasso Preserve and Walker Ranch. The county's first comprehensive plan, adopted in 1978, emphasized open space preservation, protection of environmental resources, and development of a countywide trail system. The owners of private land designated as proposed open space in the comprehensive plan can choose to develop their properties as allowed by the applicable zoning or participate in any of Boulder County's preservation programs (Boulder County 2010a).

Boulder County Parks and Open Space uses no fewer than 10 preservation methods, including land acquisition, purchase of conservation easements, and TDR. Property tax revenues generate roughly $4 million for open space preservation annually. In 1994, the voters turbocharged preservation efforts by approving a 0.25 percent open space sales and use tax. In four subsequent elections, the voters extended and increased this open space sales and use tax, and it now stands at 0.45 percent; it produced more than $17 million in preservation funding in 2008 alone. Boulder County has also received more than $5 million in preservation funding from Great Outdoors Colorado, those funds coming from the state's lottery system (Boulder County 2008).

The Boulder County TDR program has generated more voluntary interjurisdictional cooperation than any other program in the nation. In other places, TDR programs often languish because cities fail to recognize the benefit of participating in the preservation of land outside their jurisdiction. But in Boulder County, seven cities entered into intergovernmental agreements with the county, pledging to accept TDRs representing the preservation of land outside their city limits. Even though the sending areas specified in these agreements are outside the city limits, they are nevertheless of special value to these cities; they include key agricultural parcels, environmentally significant lands, greenbelts, and community separators. By accepting TDRs from land under county jurisdiction, these cities are essentially implementing their land-use goals for the surrounding countryside (Pruetz 2003).

As of 2010, Boulder County had independently preserved 84,720 acres, and the City of Boulder had separately saved 41,246 acres in parks, open space, and easements. In addition, the county had concluded joint preservation projects with the City of Boulder and other municipalities that preserved another 8,714 acres of open space (Boulder County 2010b).

The federal government protects even more land than the local governments do. The U.S. Forest Service alone holds 137,308 acres in the Roosevelt National Forest, including the James Peak Wilderness and the Indian Peaks Wilderness, which straddles the Continental Divide, forming the western boundary of Boulder County. Rocky Mountain National Park protects another 27,313 acres in the county. Adding in other public open space, protected watershed lands, and private conservation easements, there is a grand total of 324,001 acres of protected land in Boulder County (Boulder County 2010b).

In his 1910 plan, Frederick Law Olmsted Jr. cautioned that Boulder should not "spoil what a bountiful nature has provided." With more than 68 percent of its total land area permanently preserved, Boulder and Boulder County have spectacularly followed Olmsted's advice.

Figure 5-3.   Boulder County alone has preserved more than 84,000 acres of open space, including farmland.

6

BURLINGTON COUNTY, NEW JERSEY

Burlington County lies in New Jersey, the most densely populated state in the nation, 20 miles east of Philadelphia and 60 miles southwest of New York City. Despite its location, Burlington County still retains more than 111,000 acres of farmland, with almost half of that total in permanent preservation. In addition to adopting the first farmland preservation program in New Jersey and one of the most successful farmland preservation programs in the nation, Burlington County is also a leader in environmental protection and open space preservation, as shown by its County Leadership in Conservation Award from the Trust for Public Land and the National Association of Counties.

In 1977, the voters of Burlington County approved a $1 million bond to preserve a 530-acre cranberry farm in Southampton Township. Eight years later, the county board and the State of New Jersey purchased five farms in Chesterfield Township for permanent preservation. These events marked the official start of farmland preservation for both Burlington County and the state (Burlington County 2008).

Despite these initial efforts, agriculture continued to lose ground. Between 1982 and 1992, Burlington County farmland declined by 15,503 acres, or almost 14 percent. The county diagnosed that development pressure was creating "impermanence syndrome," a feeling that farmland conversion is inevitable. "If this condition takes hold, farmers in a region tend to avoid investment in their farming equipment, maintenance of farm buildings and reduce efforts towards soil and water conservation practices" (Burlington County 2008, 18).

Figure 6-1.   Chesterfield Township has the most successful municipal TDR land preservation program in the nation.

By the mid-1990s, Burlington County was losing twice as much farmland as it was saving, despite being New Jersey's leader in farmland preservation. Under the leadership of County Freeholder William S. Haines, in 1996 the voters approved a dedicated open space tax of $0.02 per $100, thereby creating a stable, long-term funding source, known as the Burlington County Farmland, Open Space and Historic Preservation Trust Fund (Burlington County 2008). Two years later, the voters doubled the tax, to $0.04 per $100 of assessed value. In the trust fund's first 11 years of operation, more than $78 million that it generated was allocated for farmland preservation. Between 2008 and 2036, the trust fund is projected to generate another $223 million for farmland preservation alone (Burlington County 2008; Trust for Public Land 2005).

In 1998, Burlington County adopted a strategic plan with one overriding goal: to preserve the greatest amount of productive agricultural land in the shortest period of time possible. The plan then proposed several ways of accomplishing that goal. In one strategy, Burlington County acquires land in fee when farms are headed for conversion and the owners have little interest in selling an easement, often due to estate ownership. After acquisition, the county leases the land for agriculture until it deed restricts and sells the farm (Burlington County 2008).

The County's Farmland Preservation Plan also promotes programs for stretching limited preservation funding. For example, the county offers farmland owners the alternative of deferred purchase with interest paid from the time that the easement is recorded until the date when the county and the landowner have agreed that full and final payment will be made. Through this approach, landowners are able to structure payments to fit their tax and retirement plans, and the county can use its finite funding to preserve more land in the near future. Roughly 40 percent of the county's preservation transactions to date have used this approach (Burlington County 2008).

The county's Farmland Preservation Program reported a total of 51,251 acres of preserved farmland as of June 2010. Of this total, 25,854 acres, or roughly half, had been preserved through the New Jersey Pinelands programs, which are discussed below. The remaining 25,397 acres had been preserved by state and county easement and fee acquisitions, as well as transfer of development rights (TDR) programs (Burlington County 2010).

Almost two-thirds of Burlington County is within the New Jersey Pinelands, the one-million-acre area that includes portions of seven counties in the southeastern quarter of the state of New Jersey. The Pinelands offers fertile ground for specialty crops, such as cranberries and blueberries, and generates roughly one-quarter of New Jersey's agricultural income. The Pinelands protects one of the largest and least polluted aquifers in New Jersey. In addition, the region is ecologically significant, providing a home for 850 species of plants and more than 350 species of birds, reptiles, mammals, and amphibians. Given its proximity to the East Coast megalopolis, the Pinelands also serves as an outdoor recreational retreat within a few hours' drive of millions of city residents.

In recognition of its importance, Congress designated the Pinelands as the first national reserve in the United States in 1978. One year later, New Jersey created the Pinelands Commission, which adopted one of the most successful regional plans in the country. The Pinelands Comprehensive Management Plan establishes nine management areas. Within the inner areas, the plan calls for preservation of ecological resources and agriculture, including specialty agriculture. In the surrounding management areas, the plan proposes various levels of future development depending on the capacity of each location to accommodate additional growth. Within Burlington County, which constitutes 36 percent of the entire Pinelands region, the plan primarily calls for preservation but designates a limited number of areas as suitable for various forms of growth, ranging from low-density rural development to villages and towns.

Under the plan, the most significant parcels are acquired in fee, primarily by federal and state funding. But the majority of the protection is accomplished by strict land-use regulations and the most ambitious TDR program in the United States. Owners of land in areas designated for preservation (sending areas) can

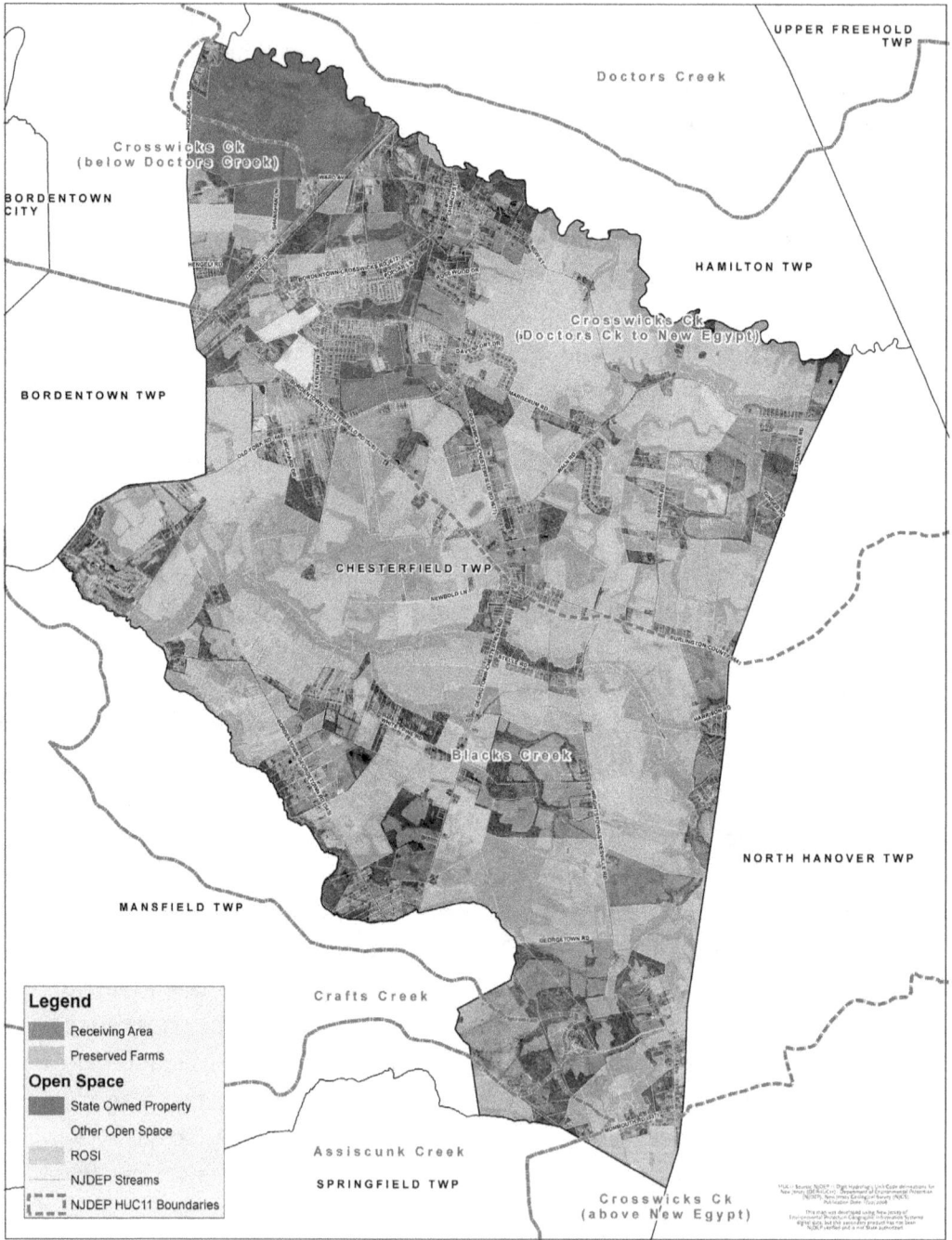

Figure 6-2. Chesterfield Township combines TDR with PDR to preserve farmland.
[Source: Clarke Caton Hintz]

permanently limit development potential in return for the issuance of transfer-able development rights, which in this program are referred to as Pinelands Development Credits (PDCs). Developers of land in areas designated for growth (receiving areas) buy these PDCs in order to achieve levels of development that would not otherwise be allowed. Consistent with the plan, 23 Pinelands munici-palities have created receiving zones that accept PDCs from other jurisdictions. This interjurisdictional transfer mechanism creates a regional market with more participating communities than any other TDR program in the country. To date, the New Jersey Pinelands PDC program has permanently preserved 58,900 acres of land, making it the second-most successful TDR program in the United States (New Jersey Pinelands Commission 2010).

In addition to the Pineland's regional TDR program, two townships in Bur-lington County operate highly successful TDR programs at the municipal level. In 1995, Lumberton Township, 20 miles east of Philadelphia, became the first community to adopt a TDR program, following passage of the Burlington County TDR Demonstration Act, a state law designed to allow municipalities in Burling-ton County to test the feasibility of TDR. Lumberton was so pleased with the success of the first phase of this TDR program that it adopted a second phase to preserve additional sending areas. The State of New Jersey was also impressed and adopted legislation in 2004 allowing communities throughout the state to use TDR (Pruetz 2003).

Chesterfield Township adopted Burlington County's second municipal TDR program. The township worked closely with developers and other stakeholders on a detailed plan for its neo-traditional receiving area, Old York Village. As of 2007, the program had saved 3,200 acres of farmland, more land than any other municipal level TDR program in the country had saved (Pruetz and Standridge 2009; Walls and McConnell 2007). The program has also won several awards, including a National Outstanding Planning for a Program Award from the Ameri-can Planning Association (Chesterfield 2011).

In addition to preserving farmland, Burlington County and its partners have achieved remarkable success at protecting natural resources, parkland, and other open space. The county's park system includes unique recreational spaces, such as Historic Smithville Park, a relatively intact 19th-century industrial town, and the Rancocas Creek Canoe Trail, connecting parks and other points of interest along 30 miles of Rancocas Creek. The parks system is supported by the county's Farm-land, Open Space and Historic Preservation Trust Fund. In addition, 14 munici-palities in Burlington County also have a dedicated tax supporting open space trust funds (Burlington County 2002).

Roughly half of the Pinelands portion of Burlington County is already protected by an assortment of government agencies and private nonprofit organizations:

- Wharton State Forest features the restored village of Batsto, which thrived from 1766 to 1867 as a bog iron and glassmaking industrial center (NJDEP 2010d).
- Brendan T. Byrne State Forest, formerly named Lebanon State Forest, is home to Whitesbog Village, the center of one of the largest cranberry plantations in New Jersey and the birthplace of the modern strain of commercial blueberries (NJDEP 2010b).
- Bass River State Forest includes a segment of the 50-mile Batona Trail that passes several ghost towns as it links Bass River State Forest with the Wharton and Brendan T. Byrne state forests (NJDEP 2010a).
- Rancocas State Park incorporates a replica of a Native American village run by the Powhatan Renape Nation (NJDEP 2010c).

To date, Burlington County has preserved more than 50,000 acres of farmland, making theirs the seventh-most successful farmland preservation program in the nation (*Farmland Preservation Report* 2010). That achievement largely resulted from a 1998 plan that prioritized farmland preservation and instituted creative ways of making finite funding go as far as possible. Based on that accomplishment, Burlington County is well positioned to reach its 2009 Farmland Preservation Plan goal of preserving another 20,000 acres by the year 2018.

Figure 6-3.   In Historic Smithville Park, Burlington County has converted a 19th-century mill pond into a sanctuary.

7

CHESTER COUNTY, PENNSYLVANIA

The idyllic landscape of Chester County, Pennsylvania, survived some of the fiercest fighting of the Revolutionary War. Today, Chester County battles the sprawl advancing from Philadelphia, only 20 miles to the east. To date, the county has preserved more than 100,000 acres of natural terrain and farmland, often accented by historic cottages and stone walls. The county has been remarkably victorious due largely to a progression of sophisticated plans implemented by land trusts, local governments, federal agencies, and state programs, as well as Chester County itself.

Chester County adopted its first open space plan in 1982 and followed that in 1987 with its first open space bond. In 1989, Chester County voters approved a $50 million open space bond that funded grants for open space planning in Chester County municipalities. The bond also allowed Chester County to put its preservation policies into action. As described below, Chester County has continued to invest in the implementation of its preservation goals using a highly collaborative approach, resulting in a 2008 County Leadership in Conservation Award from the Trust for Public Land and the National Association of Counties (Trust for Public Land 2008).

In 1996, Chester County adopted Landscapes, a policy element that established a simple land-use philosophy: Encourage development in designated urban, suburban, and rural centers rather than areas designated as rural or natural landscapes. In 2002, the county added important details to this land-use philosophy by adopting Linking Landscapes: A Plan for the Protected Open Space

Network in Chester County, Pennsylvania. As the title suggests, this plan aims to link open space of every kind, including private farmland, land trust preserves, and publicly owned parks and refuges.

Significantly, Linking Landscapes focuses on protecting open space forever. Unlike communities that rely on zoning to accomplish open space protection, in Linking Landscapes, Chester County clearly acknowledges the bitter truth that zoning is insufficient for open space preservation, because it is subject to variances and zoning amendments. To that end, Linking Landscapes takes the radical step of setting a target of permanently preserving 5,000 acres of open space *every year* (Chester County 2002).

The window of opportunity for open space preservation in Chester County is rapidly closing. Linking Landscapes offers the following calculations to justify its ambitious preservation goals. When this open space element was prepared in 2000, 15 percent of the county's land area was preserved open space, 40 percent was developed, and 5,000 acres were being converted from open space to development each year. If the county achieves its goal of preserving 5,000 acres per year, in 2020, 60 percent of the county will be developed, 35 percent will be preserved, and the remaining 5 percent will be unprotected open space. Linking Landscapes emphasizes that reaching this goal will require the combined efforts of the Agricultural Land Preservation Board, home owners associations, private land trusts, and land-acquisition programs at the federal, state, county, and municipal levels (Chester County 2002).

The Chester County Agricultural Land Preservation Board administers the Pennsylvania Agricultural Conservation Easement (ACE) Program as well as the Chester County Challenge Grant Program. In the ACE Program, the board offers to purchase development rights based on Land Evaluation and Site Assessment (LESA) rankings. In the Challenge Grant Program, Chester County pays 50 percent of the agreed-upon easement price when the remainder is paid by a municipal program, the Commonwealth of Pennsylvania, or a land trust, or is donated by the landowners themselves. As of August 2010, these two programs had preserved a total of 27,185 acres (Agricultural Land Preservation Board 2010). However, the preservation programs of municipalities and private nonprofit land trusts more than double that amount, producing a grand total of more than 58,715 acres of permanently preserved farmland (*Farmland Preservation Report* 2010).

Private nonprofit land trusts have been extremely effective protectors of open space in Chester County. In Linking Landscapes, Chester County recognizes this success by essentially relying on land trusts to meet 30 percent of its annual preservation goal, or 1,500 acres per year. Some believe that the remarkable track record of land trusts there can be traced to the example established in 1984 when the Brandywine Conservancy orchestrated the preservation of the 5,367-acre King Ranch. Most of the King Ranch is preserved by easement, but 771 acres of the

Figure 7-1.   Chester County ranks in the top five locally operated farmland preservation programs in the nation.

most environmentally significant land were donated and have since become the conservancy's Laurels Preserve (Gilmour 2009). In total, the Brandywine Conservancy holds more than 400 conservation easements on more than 43,000 acres of land in Chester County and two adjacent counties (Brandywine Conservancy 2010).

After seeing how effective private land trusts could be, Chester County created the Preservation Partnership Program, which provides funding to nonprofit conservation organizations for projects that preserve significant natural, historic, cultural, and agricultural resources. The organizations submit applications to compete for funding based on program criteria. Generally, the county grants up to 50 percent of the appraised market value of a property proposed for acquisition and

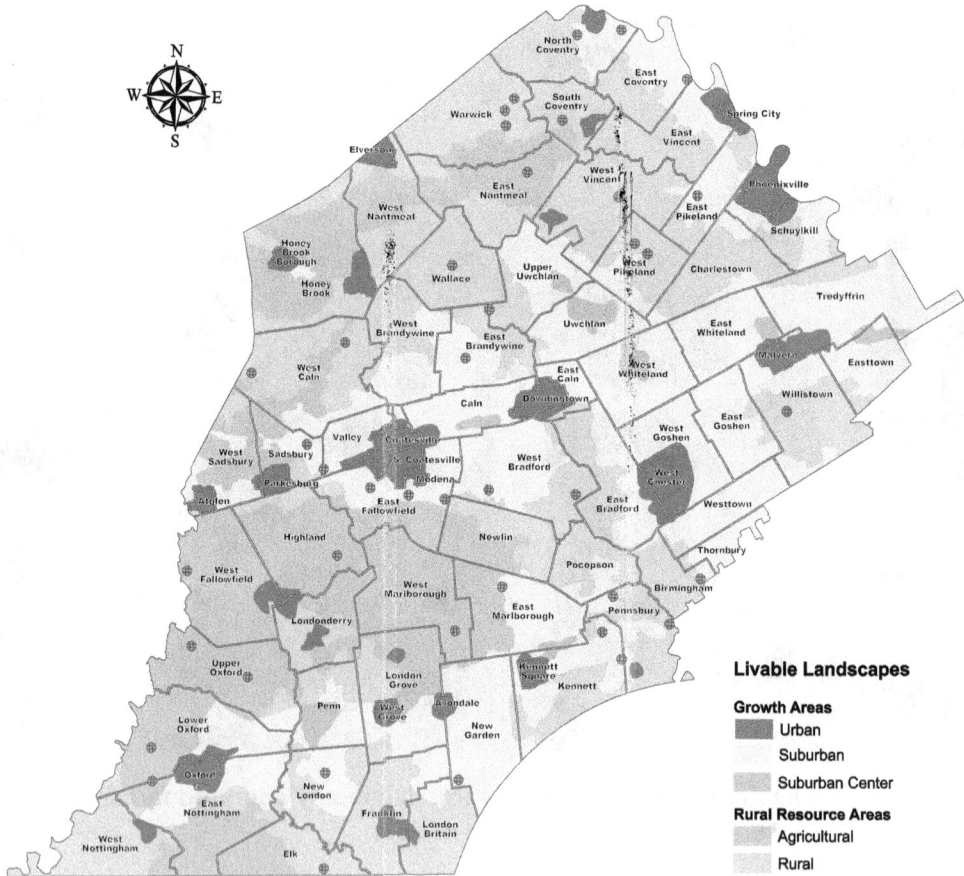

Livable Landscapes

Livable Landscapes

Growth Areas
- Urban
- Suburban
- Suburban Center

Rural Resource Areas
- Agricultural
- Rural
- Rural Center

Overlay Features
- Villages
- Municipalities

Landscapes2
Our Growth & Preservation Plan
CHESTER COUNTY | PENNSYLVANIA
http://www.landscapes2.org

For more information, please contact:
Chester County Planning Commission
http://www.chesco.org/planning
landscapes2@chesco.org

Miles
0   1.25   2.5   5

Adopted November 2009

Figure 7-2.   Chester County aims to permanently preserve 5,000 acres of open space every year. [Source: Chester County]

up to 33 percent of the appraised easement value of an agricultural easement (Chester County 2008). This program allows the county to stretch limited dollars by encouraging landowners to offer bargain sales and by matching funding from private sources as well as the municipal open space programs discussed below. Because the funding flows through private land trusts, this program is also able to preserve farms owned by Amish families, who often decline to receive funds directly from government sources (Tracy 2010).

Since 1989, the Preservation Partnership Program has preserved more than 6,200 acres of land. The county's cost has been less than $36 million, only 27 percent of the total cost of these projects. Through this program, Chester County has partnered with 16 nonprofit organizations, including the Brandywine Conservancy, the Nature Conservancy, the Natural Lands Trust, and the French and Pickering Creeks Conservation Trust (Chester County 2010a).

Formed in 1967, the French and Pickering Creeks Conservation Trust has preserved more than 9,000 acres and placed more than 60 sites in the National Register of Historic Places, and it is steadily assembling trails that link these protected properties throughout northern Chester County (French and Pickering Creeks Conservation Trust 2010). The Natural Lands Trust, formed in 1953, owns and manages 41 nature preserves in the Philadelphia region, including the 1,263-acre ChesLen Preserve, which features Stargazer's Stone, the reference point used by Charles Mason and Jeremiah Dixon, of Mason-Dixon Line fame, when they performed their historic survey from 1764 and 1768 (Natural Lands Trust 2010). To celebrate and maintain public support for the Preservation Partnership Program, Chester County's Open Space Preservation Department prepared a nature preserve guide, which maps and describes 13 properties throughout the county preserved by this groundbreaking program (Chester County 2009a).

Chester County also provides matching grants to municipalities for the acquisition and development of local parks. As of 2010, this program had awarded more than $40 million to 68 municipalities, resulting in 5,425 acres of parkland (Chester County 2010b). In total, Chester County municipal parks protect more than 8,700 acres of open space (DVRPC 2008).

Municipalities in Pennsylvania can raise money for open space preservation using the 1996 amendment to the Pennsylvania Conservation and Land Development Act, better known as Act 153, which allows cities, boroughs, towns, and townships to hold referenda so that voters can approve increases in property tax and/or earned income tax to fund the preservation of significant farmland and natural areas. As of 2009, the voters in 29 municipalities in Chester County had approved these referenda, more communities than in any other Pennsylvania county in the Philadelphia region (DVRPC 2009).

Figure 7-3.   The French and Pickering Creeks Conservation Trust has preserved more than 9,000 acres of open space.

Chester County municipalities have been very successful at leveraging their Act 153 revenue. A study of 12 municipalities revealed that an average of $5 million in annual open space taxes leveraged an additional $26 million in funding and resulted in the preservation of 6,000 acres (Brandywine Conservancy 2009). For example, the voters of East Bradford Township approved an open space tax of 0.25 percent on earned income, which generates between $1 million and $2 million per year for its open space fund. Today, roughly 40 percent of the township's land area has been preserved by matching this fund with state and county grants and by combining this public sector action with ongoing preservation work by the Natural Lands Trust, the North American Land Trust, and the Brandywine Conservancy (East Bradford Township 2009). Similarly, Franklin Township matched $825,000 of Act 153 funding with federal, state, and county grants, as well as landowner donations, succeeding in securing more than six times that amount in total preservation buying power (Tracy 2010; Brandywine Conservancy 2009).

In addition to assisting municipalities with farmland preservation and open space protection, Chester County itself has protected 5,956 acres of open space, including land in five county parks (DVRPC 2008). The county and municipal parks are supplemented by an additional 8,506 acres of open space protected by the state and federal government, including portions of French Creek State Park and Hopewell Furnace National Historic Site (DVRPC 2008).

Linking Landscapes reported the grim news that development was converting 5,000 acres of rural land in Chester County every year. That plan set a goal of permanently preserving an equal amount of land, 5,000 acres, every year through the combined efforts of the Agricultural Land Preservation Board, home owners associations, private land trusts, and land-acquisition programs at the federal, state, county, and municipal levels. Although ambitious, it is an achievable target considering that by 2006, this partnership had already preserved more than 100,000 acres, or roughly 20 percent of Chester County's total land area (Chester County 2009b).

8

COLLIER COUNTY, FLORIDA

Collier County, Florida, has recovered from some early environmental missteps to become one of the most nature-friendly jurisdictions in the United States. Today more than 80 percent of the county is protected through the efforts of the State of Florida, federal agencies, the National Audubon Society, and other conservation groups, as well as Collier County itself. Much of this success can be credited to county plans that stress the need for long-term protection of natural resources to promote health, economic vitality, and quality of life, as well as ecosystem restoration.

Collier County lies on the Gulf Coast, surrounding the City of Naples. Its natural features have been under constant threat since the 19th century, when plume hunters there killed tropical birds to supply colorful feathers for hat decorations popular at the time. For the first half of the 20th century, logging companies clear cut most of the old growth bald cypress trees that once towered over Collier County. By 1954, the only remaining groves of virgin bald cypress trees stood in Corkscrew Swamp, owned by the Lee Tidewater Cypress Company and Collier Enterprises. These owners both sold and donated much of the land that is now the Audubon Society's 13,000-acre Corkscrew Swamp Sanctuary. Today the sanctuary preserves the largest virgin bald cypress forest in North America, the biggest nesting colony of wood storks, and habitat for numerous other endangered species (Buchheister 1967).

The land that is now preserved as Collier-Seminole State Park was once owned by Barron Collier, a wealthy advertising tycoon who bought more than one million acres of southwest Florida in the early part of the 20th century. Collier funded the completion of the Tamiami Trail, the cross-Everglades highway that finally linked Florida's Atlantic and Gulf coasts in 1928. Collier originally envisioned a national park encompassing land near Naples known as Royal Palm Hammock. But the land instead became a county park and was turned over to the state in 1947. Today, the park preserves one of Florida's three original native stands of royal palm and serves as the final resting place of the Bay City Walking Dredge, the machine that built the Tamiami Trail and paved the way for Collier County's rapid growth (Florida State Parks 2008).

The county's population, which now exceeds 315,000, more than doubled in the 1960s. At the peak of the real estate fever, the Gulf American Land Corporation, then the largest land sales firm in the United States, broke ground on Golden Gates Estates, which was supposed to become America's largest subdivision. Before going bankrupt, Gulf American dug 48 miles of canals and built 290 miles of roads. These "improvements" disrupted the natural flow of water and left a distressed landscape that was prone to flooding in the rainy season yet susceptible to invasive species and wildfires. Due to aggressive and deceptive sales practices, these pieces of the Florida dream were sold to thousands of small property owners, who ultimately had little to show for their investment. In addition to prompting some of the massive open space acquisition programs described below, this episode of recklessness set the stage for a new era of planning in Collier County (Florida Division of Forestry 2010).

To avoid future environmental disasters, Collier County planners considered ways of preserving natural areas for their ecosystem services while respecting private property rights. As one solution, the county adopted one of the first environmental-preservation transfer of development rights (TDR) programs in the United States in 1974. This program applies Special Treatment (ST) regulations to critical natural resources, such as barrier islands, mangroves, marshes, beaches, and other types of environmentally sensitive land. Affected landowners can get relief from these ST requirements by transferring development potential to sites that are appropriate for growth (Spagna 1979).

The 1983 Collier County Comprehensive Plan established a land-use strategy that is still the foundation of the Growth Management Plan in effect in 2010. The current Future Land Use Element begins by establishing the underlying concept of natural resource system preservation and demonstrating how that concept guides most significant land-use decisions. Specifically, areas designated as urban absorb concentrated growth and allow for the protection of areas of greatest environmental sensitivity. Just beyond the urban areas lie the Rural Fringe Mixed Use District and the Rural Lands Stewardship Area, which offer additional TDR mechanisms, discussed below, to protect critical resources identified as natural resource protection area overlays, flow way stewardship areas, and habitat stewardship areas. As shown on the Future Land Use Map, the natural resource systems generally lying beyond the Rural Fringe and the Rural Lands Stewardship Area have largely been protected by state and federal preservation programs, as discussed below (Collier County 2010a).

In 1985, a plan was established to buy part of the abandoned South Golden Gate Estates from 17,000 landowners, using Florida's Conservation and Recreation Lands (CARL) funds, supplemented by $25 million from the federal government. Today, the Picayune Strand State Forest preserves 78,615 acres of land in the heart of the Big Cypress Basin. A program to repair the hydrological damage caused by Gulf American's ill-conceived canals and roads will benefit the ecological integrity of the nearby Ten Thousand Islands National Wildlife Refuge and Rookery Bay National Estuarine Research Reserve, as well as the Picayune Strand (Florida Division of Forestry 2010).

The Big Cypress watershed was originally supposed to be part of Everglades National Park even though Big Cypress has a slightly different topography and ecosystem from the neighboring Everglades. However, when Everglades National Park was finally dedicated in 1947, Big Cypress was not included. For the next two decades, the private owners of Big Cypress Basin logged most of the remaining timber, began drilling for oil, and engaged in land speculation as the Gulf American Land Corporation dredged canals and built roads for its doomed South Golden Gate subdivision to the west. In 1968, swampland prices jumped tenfold at the unveiling of plans to build the world's largest airport there, with an adjoining city for 150,000 people. Newspapers and magazines wrote extensively about the airport's impacts. Average Americans paid attention to these concerns since the United States was passing through a phase of heightened environmental consciousness, as demonstrated by the adoption of the National Environmental Policy Act in 1969 and the first Earth Day in 1970. In 1973, Florida pledged $40 million toward the preservation of this fragile land. And in 1974, the U.S. Congress authorized an additional $150 million. Today, Big Cypress National Preserve protects 728,000 acres, of which 574,848 acres are within Collier County (Butcher 2010).

Fakahatchee Strand is one of the best examples of a subtropical strand swamp in the country, featuring the greatest concentration and diversity of native orchids on the continent as well as numerous endangered species. The area was logged by the Lee Tidewater Cypress Company and then purchased in 1966 by Gulf American Land Company for the ill-fated South Golden Gate Estates. In 1972, Florida voters approved a $240 million open space bond and launched the state's first major environmental land preservation effort: the Environmentally Endangered Lands (EEL) program. In addition to acquisition efforts throughout the state, the EEL program acquired 34,727 acres in the Fakahatchee Strand. Additional funding came from Florida's CARL program and passage of Preservation 2000, a 10-year, $3 billion land preservation fund started in 1990. In 2000,

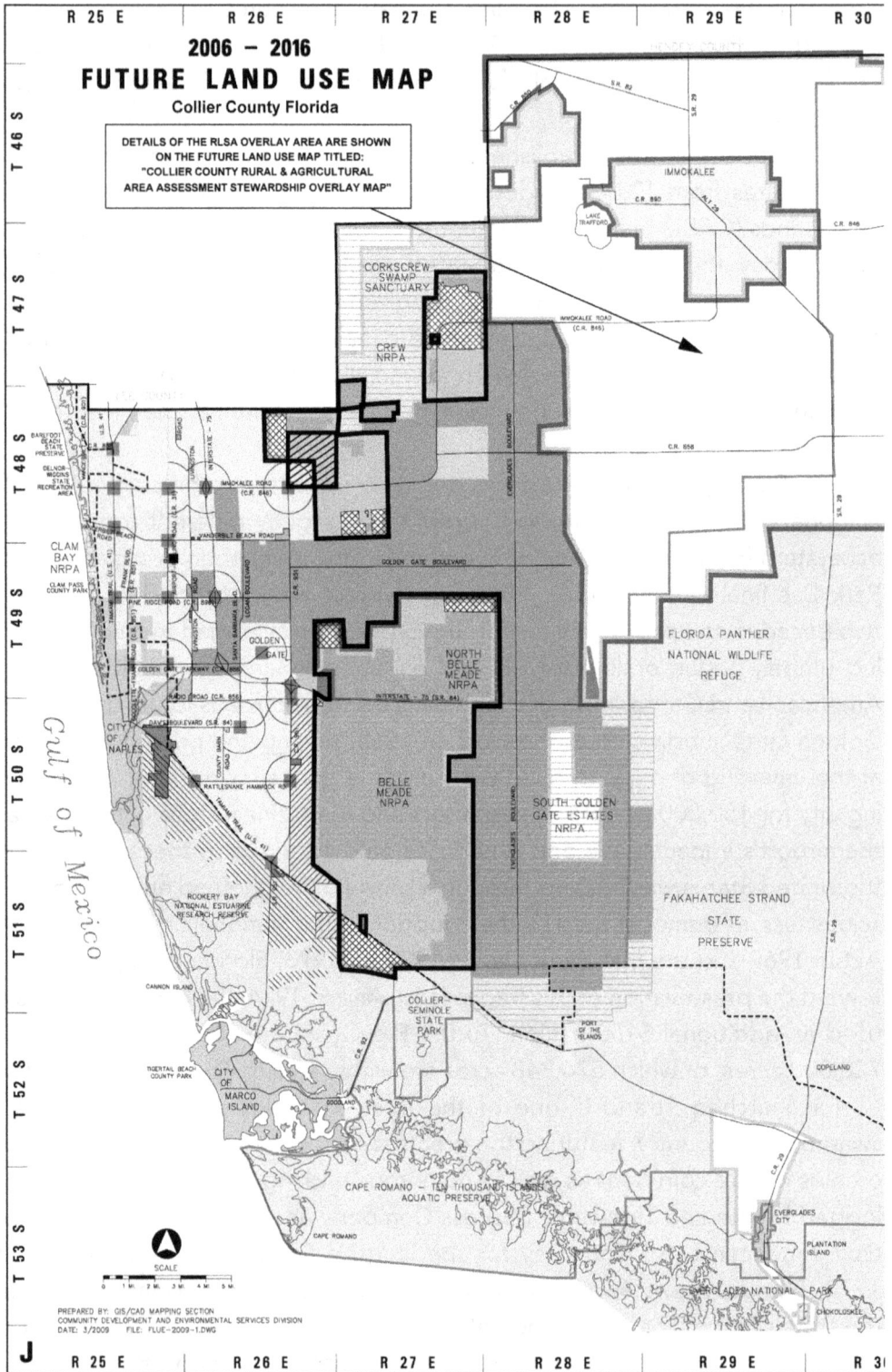

Figure 8-1. Collier County's growth management plan promotes natural resource conservation and uses preserved open space to maintain compact urban areas. *[Source: Collier County]*

URBAN DESIGNATION

MIXED USE DISTRICT

- URBAN RESIDENTIAL SUBDISTRICT
- RESIDENTIAL DENSITY BANDS
- URBAN COASTAL FRINGE SUBDISTRICT
- URBAN RESIDENTIAL FRINGE SUBDISTRICT

BUSINESS PARK SUBDISTRICT
OFFICE AND INFILL COMMERCIAL SUBDISTRICT
PUD NEIGHBORHOOD VILLAGE CENTER SUBDISTRICT
RESIDENTIAL MIXED USE NEIGHBORHOOD SUBDISTRICT

- ORANGE BLOSSOM MIXED USE SUBDISTRICT
- VANDERBILT BEACH / COLLIER BLVD. COMMERCIAL SUBDISTRICT
- HENDERSON CREEK MIXED USE SUBDISTRICT

RESEARCH AND TECHNOLOGY PARK SUBDISTRICT

- BUCKLEY MIXED USE SUBDISTRICT

COMMERCIAL MIXED USE SUBDISTRICT

- DAVIS BOULEVARD / COUNTY BARN ROAD MIXED USE SUBDISTRICT
- LIVINGSTON ROAD / RADIO ROAD COMMERCIAL INFILL SUBDISTRICT
- VANDERBILT BEACH ROAD NEIGHBORHOOD COMMERCIAL SUBDISTRICT
- COLLIER BOULEVARD COMMUNITY FACILITY SUBDISTRICT

INDUSTRIAL DISTRICT

BUSINESS PARK SUBDISTRICT
RESEARCH AND TECHNOLOGY PARK SUBDISTRICT

COMMERCIAL DISTRICT

- MIXED USE ACTIVITY CENTER SUBDISTRICT
- INTERCHANGE ACTIVITY CENTER SUBDISTRICT
- LIVINGSTON / PINE RIDGE COMMERCIAL INFILL SUBDISTRICT

BUSINESS PARK SUBDISTRICT
RESEARCH AND TECHNOLOGY PARK SUBDISTRICT

- LIVINGSTON ROAD / EATONWOOD LANE COMMERCIAL INFILL SUBDISTRICT
- LIVINGSTON ROAD COMMERCIAL INFILL SUBDISTRICT

COMMERCIAL MIXED USE SUBDISTRICT

- LIVINGSTON ROAD / VETERAN'S MEMORIAL BLVD. COMMERCIAL INFILL SUBDISTRICT
- GOODLETTE / PINE RIDGE COMMERCIAL INFILL SUBDISTRICT
- ORANGE BLOSSOM / AIRPORT CROSSROADS COMMERCIAL SUBDISTRICT

AGRICULTURAL / RURAL DESIGNATION

- AGRICULTURAL/RURAL MIXED USE DISTRICT

RURAL COMMERCIAL SUBDISTRICT

- CORKSCREW ISLAND NEIGHBORHOOD COMMERCIAL SUBDISTRICT

RURAL FRINGE MIXED USE DISTRICT

- RECEIVING LANDS
- SENDING LANDS
- NEUTRAL LANDS

- RURAL SETTLEMENT AREA DISTRICT
- RURAL INDUSTRIAL DISTRICT

ESTATES DESIGNATION

CONSERVATION DESIGNATION

OVERLAYS AND SPECIAL FEATURES

- INCORPORATED AREAS
- COASTAL HIGH HAZARD AREA
- TRAFFIC CONGESTION BOUNDARY
- AREA OF CRITICAL STATE CONCERN OVERLAY
- AIRPORT NOISE AREA OVERLAY
- NATURAL RESOURCE PROTECTION AREA (NRPA) OVERLAY
- BAYSHORE/GATEWAY TRIANGLE REDEVELOPMENT OVERLAY
- RURAL LANDS STEWARDSHIP AREA OVERLAY
- URBAN-RURAL FRINGE TRANSITION ZONE OVERLAY
- NORTH BELLE MEADE OVERLAY

NOTE :

(1) THIS MAP CAN NOT BE INTERPRETED WITHOUT THE GOALS, OBJECTIVES AND POLICIES OF THE COLLIER COUNTY GROWTH MANAGEMENT PLAN.
(2) THE FUTURE LAND USE MAP SERIES INCLUDES NUMEROUS MAPS IN ADDITION TO THIS COUNTYWIDE FUTURE LAND USE MAP; THESE MAPS ARE LISTED AND LOCATED AT THE END OF THE FUTURE LAND USE ELEMENT TEXT.
(3) MOST SUBDISTRICTS AS DEPICTED MAY NOT BE TO SCALE. THE FUTURE LAND USE MAP SERIES DEPICTS THESE SUBDISTRICTS TO SCALE.
(4) THE CONSERVATION DESIGNATION IS SUBJECT TO CHANGE AS AREAS ARE ACQUIRED AND MAY INCLUDE OUTPARCELS.
(5) REFER TO THE GOLDEN GATE AREA MASTER PLAN AND THE IMMOKALEE AREA MASTER PLAN FOR FUTURE LAND USE MAPS OF THOSE COMMUNITIES.

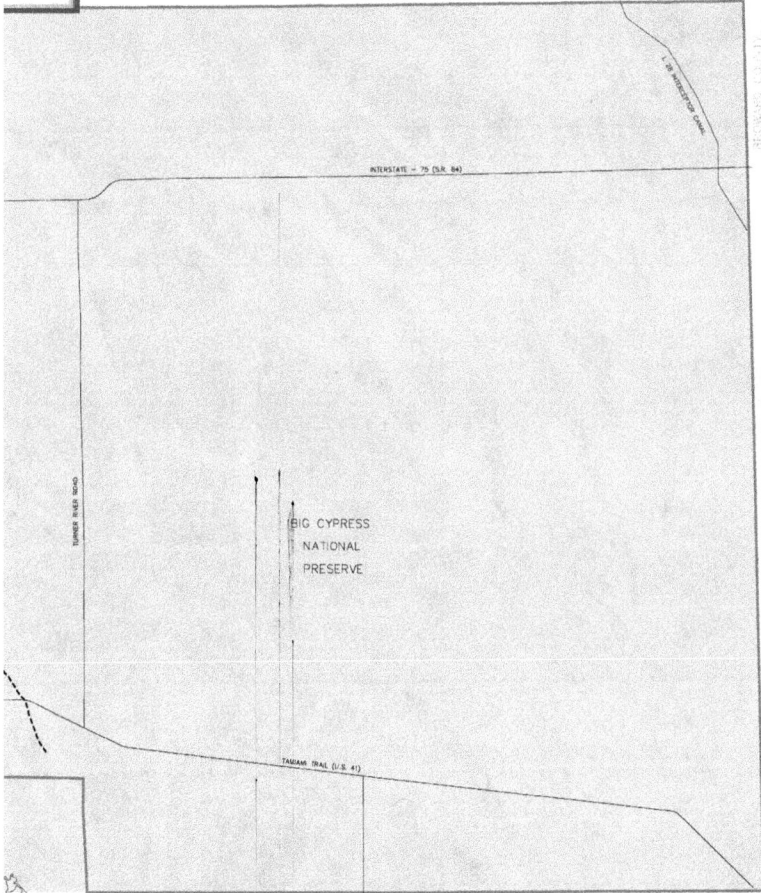

INTERSTATE - 75 (S.R. 84)

BIG CYPRESS NATIONAL PRESERVE

TAMIAMI TRAIL (U.S. 41)

FUTURE LAND USE MAP	
ADOPTED –	JANUARY, 1989
AMENDED –	JANUARY, 1990
AMENDED –	FEBRUARY, 1991
AMENDED –	MAY, 1992
AMENDED –	MAY, 1993
AMENDED –	APRIL, 1994
AMENDED –	OCTOBER, 1997
AMENDED –	JANUARY, 1998
AMENDED –	FEBRUARY, 1999
AMENDED –	FEBRUARY, 2000
AMENDED –	MAY, 2000
AMENDED –	DECEMBER, 2000
AMENDED –	MARCH, 2001
AMENDED –	MAY 14, 2002 (Ord. No. 2002-24)
AMENDED –	JUNE 19, 2002 (ORD. NO. 2002-32)
AMENDED –	OCTOBER 22, 2002 (Ord. No. 2002-54)
AMENDED –	FEBRUARY 11, 2003 (Ord. No. 2003-7)
AMENDED –	SEPTEMBER 9, 2003 (Ord. No. 2003-43)
AMENDED –	SEPTEMBER 10, 2003 (Ord. No. 2003-44)
AMENDED –	DECEMBER 16, 2003 (Ord. No. 2003-67)
AMENDED –	OCTOBER 26, 2004 (Ord. No. 2004-71)
AMENDED –	JUNE 7, 2005 (Ord. No. 2005-25)
AMENDED –	JANUARY 25, 2007 (Ord. No. 2007-18)
AMENDED –	DECEMBER 4, 2007 (Ord. No. 2007-78,79,81)
AMENDED –	OCTOBER 14, 2008 (Ord. No. 2008-57,58,59)

T 46 S   T 47 S   T 48 S   T 49 S   T 50 S   T 51 S   T 52 S   T 53 S

Figure 8-2.   An epiphyte clings to a tree in Rookery Bay National Estuarine
                Research Reserve.

Florida continued the success of Preservation 2000 with another 10-year, $3 billion land acquisition fund named Florida Forever. Gulf American Land Company also transferred title to almost 10,000 acres of the Fakahatchee Strand as part of a settlement agreement rising out of allegations that the company had committed dredging violations in another part of the state. As of 2007, 75,000 acres were preserved in this park (Friends of Fakahatchee Strand State Preserve 2005; Florida Department of Environmental Protection 2010).

Rookery Bay is one of only 25 national estuarine reserves in the United States. Together with two adjacent Florida aquatic preserves, Rookery Bay protects the habitat of the manatee and other endangered species within 112,000 acres of relatively undisturbed mangrove forest on Collier County's southwest coast (Florida Department of Environmental Protection 2009). Preservation efforts began there in 1964, when a proposed road through Rookery Bay roused citizens and prompted the formation of the Conservancy of Southwest Florida. The conservancy led repeated fundraising campaigns, orchestrated land swaps, and was largely responsible for the 1978 designation of Rookery Bay as a national estuarine reserve (Rookery Bay National Estuarine Research Reserve 2010).

In 1996, the Arizona-Florida Land Exchange Act was used to swap property in Arizona for 108,000 acres of land in Collier County. Of that total, 35,000 acres were used to create Ten Thousand Islands National Wildlife Refuge, which now preserves part of the largest remaining mangrove forest in North America (U.S. Fish and Wildlife Service 2010). Another portion of the exchange expanded Big Cypress National Preserve, and the remainder was used to enlarge the Florida Panther National Wildlife Refuge, where the number of these endangered cats has slowly been increased from 50 to 80 individuals (U.S. Fish and Wildlife Service 2005).

In 1999, litigation loomed that would decide the fate of 300 square miles of land in northeastern Collier County surrounding the city of Immokalee. The county resolved the controversy between landowners and environmentalists by adopting a sophisticated form of TDR called rural lands stewardship. In this approach, transferable development credits are issued based on the level of preservation chosen by the property owner and the significance of each specific acre for habitat, flow way, and other environmental benefits. To date, this technique has preserved more than 54,000 acres of land, and developers have used the credits generated by this preservation to build the smart-growth new town of Ave Maria, which is already the home to a university and is planned to ultimately accommodate 11,000 dwelling units (Collier County 2011a). In 2004, Collier County added a third TDR program, designed to restore as well as preserve wetlands, habitat, and other environmentally sensitive land in the Rural Fringe District, which covers roughly 90,000 acres of land. To date, the rural fringe TDR program has preserved more than 3,500 acres (Collier County 2011b).

Figure 8-3.   Tigertail Beach County Park is one of the best birding sites in southwestern Florida.

Despite the vast amount of publicly protected open space in Collier County, the citizens voted in 2002 to increase their property taxes for 10 years to support Conservation Collier, a program to protect rare and threatened ecosystems, particularly in western parts of the county. In 2006, the voters repeated their support for Conservation Collier by removing the original funding limits, thereby allowing the enhanced tax to raise an estimated $189 million. To date, this program has spent more than $100 million preserving more than 4,000 acres of environmentally sensitive land in 19 separate preserves (Collier County 2010b).

Collier County's open space inventory also includes a 26,000-acre portion of Everglades National Park, a 1,780-acre county-and-city park system, regional watersheds, a state forest, and Delnor-Wiggins Pass State Park, which protects a beloved beach and estuary complex north of Naples. When the land protected by Conservation Collier, TDR programs, and private conservancies are added in, the open space under permanent protection exceeds one million acres in total (Collier County 2010c). With roughly 80 percent of its total land area now permanently preserved, Collier County has come a long way since the 1960s, when it was one of America's most endangered places.

9

CONTRA COSTA COUNTY, CALIFORNIA

One-fifth of Contra Costa County's total land area is preserved by parks, watershed lands, and conservation easements, a remarkable achievement considering the county's location on "the opposite shore" from the City of San Francisco, at the center of a booming nine-county region with a population of more than seven million people. Much of the credit goes to the East Bay Regional Park District, the largest regional park agency in the United States and the recipient of American Planning Association's National Planning Landmark Award. Additional contributions to the county's open space inventory, including Mount Diablo State Park, have come from a multispecies habitat conservation plan and from the State of California. Land preservation efforts by all levels of government have been greatly facilitated by a succession of plans that establish and maintain a county-wide urban limit line (ULL) reserving most of the county's land for agriculture, open space, wetlands, parks, and other nonurban uses.

Mount Diablo is Contra Costa County's most prominent natural landmark and the main target of early land preservation efforts here. Despite a relatively modest elevation (3,849 feet), Mount Diablo is nevertheless taller than the surrounding landscape, creating a spectacular viewshed. Native Americans considered Mount Diablo sacred and made pilgrimages to its summit for ceremonies. After California achieved statehood in 1850, curiosity seekers scaled it for views of the Coast Ranges, San Francisco Bay, and on a clear day, California's Central Valley and the Sierra Nevada mountain range. By 1874, stagecoaches were carrying tourists to the Mountain House Hotel, three miles from the top. In 1921, the state

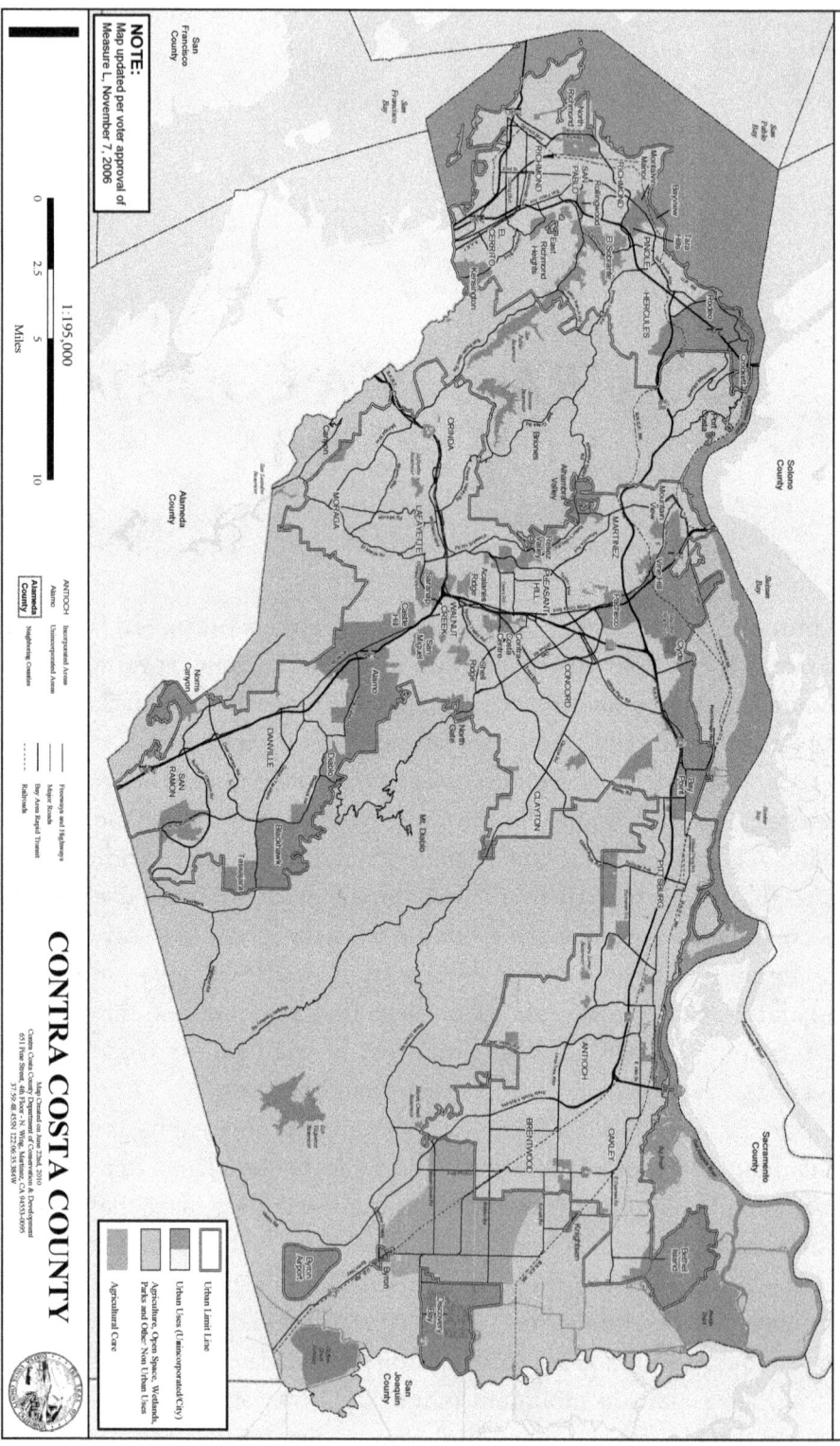

Urban Limit Line

1:195,000

0   2.5   5   10
Miles

CONTRA COSTA COUNTY

Map Created on June 22nd, 2010
Contra Costa County Department of Conservation & Development
651 Pine Street, 4th Floor, N. Wing, Martinez, CA 94553-0095
37.59.48.835N 122.06.53.384W

Urban Limit Line

Urban Uses (Unincorporated City)

Agriculture, Open Space, Wetlands, Parks and Other Non Urban Uses

Agricultural Core

ANTIOCH   Incorporated Areas
Alamo   Unincorporated Areas
Alameda County   Neighboring Counties

Freeways and Highways
Major Roads
Bay Area Rapid Transit
Railroads

Figure 9-1. A countywide urban limit line designates 35 percent of Contra Costa County's land for urban development and 65 percent for the preservation of natural resources, farmland, and rural open space. [Source: Contra Costa County]

began acquiring land on the mountain; it had assembled almost 7,000 acres by 1971. In that year, the grassroots organization Save Mount Diablo was formed; it led the effort to almost triple the size of Mount Diablo State Park over the next 40 years. Today the park's 20,000 acres are home to more than 400 species plus more than 60 miles of hiking and mountain-biking trails (California Department of Fish and Game 2010; California State Parks 2000; California State Parks 2010; Save Mount Diablo 2010).

In 1934, Contra Costa County was predominantly rural, and the board of supervisors declined to participate in the initial formation of the East Bay Regional Park District, fearing an erosion of the county's tax base (Ahrens 2006). As detailed in chapter 2, William Penn Mott Jr. took the helm of the East Bay Regional Park District in 1962, when its landholdings totaled 7,400 acres in adjacent Alameda County. Mott persistently worked with the district's public information director, Richard Trudeau, and Contra Costa County attorney John Nejedly to overcome the Contra Costa County Board of Supervisors' aversion to a separately elected park board with taxing authority. Finally, the supervisors gave a green light to putting expansion of the park district on the ballot. In 1964, the voters of western Contra Costa County agreed to join the district (McCreery 2010).

Immediately following this successful ballot measure, the district acquired significant properties in Contra Costa County, including the 6,117-acre Briones Regional Park and 5,342-acre Las Trampas Regional Wilderness. By the time William Penn Mott Jr. left to become the director of the California State Parks department in 1967, the district had grown to 22 parks with more than 17,000 acres in two counties (McCreery 2010). Under its new general manager, Trudeau, the district continued acquiring properties in Contra Costa County, including land for its 5,375-acre Black Diamond Mines Regional Preserve, which safeguards the remnants of five coal-mining towns that operated in the last half of the 19th century. In 1981, the eastern portion of Contra Costa County was annexed to the district (East Bay Regional Park District 2010a; McCreery 2010).

The East Bay Regional Park District has skillfully used its planning process to build public support for open space preservation. The proposed acquisitions in the district's 1989 master plan motivated voters to approve Measure AA, a $225 million parks bond that secured more than 34,000 acres and added more than 100 miles to the district's trail system. To finance the district's 2007 plan, the voters approved Measure WW, the largest local park bond measure in the United States, generating an additional $500 million for open space preservation (East Bay Regional Park District 2010a; Kent 2009; McCreery 2010). With the passage of Measure WW, the district is well positioned to retain its title as the largest regional park system in the nation, offering roughly 50,000 acres of parkland in Contra Costa County alone (East Bay Regional Park District 2000; East Bay Regional Park District 2010b).

In addition to the state and the East Bay Regional Park District, other agencies are also preserving Contra Costa County land. The National Park Service manages the Rosie the Riveter / World War II Home Front National Historic Park as well as two national historic sites. One historic site near the town of Danville preserves the home of playwright Eugene O'Neill. The other, in the city of Martinez, preserves the Victorian home of naturalist John Muir (National Park Service 2010).

Despite their remarkable successes, park agencies alone could not independently control the overwhelming growth pressure generated in the San Francisco

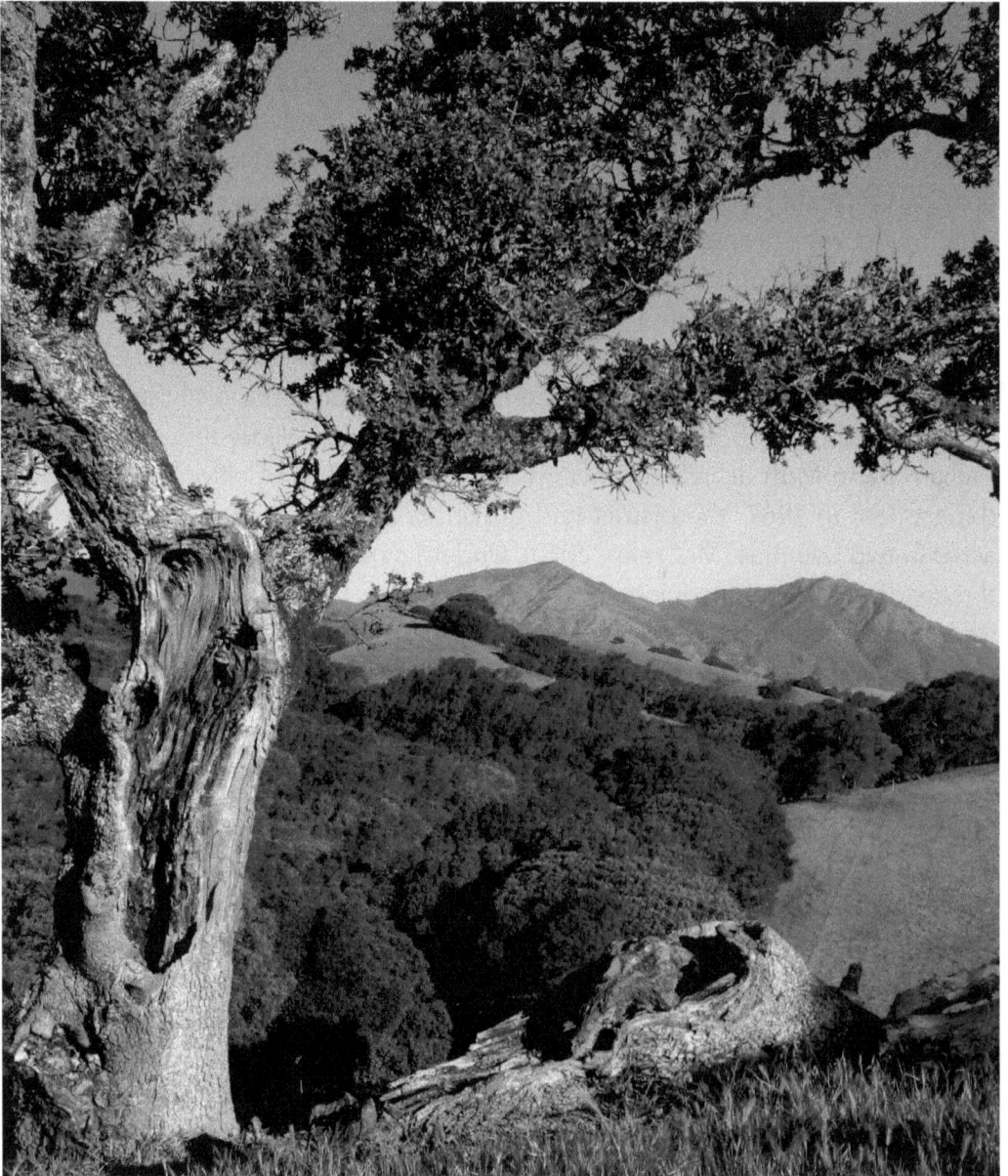

Figure 9-2.   Morgan Territory Regional Preserve offers distant views of Mount Diablo.

Bay region. Between 1971 and 1996, Contra Costa County lost one-half of its prime agricultural land. In 1984, county officials were urged to update the 1963 general plan by a coalition of conservation groups and the organization that later became the Greenbelt Alliance. The Contra Costa County Board of Supervisors started a comprehensive process known as the General Plan Congress that ultimately resulted in the 1990 general plan. The board also won voter approval for Measure C-1990, which created a countywide ULL designating 35 percent of the county's land area for urban development and 65 percent for rural preservation. The Greenbelt Alliance objected to several aspects of Measure C-1990, including the fact that the ULL could be expanded every five years by a four-to-one vote of the supervisors. However, in response to increasing antisprawl sentiment, a 2000 revision actually tightened the ULL, moving 14,000 acres in eastern Contra Costa County from the urban to the rural designation. As a result, the Trust for Public Land was able to transfer the Cowell Ranch, near Brentwood, to the California State Parks department (Greenbelt Alliance 2003).

The General Plan updates of 1995 and 2005 continued to follow the framework established in the 1990 general plan, with a countywide ULL and a mandate that at least 65 percent of all land in the county be preserved for agriculture, open space, wetlands, parks, and other nonurban uses (Contra Costa County 2005). In 2006, Measure L was approved, extending the ULL to 2026 and requiring voter approval to expand the ULL by more than 30 acres (League of Women Voters 2007).

Contra Costa County, the East Bay Regional Park District, and four cities have joined together to form the East Contra Costa County Habitat Conservation Plan Association (East Contra Costa County HCPA). By 2007, the East Contra Costa County Habitat Conservation Plan/Natural Community Conservation Plan was adopted, and the jurisdictions within its 175,000-acre planning area approved the ordinances needed for implementation. Under this plan, up to 30,300 acres will be preserved as habitat for 28 species, including the San Joaquin kit fox, Western burrowing owl, and California red-legged frog (East Contra Costa County Habitat Conservancy 2010). Over its 30-year life, this plan could cost more than $350 million. A large portion of this total will be funded by development fees ranging from $6,000 to $24,000 per acre of land developed (East Contra Costa County HCPA 2006).

To date, more than 100,000 acres of open space have been preserved in Contra Costa County through the East Bay Regional Park District, the California State Park system, other public agencies, and private conservation organizations, as well as the county itself. In addition, the county and four cities have recently teamed up to implement the largest habitat conservation plan in northern California (McCreery 2010). With more than 20 percent of its land area preserved so far, Contra Costa County is already a national conservation leader. Moreover, the stability of the county's general plan and ULL create a promising environment for future preservation efforts.

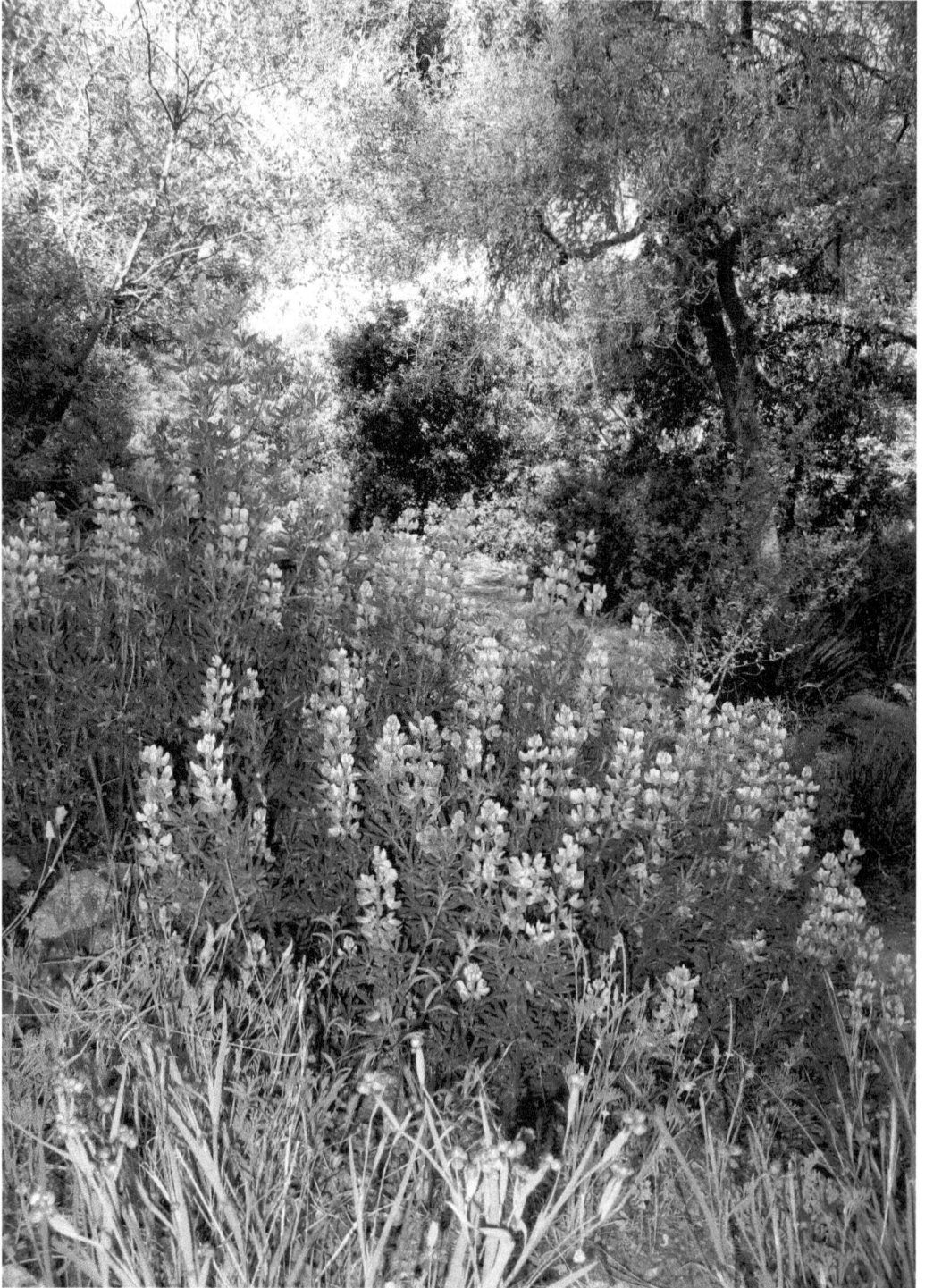

Figure 9-3.   Half of the parkland preserved by the East Bay Regional Park District lies within Contra Costa County.

10

DANE COUNTY, WISCONSIN

We abuse land because we regard it as a commodity belonging to us. When we see land as a community to which we belong, we may begin to use it with love and respect. There is no other way for land to survive the impact of mechanized man, nor for us to reap from it the esthetic harvest it is capable, under science, of contributing to culture. (Leopold 1949, xi)

These thoughts launch *A Sand County Almanac*, written by Aldo Leopold when he was a professor of ecology at the University of Wisconsin in the 1940s. Since then, newcomers have flocked to Madison for the campus, the state capital, and the beauty of surrounding Dane County's farms, lakes, and glacially carved terrain. Between 1950 and 2010, Dane County's population almost tripled. But despite this intense growth pressure, respect for the land is still alive and well there, as demonstrated by the preservation plans adopted and implemented by private conservation organizations and public agencies as well as Dane County itself.

In 1935, the Dane County Parks Division was formed and bought the first county park. By 2005, the system contained 25 parks, including the intriguingly named Nine Springs E-Way. The *E* in "E-Way" signifies the goal of promoting an understanding of educational, environmental, esthetic, and ecological concerns (Dane County 2006). Envisioned by Phil Lewis, emeritus professor of landscape architecture at the University of Wisconsin, the E-Way is a seven-mile corridor that incorporates wetlands, sedge meadows, native forests, and numerous other natural as well as man-made features (Dane County 2009).

In 1970, the same year that one of Wisconsin's U.S. senators, Gaylord Nelson, organized the first Earth Day, Dane County adopted its first Parks and Open Space Plan. In addition to traditional assessments of recreational needs, this plan created goals for the protection of Natural Resource Areas, places where valuable environmental land is preserved primarily for habitat protection and open space preservation. The county's comprehensive plan also looks to open space preservation as a means of connecting recreational nodes, separating communities, and guiding urban growth (Dane County 2007a).

The 1970 Parks and Open Space Plan identified two Natural Resource Areas: Cherokee Marsh, the largest wetland in Dane County; and Token Creek, a major tributary to Madison's iconic chain of lakes (Dane County 2006). Over time, the county's environmental protection goals have expanded significantly. The 2006–2011 plan identifies 25 Natural Resource Areas encompassing a total of 70,797 acres within the designated project area boundaries. The project area boundary for one resource area alone includes 11,630 acres of the watershed drained by Black Earth Creek, a nationally recognized trout stream. The county currently owns 3,379 acres of those 11,630 acres, with additional land in three county forests and two historical sites, including the Schumacher Farm, an outdoor museum depicting farm life in the early 20th century (Dane County 2006). In total, more than 35,000 acres of open space in Dane County are owned by public agencies, including more than 14,000 acres in state wildlife areas and more than 9,000 acres in city, town, and village parks (Wisconsin DNR 2005b).

The Wisconsin Department of Natural Resources (DNR) conducted a three-year inventory of the special natural places that, as the report puts it, make Wisconsin *Wisconsin*. The resulting *Wisconsin Land Legacy Report* identified 229 legacy places throughout the state, with 11 in Dane County, including several areas already targeted for preservation by Dane County's Natural Resource Area program (Wisconsin DNR 2005a). Dane County is working with the Wisconsin DNR and several other partners on two projects of regional scope identified in the *Land Legacy Report*. The Southwest Grasslands project aims to protect and conserve cultural and historic resources as well as grassland, savanna, streams, and rural farmland throughout southwestern Wisconsin, including portions of the townships of Blue Mounds and Perry, in western Dane County. Part of this work has already been initiated by the Nature Conservancy and others, as described below. The Glacial Heritage Area project proposes to protect similar resources in eastern Dane County as well as three adjacent counties (Dane County 2006).

Through its Conservation Fund Grant Program, Dane County coordinates with a coalition of environmental groups dedicated to preserving the Military Ridge Prairie Heritage Area (MRPHA). The 50,000-acre MRPHA gets its name from a prominent ridge that is now the site of the 40-mile Military Ridge State Trail connecting Dodgeville, Wisconsin, with the western suburbs of Madison.

Figure 10-1. Wildflowers line the Ice Age Trail as it crosses Badger Prairie Park.

The MRPHA is the highest priority grassland landscape for management and protection in the state of Wisconsin (MRPHA Partnership 2010). The Nature Conservancy accepted its first land donation there in 1964 and has since preserved almost 1,500 acres, including the Thomson Memorial Prairie, one of the few dry prairies remaining in Wisconsin (Nature Conservancy 2010).

The 2006 Parks and Open Space Plan maintains Dane County's support for the continuing development of the Ice Age Trail, the 1,200-mile route that traces the terminus of the Wisconsin Glacier, which retreated a mere 15,000 years ago. Even though this sheet of ice once covered most of the northern United States, its deposits and depressions are most evident in Wisconsin. The Ice Age Trail travels through towns as well as countryside, giving hikers a lesson about the moraines, eskers, drumlins, and kettles formed by our last bout with climate change. Envisioned by Milwaukee attorney Ray Zillmer and promoted by U.S. Congressman Henry Reuss, the route was designated as the Ice Age National Scientific Reserve in 1971 and subsequently became a National Scenic Trail, one of only 11 in the entire country (Ice Age Trail Alliance 2010).

Dane County's Parks and Open Space Plan responds to strong public demand for more trails on water as well as land. The county partners with Capitol Water Trails to establish recreational navigation on 83 miles of Dane County's rivers and streams (Capitol Water Trails 2010). Water trail opportunities already exist on nine Dane County rivers and the Yahara Waterways, a chain of six lakes joined by the Yahara River, allowing canoeists and kayakers to travel from Cherokee Marsh though the heart of the city of Madison, a distance of more than 30 miles (Dane County 2007b).

For ambitious paddlers, the Wisconsin River remains free-flowing from the northwestern corner of Dane County to its confluence with the Mississippi River, 92 miles downstream at Prairie du Chien, Wisconsin. In 1989, the state formed the Lower Wisconsin State Riverway Board to regulate development and guide land preservation on 80,000 acres of shoreland in this seven-county area (Lower Wisconsin State Riverway Board 2005). The Mazomanie Bottoms of the Lower Wisconsin Riverway lies in Dane County, protecting an oak barrens and a floodplain forest used by bald eagles in winter (Wisconsin DNR 2010).

The county developed the hugely successful Capital City State Trail for walking, jogging, rollerblading, stride skiing, and bicycling. Based on the enthusiastic public response, the county's 2006 Parks and Open Space Plan calls for eight more multiplepurpose recreation trails, including a path between McCarthy County Park and Patrick Marsh that would pass the original homestead of Georgia O'Keeffe and travel through the countryside that inspired many of her paintings (Dane County 2006). These county trails augment the rail trails already developed by the state, including the Glacial Drumlin State Trail linking Madison suburbs with the City of Waukesha, 52 miles to the east.

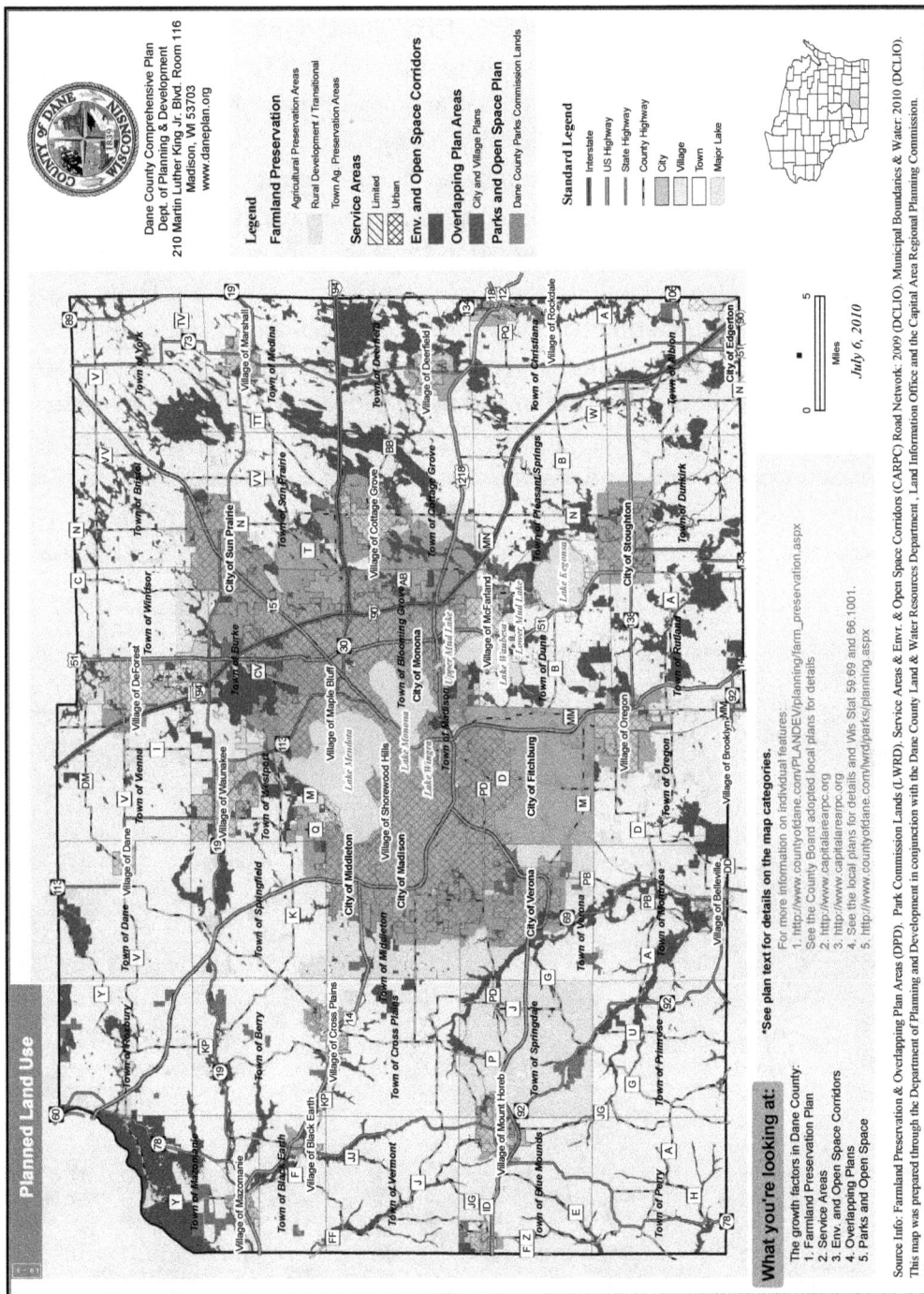

Figure 10-2. The Dane County Comprehensive Plan promotes large agricultural preservation areas. [Source: Dane County]

In 1990, Dane County launched the Conservation Fund Grant Program, which acquired more than $14 million worth of land by the year 2006. In 1999, Dane County voters overwhelmingly approved an advisory referendum for an accelerated program intended to triple the historic rate of land preservation. Specifically, an additional $30 million of funding was applied over the next 10 years. The county uses most of the conservation fund to buy land or easements directly from the owners of qualifying land. But 20 percent is reserved for grants to local governments and nonprofit organizations that acquire land identified in the county's Parks and Open Space Plan (Dane County 2006).

Dane County is the most agriculturally productive county in Wisconsin, generating the highest value of agricultural products, both in crops and livestock (USDA 2007). The county has also been a leader in food security and food system planning. In 2005, the Dane County Board of Supervisors created the Dane County Food Council, the first food council in Wisconsin. Food councils aim to use local food systems as an economic development strategy, a means of resource stewardship, and a vehicle to give children and the disadvantaged improved access to fresh food. To promote coordination, drafts of the Dane County Comprehensive Plan call for support of the food council's work (Dane County 2007a). In 2009, the food council joined the county's Sustainable Agricultural Subcommittee in brainstorming ways to improve the local food system, including help for beginning

Figure 10-3.   This farm was preserved by the Town of Dunn's PDR program.

farmers, new strategies for farm profitability and food security, and of course, farmland preservation. Along with many other suggestions, the subcommittee's 2010 report recommended facilitation of the county's transfer of development rights (TDR) program, which was adopted in February 2010 (Dane County Food Council 2010).

While TDR is just getting started in Dane County, preservation through the purchase of development rights (PDR) has a longer history. In 1996, the voters of the Town of Dunn, four miles south of the Wisconsin State Capitol, approved a property tax increase of 0.5 percent to fund the acquisition of agricultural easements from willing landowners. In 1997, this program protected its first property, the Sinaiko Farm. As of August 2009, the Dunn PDR program had permanently protected 24 farms, with a total of 2,835 acres. Additional properties preserved by other public agencies and the Nature Conservancy increase the total to almost 5,500 acres, roughly 25 percent of the town's land area (Dunn 2010).

Nonprofit organizations are also preserving farmland and natural areas in Dane County. The Natural Heritage Land Trust (NHLT), originally known as the Dane County Natural Heritage Foundation, has protected more than 6,500 acres of land since its formation in 1983. In one example, the trust secured a conservation easement that protects the setting for Cave of the Mounds, which is listed as a National Natural Landmark by the National Park Service (NHLT 2010).

In his foreword to *A Sand County Almanac*, Aldo Leopold wrote, "That land is a community is the basic concept of ecology, but that land is to be loved and respected is an extension of ethics" (Leopold 1949, xi). The wide array of preservation plans and programs in Dane County strongly suggest that Leopold's land ethic has taken root there.

11

KING COUNTY, WASHINGTON

King County, which surrounds Seattle and its suburbs, deserves its reputation as an undisputed leader in open space preservation. It has saved more land through transfer of development rights (TDR) than any other jurisdiction in the country. It supplements TDR with other conservation tools, and the Greenprint for King County has won awards from American Planning Association (APA) and the Planning Association of Washington. When the holdings of the state of Washington and the federal government are added to public lands conserved by local jurisdictions, King County already permanently preserves more than half of its total land area, a remarkable achievement for a county with a population of 1.9 million located within a four-county region with 3.7 million people.

King County had acquired roughly 4,000 acres of parkland by the mid-1960s. In 1964, the county adopted its first comprehensive plan. It supplemented the plan one year later with the Ten Year Program for Open Space Acquisition. This set the stage for a regional open space program known as Forward Thrust, supported by a $49.2 million bond that doubled the size of the county's park system. King County recognized the growing popularity and synergistic benefits of trail systems earlier than most jurisdictions, adopting the Urban Trails Plan and General Bicycle Plan in 1976 (King County 2010d; King County 2010e).

In 1985, King County adopted a new comprehensive plan featuring the first urban growth boundary in the state of Washington and a goal of preserving resource lands, habitat, and open space in general. To implement that plan, the voters approved a $117 million open space bond in 1989. This was followed in

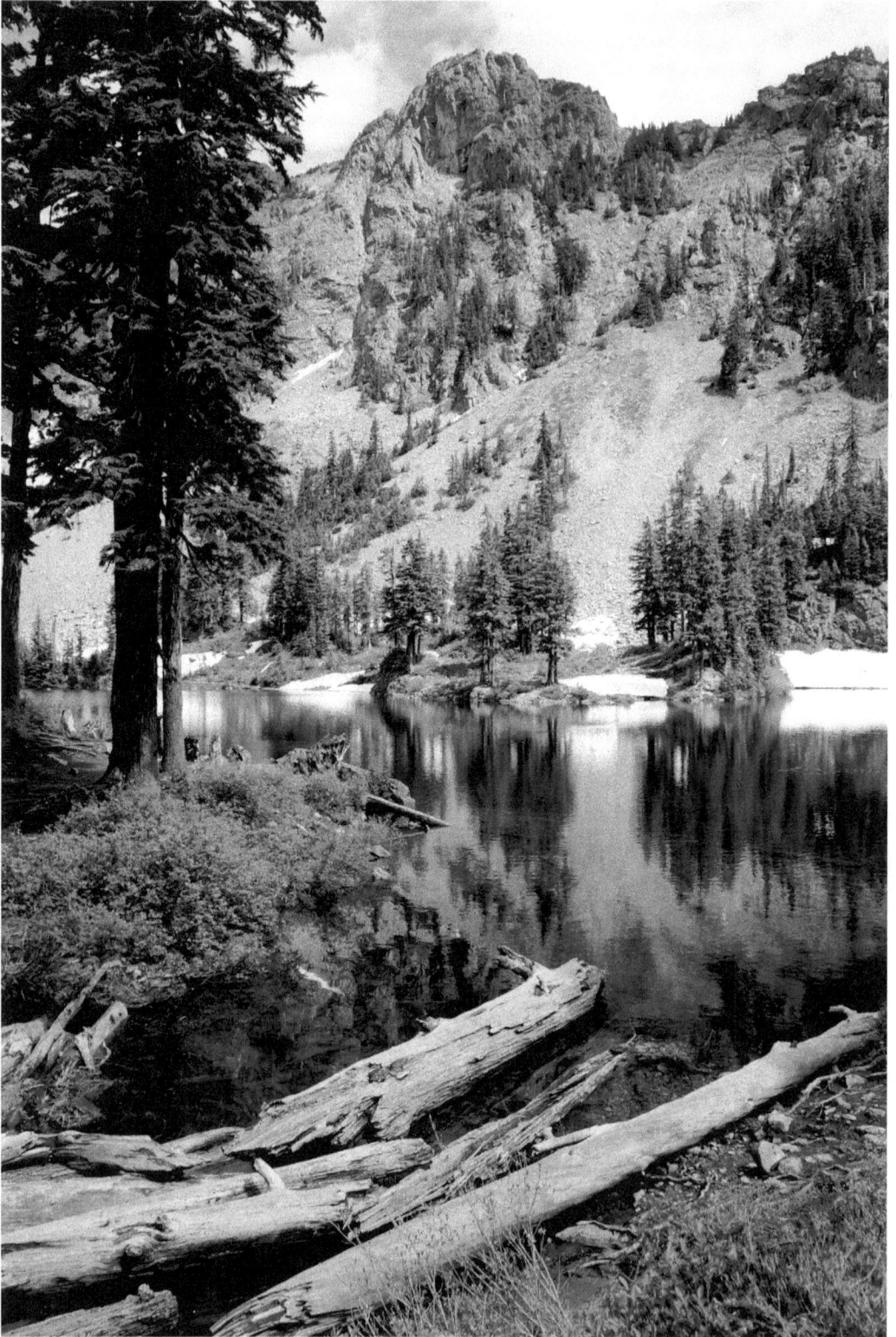

Figure 11-1. Melakwa Lake is one of more than 700 small mountain lakes in the Alpine Lakes Wilderness.

1993 by the creation of the $60 million Conservation Futures Bond Acquisition Program, allowing the preservation of large open space areas for passive recreation, including the 3,115-acre Cougar Mountain Regional Wildland Park (King County 2010d; King County 2010e).

King County's 1994 comprehensive plan was the first to comply with the state of Washington's Growth Management Act. One year later, King County implemented that plan with new development regulations, including the rezoning of more than 33,000 acres of land from urban to rural designations. In 1999, Puget Sound chinook salmon and bull trout were listed as threatened species, prompting greater emphasis on watershed protections. In addition, a 2002 plan refocused the county's park system on significant ecological lands, trails, and regional open space areas. Consistent with that plan, the King County Parks system now protects 25,000 acres of open space in 180 parks with 175 miles of trails (King County 2010c; King County 2010d; King County 2010e).

King County was also an early practitioner of farmland preservation. In 1979, the county's voters approved a $50 million farmlands preservation bond, making King County the first jurisdiction in the nation in which voters agreed to tax themselves to preserve farmland. Although the original funding has been depleted, the county continues to buy development rights from high-priority farms. To date, this program has preserved 13,200 acres of farmland (Buckland 1987; King County 2010b).

In 2004, King County recognized the need for a comprehensive land conservation strategy to address multiple issues, including growth management and climate change as well as the conservation of habitat, farmland, forests, and watersheds. In partnership with the Trust for Public Land, King County created a geographic information systems (GIS) model to help identify the highest conservation priorities. The resulting Greenprint also demonstrated how the county could achieve ambitious preservation goals using multiple funding sources, including continued use of its real estate excise tax and conservation futures tax, a dedicated portion of property tax that generates more than $10 million per year for open space preservation (King County 2010a; Trust for Public Land 2004).

King County's TDR program has now saved more land than any other TDR program in the United States. This success partly stems from the willingness of some cities within King County to accept transferred development rights from land under county jurisdiction in accordance with interjurisdictional agreements. The City of Seattle, for example, allows developers in a downtown neighborhood to gain additional floor area within new buildings by buying TDRs transferred from sending areas that are often more than 25 miles away. This cooperation reflects an understanding of the interdependence between urban and surrounding rural areas that is sadly lacking in many parts of the United States (King County 2010f).

King County TDR Program Sending and Receiving Areas

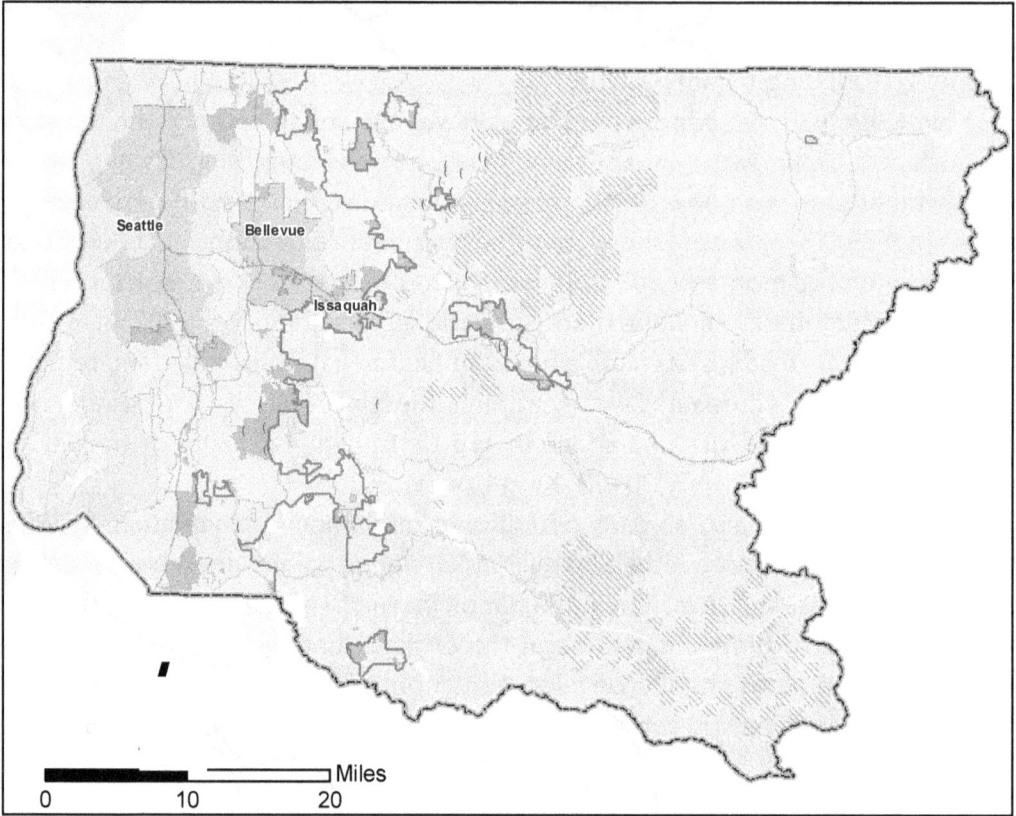

King County TDR Program

- Eligible Sending Areas*
- —— Urban Growth Area Boundary
- Eligible Receiving Areas (Unincorporated Urban Areas)
- Partner Cities (Contain Eligible Receiving Areas)
- Other Cities
- Enrolled TDR Sending Sites (Large Properties)
- Enrolled TDR Sending Sites (Small Properties)

Sending sites eligible by zoning must also meet public benefit criteria to enroll in the program.

Map by Michael Murphy, King County TDR Program. May

Washington State

King County

Figure 11-2. Three cities have voluntarily agreed to accept transferred development rights from sending areas under King County jurisdiction that are sometimes more than 25 miles away. [Source: King County TDR Program]

King County has been extremely skillful in using its TDR program to leverage preservation funding. Most counties in Washington simply use their conservation futures tax revenue to buy land or easements and do not resell the resulting development potential. In contrast, King County sometimes uses its conservation futures tax to buy transferred development rights. The county deposits these in its TDR bank and resells them, thereby creating an ongoing revolving fund for preservation from what would otherwise be a one-time acquisition. The wisdom of this approach is demonstrated by the fact that King County's program has preserved 141,500 acres so far, more than twice the next-most successful TDR program in the country (King County 2010f; Pruetz and Standridge 2009).

In addition to the land preserved directly by King County, roughly 43 percent of the county's total area is protected by other levels of government, with federal agencies accounting for 354,000 acres, municipalities adding 142,900 acres, and the state contributing 97,500 acres (Trust for Public Land 2005). The Mt. Baker–Snoqualmie National Forest alone protects most of the eastern third of King County and features the Alpine Lakes Wilderness Area. Providing more than 700 mountain lakes and a 615-mile trail system within an hour's drive of half of the population of the state, Alpine Lakes is one of the most popular wilderness areas in the nation (U.S. Forest Service 2010).

Many of King County's most successful preservation efforts have been facilitated by the Cascade Land Conservancy (CLC), the largest independent land conservation and stewardship organization in Washington state. The CLC spearheaded the preservation of more than 163,000 acres of land and launched the Cascade Agenda, an ambitious regional planning and preservation strategy implemented largely by market-based mechanisms. Rather than focus on a typical 20-year horizon, the Cascade Agenda looks ahead 100 years to a four-county region that is double its present population. This 100-year horizon generates idealism and cooperation, because the work is clearly aimed at future generations. Optimism is also critical since the Cascade Agenda proposes the preservation of no less than one million additional acres of privately held land with conservation easements and the purchase of another 265,000 acres for public parks, natural areas, and shorelines. Of the estimated $7 billion total price tag, $4 billion is projected to be supplied by the aggressive use of TDR (CLC 2010).

The goal of saving nearly 1.3 million acres of land might seem overly optimistic in most U.S. regions. But King County has already proven its capabilities: More than half of its land area is permanently preserved, and it has the most successful TDR program in the nation. Perhaps more importantly, leaders and the general public alike recognize that the future of the region's neighborhoods and cities is closely interconnected with the health of the surrounding countryside. This recognition was well expressed by Ada Healy in the following quote from the Cascade Agenda Progress Report of 2008: "But think of that classic Seattle postcard: the Space needle framed by snow-capped peaks and a sparkling Puget Sound. We need to all see that connection in everything we build: we have to grow our families, make our homes and expand our businesses while sustaining this region's lands and waters" (CLC 2008, 13).

Figure 11-3.   King County's TDR program has preserved 141,500 acres of land, including the 90,000-acre Snoqualmie Forest, shown here.

12

LANCASTER COUNTY, PENNSYLVANIA

Despite its proximity to Philadelphia, Lancaster County has largely succeeded in retaining its storybook landscape of prosperous farms, historic villages, rustic covered bridges, and horse-drawn buggies. Since 1975, plans there have stressed the need for urban–rural balance, and the county has followed through with a full suite of implementation tools. In recognition of this achievement, the U.S. Environmental Protection Agency gave Lancaster County its 2009 National Award for Smart Growth Achievement. More importantly, Lancaster County has permanently preserved more than 85,510 acres of farmland, a greater amount than any other county in the nation.

Just 80 miles west of Philadelphia and 70 miles north of Baltimore, Lancaster County could easily be swallowed by the Boston–Washington megalopolis. Its population, which now tops 500,000, grew by more than 100,000 between 1970 and 1990 (U.S. Census Bureau 1995). High growth rates prompted the World Monuments Fund to place Lancaster County on its watch list of endangered places in 1998 and 2000 (World Monuments Fund 2010).

But Lancaster County has three formidable resources on its side in the war on sprawl. First, the productivity of farmland in Lancaster County is not in dispute. More than half of the county is classified as prime farmland by the Natural Resources Conservation Service (Lancaster County 2006). Farm sales exceed $1 billion annually, which ranks Lancaster County first in Pennsylvania and 18th in the nation (USDA 2007). Agriculture accounts for 20 percent of the jobs in Lancaster

County, forming a sizeable constituency for the preservation of farming (Blue Ribbon Commission 2005).

Second, more than 40 percent of the farms in Lancaster County are owned by members of Plain Sect communities: Amish, Mennonite, and Brethren. These families are part of the larger Pennsylvania Dutch community composed of the descendants of Germanic immigrants who first settled Pennsylvania in the 18th century. Farming is central to Plain Sect communities, and children often follow in their parents' footsteps, choosing not only to stay in farming but to maintain traditional farming methods, including the use of horse-drawn farm equipment. Between 1984 and 2003, the number of Amish farms in the county grew from 1,116 to 1,432, representing an increase of 21,659 acres (Lancaster County 2006). This confidence in the future of farming creates fertile ground for preservation.

Third, tourists are irresistibly attracted to this idyllic countryside inhabited by women in white caps and men in straw hats who use draft horses to power farm machinery from another century. Particularly appealing is that this is not a staged pageant in a theme park but real people going about their lives in a working landscape. Directly and indirectly, tourism generates almost $4 billion annually for Lancaster County and supports more than 20,000 jobs (Lancaster County 2005). Everyone there understands the need to preserve the culture and the land that make this possible.

Fortunately, the people of Lancaster County have long recognized the vulnerability as well as the significance of their rural heritage. In 1975, Lancaster County adopted a plan that recognized the threat that urbanization posed and called for the preservation of 278,000 acres, more than 45 percent of the county's total land area (Maynard 1998). Lancaster County followed through with an implementation strategy that included a wide array of tools, including agricultural zoning, purchase of development rights (PDR), and urban growth boundaries (UGBs).

Instituting meaningful agricultural zoning in Pennsylvania is not easy since land-use decisions are all controlled at the local government level, which in Lancaster County means 41 separate townships. In order to implement agricultural preservation plans, the Lancaster County commissioners must convince these local governments to act as one. In 1976, the first township agricultural zone in Lancaster County was adopted. By 2000, 39 townships had adopted agricultural zoning, thereby providing temporary protection for 320,000 acres of land, more than half of the county's land area. Importantly, agricultural zoning in Lancaster County imposes meaningful restrictions, typically limiting residential density to one dwelling unit per 25 acres or, in the case of two townships, to one dwelling per 50 acres (Daniels 2000).

In 1980, the Lancaster County Board of Commissioners appointed an Agricultural Preserve Board to designate agricultural preserves and manage a voluntary deed restriction program. The board accepted donated easements on 5,500

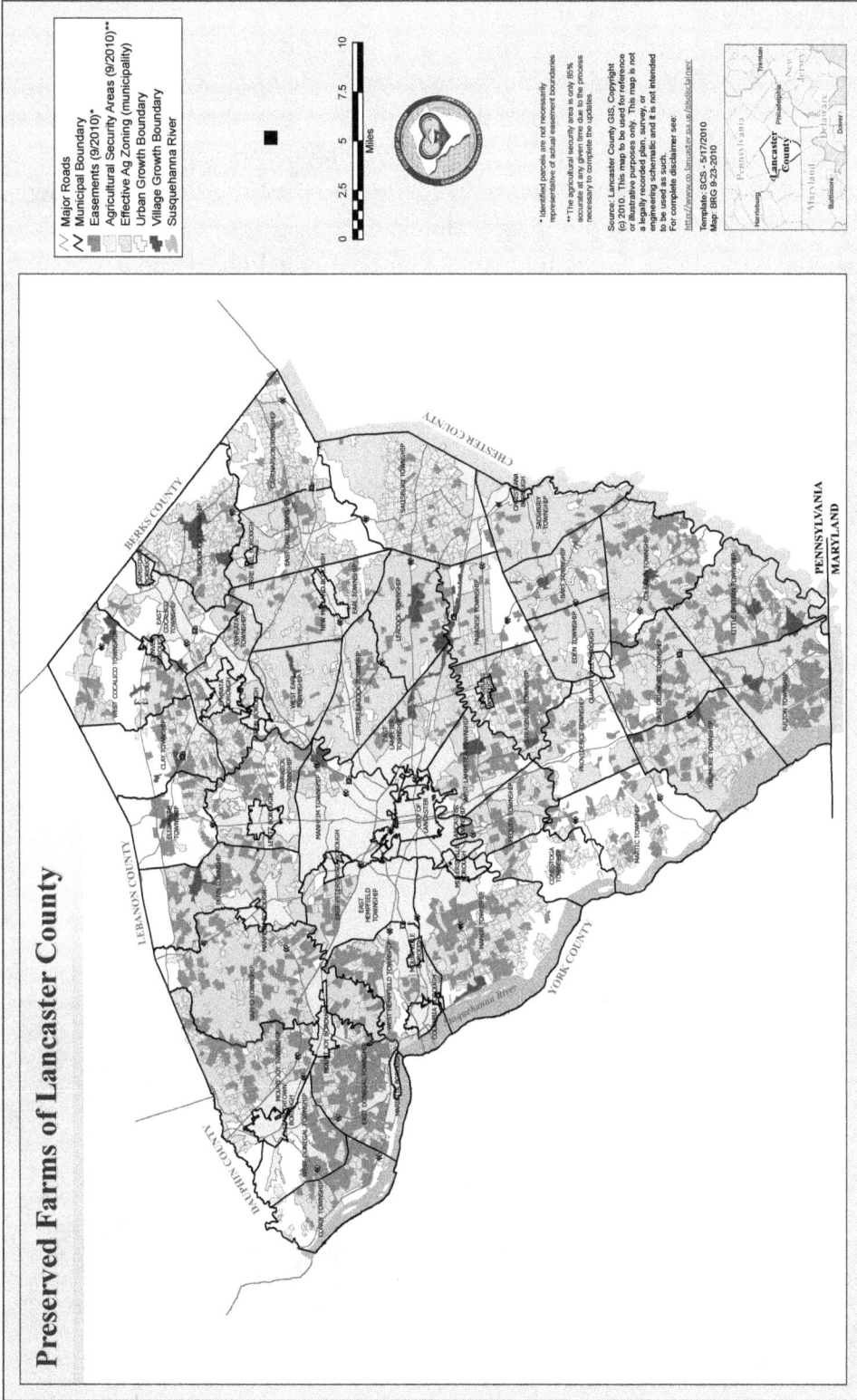

Figure 12-1. Lancaster County has permanently preserved more than 85,510 acres of farmland, a greater amount than any other county in the nation. [Source: Lancaster County]

acres of farmland before this program began receiving money from the Pennsylvania PDR program in 1989 (Daniels 1991).

The Pennsylvania PDR program was initially funded by a voter-approved $100 million bond and subsequently by cigarette taxes. In the first 10 years of the state program, Lancaster County accounted for more than one-third of all the easements purchased in Pennsylvania (Maynard 1998), receiving $20 million of state funding by 1996 (Daniels and Bowers 1997). In addition, the Lancaster County Board of Commissioners appropriated almost $1 million per year for farmland preservation in the 1990s, more than any other county in Pennsylvania.

The PDR program was blessed with good timing. In 1991, a prominent farming family preserved its land, demonstrating confidence in the benefits of preservation as well as the sustainability of Lancaster County agriculture. Following that lead, farmers flooded the county with applications for preservation funding (Daniels 2011). By 1998, 23,000 acres had been preserved by the PDR program, and another 5,000 acres had been saved by the Lancaster Farmland Trust (Daniels 2000).

Lancaster County also encourages its municipalities to create UGBs. These boundaries literally draw the line between urban areas (where growth will be accommodated) and rural areas (where communities will not extend water, sewer, or other urban infrastructure). In 1993, the first UGB in Pennsylvania was adopted in Lancaster County, seven years before UGBs were explicitly enabled by the

Figure 12-2.   Plain Sect farms continue to thrive and expand in Lancaster County.

Pennsylvania Municipalities Planning Code. As it does with zoning and other land-use authorities, the Lancaster County Growth Management Plan proposes rather than mandates UGBs. Then the Lancaster County Planning Commission promotes voluntary adoption, often through community planners who work one-on-one throughout the planning and implementation process with the county's separate municipalities. Between 1993 and 2004, 13 urban growth areas and 26 village growth areas were created around villages and cities in Lancaster County (Jaffe 2005).

In addition to comprehensive planning, agricultural zoning, PDR, and UGBs, Lancaster County uses agricultural districts, preferential farmland taxation, relief from sewer and water assessments, right-to-farm laws, and economic development strategies such as farmers markets and agritourism (Daniels and Bowers 1997). This comprehensive approach allowed Lancaster County to rein in the rate of farmland loss, which declined from an average of 3,000 acres per year in the 1980s to 1,500 acres per year in the 1990s (Daniels 2000).

However, Lancaster County was not content merely to reduce the rate of farmland conversion. In 2005, the Blue Ribbon Commission for Agriculture in Lancaster County, Pennsylvania, was formed to make recommendations for an update of the growth management element of the county's comprehensive plan. In the course of 18 "listening sessions," the commission heard, loud and clear, that it was essential to maintain a critical mass of farmland to permanently sustain the county's agrarian heritage. The commission's report, aptly titled *Keep Lancaster County Farming*, concluded that farming in Lancaster County was at a crossroads.

In addition to recommendations for agricultural economic development, advocacy, tax reform, and zoning improvements, the commission's report urged a recommitment to farmland preservation. Specifically, the report noted that funding for the PDR program could not buy all the development rights that Lancaster County farmers wanted to sell. For example, in 2005, the PDR program had a list of 200 farmers waiting for funding. Not surprisingly, the report recommended increased financial support for the PDR program. In addition, the Blue Ribbon Commission recommended other ways of achieving permanent preservation, including the creation of multi-jurisdictional transfer of development rights (TDR) programs throughout the county and even the establishment of a countywide TDR program (Blue Ribbon Commission 2005).

In 2006, Lancaster County adopted an updated growth management element in its comprehensive plan, entitled Balance, designed to help achieve and sustain a "balanced community where urban centers prosper, natural landscapes flourish, and farming is strengthened as an integral component of our diverse economy and cultural heritage" (Lancaster County 2006, xv). As promised by its title, Balance features a rural strategy as well as an urban growth area strategy. The Urban Growth Area Strategy sets targets for capturing most new development at smart-growth densities. Significantly, the Rural Strategy is as detailed and comprehensive as the Urban Growth Area Strategy, thereby enhancing the status of rural areas and adding a sense of urgency to their protection, as recommended by the Blue Ribbon Commission.

For Balance to succeed, Lancaster County's municipalities must be fully engaged in the implementation of the growth management plan. Balance calls for ongoing citizen outreach, increased funding, and the development of a smart-growth toolbox. This toolbox is now online, providing a place for Lancaster County to honor its smart-growth award winners as well as offer guidelines, handbooks, and other implementation aides, including a model ordinance for farmers markets, U-pick orchards, farm stays, and other forms of agritourism. Similarly, the 168-page Lancaster County TDR Practitioner's Handbook offers step-by-step guidance in preparing and implementing a TDR program (Brandywine Conservancy 2008; Lancaster County 2009).

Not all of the tools in Lancaster County's Smart Growth Toolbox are new. Prior to the adoption of Balance, three Lancaster County townships were already

Figure 12-3.   Warwick Township's TDR program has preserved more than 1,300 acres, including this farm.

using TDR. In 1991, Manheim Township became the first municipality in Lancaster County to adopt TDR. Manheim uses money from its own general fund to buy transferred development rights, which it deposits in the township's TDR bank. When these are sold to developers, the proceeds become a revolving fund and are used to make additional TDR purchases (Brandywine Conservancy 2008).

Warwick Township runs Lancaster County's most successful TDR program. Warwick uses its own general fund money to match funds from the county's PDR program. The resulting preservation creates TDRs, which the county allows Warwick to keep and deposit in the Warwick TDR bank. When developers buy those, the proceeds are used to fund additional farmland preservation. As of 2010, Warwick had preserved 1,318 acres of farmland using the TDR program alone (Warwick Township 2010).

The Lancaster Farmland Trust is a private nonprofit organization formed in 1988 to assist in farmland preservation. Many Plain Sect farmers resist government programs, but they will work with a private organization such as the trust (as well as selling transferable development rights to developers). Partly for that reason, the trust has been an invaluable partner in farmland protection. As of 2008, the trust had preserved 20,000 acres of farmland. The trust often collaborates with municipalities to stretch limited preservation dollars. For example, the trust and Warwick Township partner in buying TDRs from Warwick farms, which they then hold for later resale. In 2008, the trust assisted West Lampeter Township with its TDR program, successfully preserving the first four farms under that program, and it has worked with seven other jurisdictions on the development of additional TDR programs (Lancaster Farmland Trust 2009).

As of 2010, all of these programs combined had saved 85,510 acres, making Lancaster County the number one locally operated farmland preservation program in the United States (*Farmland Preservation Report* 2010). Despite the growth pressures common to communities throughout the Mid-Atlantic states, Lancaster County is steadily accomplishing its key planning goal to "keep Lancaster County farming."

13

LEXINGTON–FAYETTE COUNTY, KENTUCKY

Lexington–Fayette County, Kentucky, calls itself the Horse Capital of the World. The countryside is a picture postcard of rolling hills carpeted with Kentucky bluegrass and accented by stately horse barns and white rail fences. The protection of this pastoral paradise dates back to 1958 and the formation of the first urban growth boundary (UGB) in the United States. In response to relentless growth pressure, the unified city-county government adopted its Rural Land Management Plan in 1999 and implemented it with a widely studied purchase of development rights (PDR) program. After only 10 years of operation, that program has already reached half of its land preservation goal.

Lexington–Fayette County forms the heart of Kentucky's Bluegrass region, named for the famous forage that has nourished generations of Thoroughbreds, including numerous winners of the Kentucky Derby (Slayman 2007). Despite a population of more than 280,000, Lexington–Fayette County maintains a strong agricultural economy and an even stronger tourism industry, generating $880 million annually and more than 13,000 jobs (Lexington–Fayette County 2005). In 2010, Lexington–Fayette County hosted the World Equestrian Games, an event that alone was estimated to generate $116 million (Fayette Alliance 2011). Clearly, preservation of the countryside is critical to the local economy as well as community character and way of life.

Early in the 20th century, the City of Lexington and Fayette County recognized the need to cooperate for the mutual benefit of the urban core and its surrounding countryside. The city and county did not formally consolidate until 1974, but

Figure 13-1.   Farmland preservation is critical to tourism as well as agriculture in Lexington–Fayette County.

the two governments formed a joint city-county planning department and commission in 1928. In 1958, the two governments designated an urban service area (where sewer, water, and other urban infrastructure would be provided) and a rural service area (which would be reserved for farming and other rural activities). The Urban Service Area currently constitutes about 30 percent of the county's total land area, and the Rural Service Area encompasses the remaining 70 percent.

This division of the county into urban and rural service areas essentially created the first UGB in the United States. In the following 50 years, the UGB expanded by only 23 percent even though the population of Lexington–Fayette County more than doubled (Slayman 2007). This contrasts with the sprawl experienced in most U.S. metro areas. For example, between 1982 and 1997, the amount of urbanized land in the United States grew by 47 percent even though population grew by only 17 percent (Fulton 2001). In recognition of Lexington–Fayette County's success, the American Planning Association honored the county in 1991 with a National Planning Landmark Award.

But the UGB alone could not stop the development of septic-system subdivisions on one-acre lots in the Rural Service Area. Unless additional controls were imposed, the countryside would ultimately be suburbanized with developments named for the horse farms they had replaced. So in 1964, the county instituted a 10-acre minimum size requirement for all new lots using septic systems. By the late 1960s, the 10-acre minimum lot size was adopted in the Zoning Ordinance and Subdivision Regulations (Lexington–Fayette County 1999).

The 10-acre-minimum lot requirement slowed but did not halt rural development. Between 1990 and 1998 alone, more than 400 ten-acre lots were developed. In fact, the process of converting land to 10-acre lots in that nine-year period consumed more land than the area used by all other development (residential, commercial, and industrial) within the Urban Service Area during the same time frame. Growing recognition of the vulnerability of the countryside spurred three years of studies and public meetings, which culminated in 1999 with the adoption of the Rural Service Area Land Management Plan.

The plan builds support for preserving the countryside as a whole by assembling the individual features of the countryside and demonstrating how they are interrelated and mutually supportive. Preserving farmland is naturally a key goal, and the plan emphasizes the importance of agriculture to the local economy. For example, Lexington–Fayette County produced $504 million in farm sales in 2007, making it the highest-ranking county in Kentucky for farm sales (USDA 2010).

In addition to farmland, roughly 30 percent of the Rural Service Area consists of floodplains, stream corridors, wetlands, wildlife habitat, steeply sloped land, aquifer recharge zones, and other environmentally sensitive areas (ESAs). The most notable concentration of ESAs occurs in the rugged terrain in the southern part of the county, near the Kentucky River. The plan also singles out 5,400 contiguous acres of land north of the Urban Service Area as the recharge zone for the Royal Spring Aquifer, which supplies drinking water to 7,000 customers in adjacent Scott County. This aquifer is especially vulnerable because the limestone bedrock produces sinkholes, caverns, and underground streams that allow contaminants as well as water to travel several miles in a matter of hours (Lexington–Fayette County 1999).

But remarkably, most of the 38,261 acres categorized as ESAs are spread throughout the Rural Service Area in a spiderweb pattern that generally follows dozens of streams and minor drainages. As a result, most rural farms are either close to, if not crossed by, ESAs. Consequently, ESA protection is linked to the preservation of the rural area as a whole, which is ultimately a key recommendation of the Rural Service Area Land Management Plan.

The Rural Service Area also features 15 rural settlements, one local historic district, and five historic districts in the National Register of Historic Places. The Rural Service Area Land Management Plan notes that these historic districts and rural settlements are an integral part of the unique natural and cultural landscape of Fayette County. Consequently, the plan calls for detailed study of each district and settlement to evaluate their development capacity and determine what additional development, if any, could occur without harming their historic features and rural character (Lexington–Fayette County 1999).

Rural roads, with their tree canopies and stone fences, are essential to Fayette County's pastoral charm. One of these roads, the Paris Pike, was the scene of a protracted war over a 1969 proposal to improve safety by widening the highway to four lanes. The controversy led to a 1979 federal court injunction that delayed the

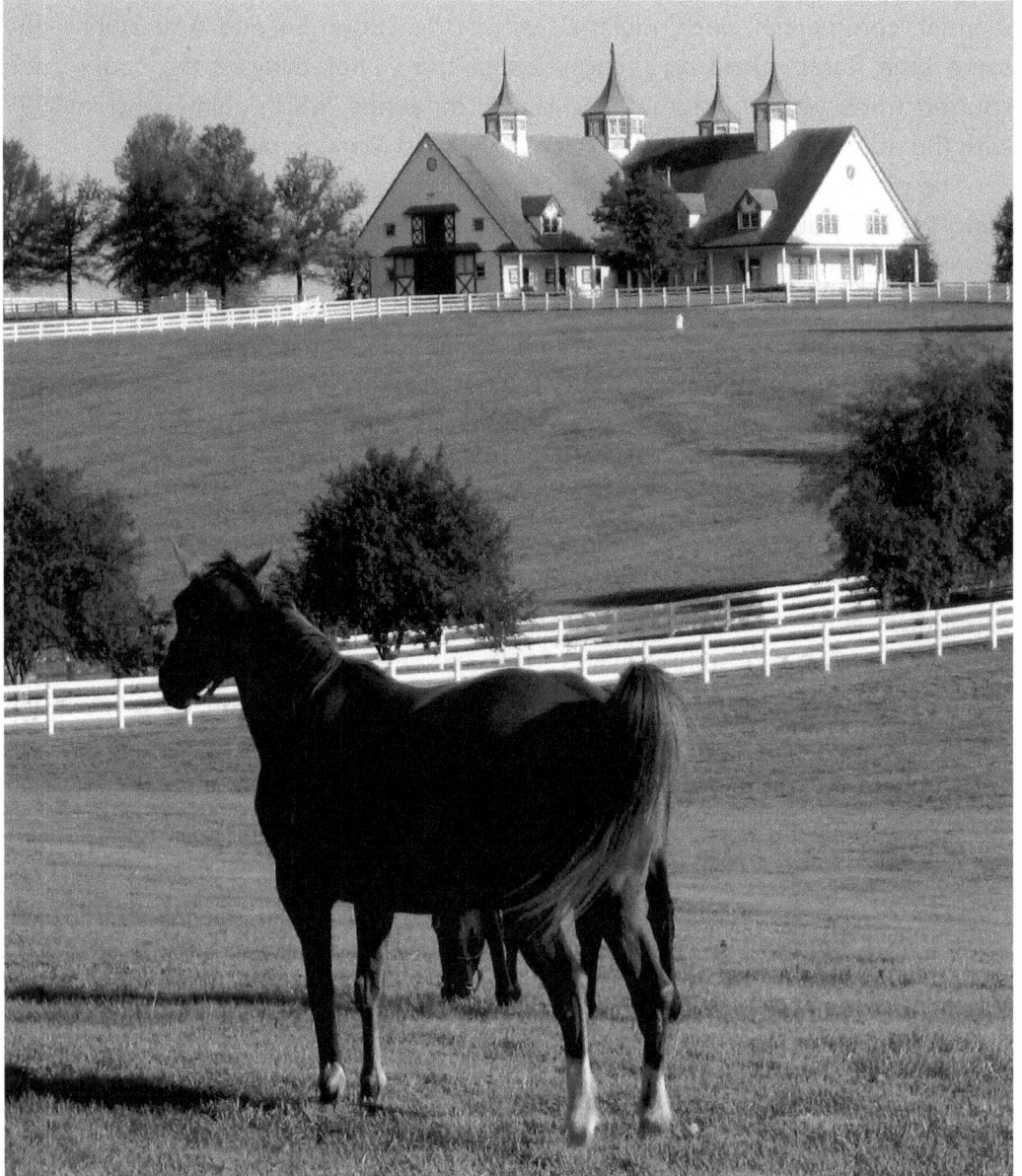

Figure 13-2.   "Great City Life in a Productive Rural Paradise" exemplifies the goals generated by Lexington–Fayette County's latest visioning project.

final design until 1994, allowing planners 14 years to study various ways of keeping construction from destroying the character of the countryside. During this period, planners completed a comprehensive inventory of stone fences throughout the county, and in 1994, Lexington–Fayette County adopted new protections for stone fences in all public rights-of-way. One year later, Lexington–Fayette County also adopted overlay zoning that reduces density and increases building setbacks on land flanking the Paris Pike. Widening of the Paris Pike was ultimately completed in 2003 at a cost of almost $7 million per mile. But the time and expense produced a highway project that is widely regarded as a national model for context-sensitive highway design (Lexington–Fayette County 1999; Schneider 2003).

Many of the issues raised during the Paris Pike battle resurfaced in the 1999 Rural Service Area Land Management Plan. That plan, for example, advocates further protection for trees and iconic views as well as stone fences flanking the county's 18 historic turnpikes and 33 scenic roads. But most significantly, the 1999 plan called for reducing the potential for future development. That response is perfectly logical since future development potential creates the need to mitigate impacts to all the rural resources that the plan aims to protect: agriculture, environmentally sensitive areas, historic landmarks, scenic views, and the trees and stone fences lining rural roadways. Consequently, Lexington–Fayette County ultimately rejected planning alternatives that would fragment the rural area, such as clustered development and new "crossroads communities." As adopted, the plan maintains the 10-acre minimum lot size on only 2,706 acres of the 125,208 undeveloped acres in the Rural Service Area. The minimum parcel size on the remaining 122,502 acres was changed from 10 acres to 40 acres, safeguarding agriculture, protecting nature, minimizing traffic, and reducing the need for costly extensions of infrastructure, including roadway widening (Lexington–Fayette County 1999).

The plan also promotes appropriate ways for urban residents and visitors to experience the countryside. The absence of places to park on the narrow rural roadways can have the unfortunate effect of forcing many people to see the horse country only through their car windshields. So the plan proposes the creation of strategically placed staging areas where people can leave their cars behind and enjoy the scenic roadways on foot or by bicycle.

Similarly, the plan seizes on the greenway concept as a way to promote non-motorized appreciation of the countryside and perhaps reinforce the rural-urban interaction that undoubtedly makes land preservation not just palatable but politically popular. Specifically, the plan proposes to use selected floodplains as greenways, environmental corridors that double as a trail system. The plan identifies five focus areas, including three that extend from the Urban Service Area to the county limits. Ultimately, these greenways will make it possible for city residents to hike or bike into the countryside. One of these focus areas contains

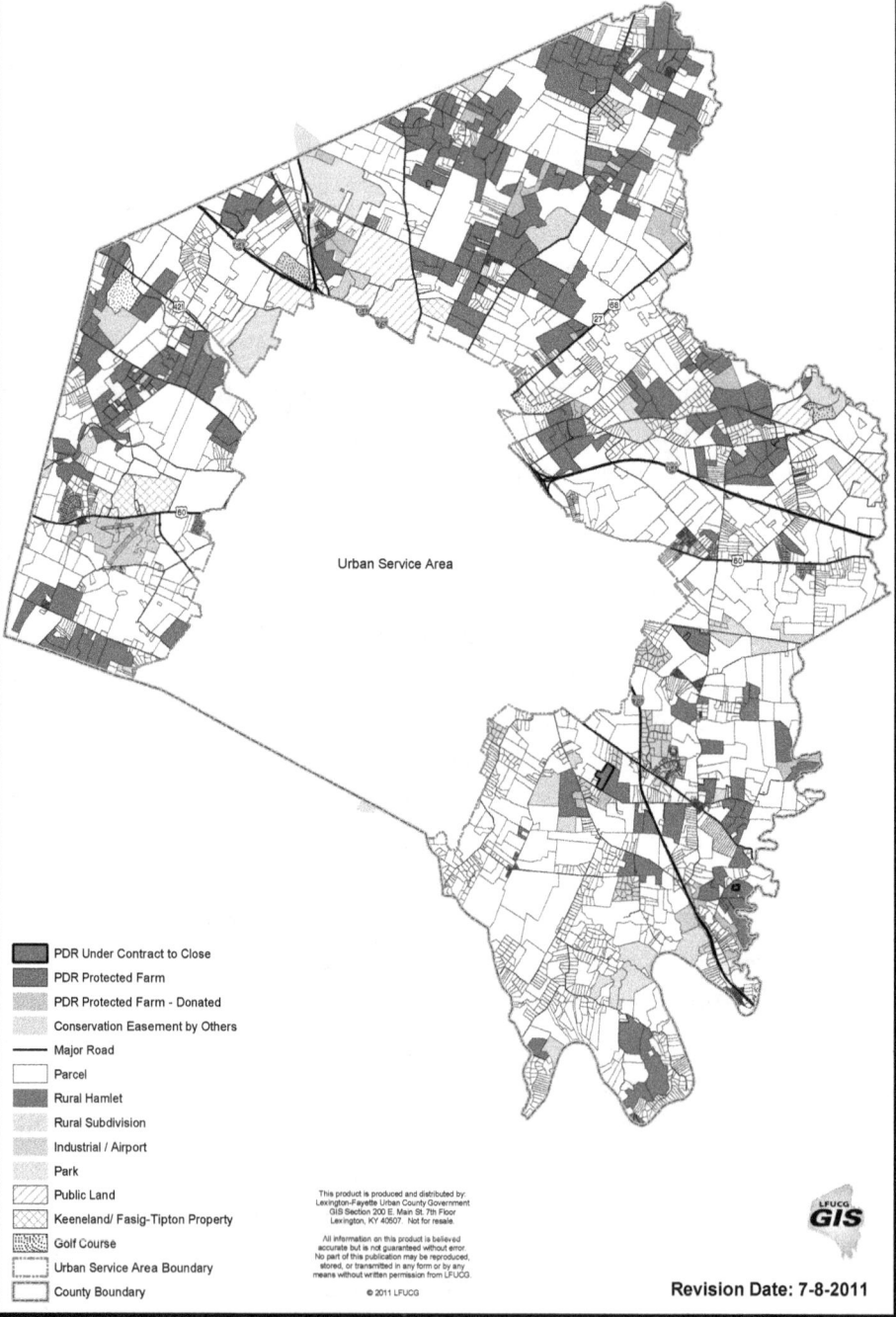

PDR Protected Farms, Accepted Offers, Other Protected Farms, and Other Public Lands

25,424 acres of preserved farmland now protected by PDR
50,000 acres of farmland is the goal of PDR.
Lexington-Fayette County, Kentucky

Urban Service Area

PDR Under Contract to Close
PDR Protected Farm
PDR Protected Farm - Donated
Conservation Easement by Others
Major Road
Parcel
Rural Hamlet
Rural Subdivision
Industrial / Airport
Park
Public Land
Keeneland/ Fasig-Tipton Property
Golf Course
Urban Service Area Boundary
County Boundary

This product is produced and distributed by:
Lexington-Fayette Urban County Government
GIS Section 200 E. Main St. 7th Floor
Lexington, KY 40507. Not for resale.

All information on this product is believed
accurate but is not guaranteed without error.
No part of this publication may be reproduced,
stored, or transmitted in any form or by any
means without written permission from LFUCG.

© 2011 LFUCG

LFUCG
GIS

Revision Date: 7-8-2011

Figure 13-3. Lexington–Fayette County is halfway to its goal of preserving 50,000 acres of land in its Rural Service Area. [Source: Lexington–Fayette County]

Raven Run Nature Sanctuary, which already protects 734 acres of land along the Kentucky River and has a 10-mile trail system.

In 2000, Lexington–Fayette County adopted a PDR program that aims to permanently preserve about 50,000 acres of rural land, roughly 27 percent of the county's total land area. Owners who apply to sell their development rights submit applications that are scored based on how well they achieve the multiple goals of the Rural Service Area Land Management Plan, such as agricultural productivity, environmental sensitivity, and scenic value. Extra points are also awarded when the landowners offer to sell the rights at less than their appraised value (Lexington–Fayette County 2011).

Local funding for the PDR program was jump-started in 2000 with a $25 million bond, to be paid off by the Lexington–Fayette County general fund. Program start-up was greatly assisted by a $15 million grant from the Kentucky Agricultural Development Board's tobacco settlement money (Boone County 2001). The Natural Resources Conservation Service of the United States Department of Agriculture also chipped in $11 million (USDA 2008).

The PDR program started acquiring easements in 2001, becoming the first agricultural easement program adopted by a local government in the Commonwealth of Kentucky. As of early 2010, $57.6 million had been spent on the program, with $31.5 million coming from state and federal grants (Eblen 2010). More importantly, 228 farms with a total of 25,423 acres had been preserved by 2011, putting the PDR program halfway to its 50,000-acre goal within its first 10 years in operation (Lexington–Fayette County 2011).

Lexington–Fayette County gets open space preservation assistance from the Commonwealth of Kentucky. In 1972, the commonwealth bought more than 1,200 acres of land in northern Fayette County that had been used to raise Thoroughbred horses long before the Civil War. Today, the Kentucky Horse Park is essentially a theme park devoted to horses, offering horse museums, horse-drawn trolley rides, horse barns, horse monuments, horse shows, and special events of all kinds as long as they involve horses. Kentucky also preserves two historic sites in Fayette County: Waveland, an early 19th-century plantation, and Boone Station, the settlement that pioneer Daniel Boone called home between 1779 and 1782.

Preservation organizations are also working to preserve Lexington–Fayette County land. The Bluegrass Conservancy alone holds conservation easements on 11,279 acres in the 9-county Inner Bluegrass Region, including approximately 2,000 acres in Lexington–Fayette County (Bluegrass Conservancy 2010). The World Monuments Fund designates 1.2 million acres in seven Kentucky counties as the Bluegrass Cultural Landscape of Kentucky. This region lost 80,000 acres of farmland to development during a 10-year period, prompting the fund to place the Bluegrass Cultural Landscape of Kentucky on its 2006 watch list of the 100 most endangered sites on Earth (Slayman 2007).

Thankfully, the people of Lexington–Fayette County recognize the uniqueness of their portion of this endangered region and are taking steps to protect it permanently. Destination 2040: Choosing Lexington's Future is a recent visioning project that reconfirms public understanding of the need to integrate the urban and rural spheres of this community. This understanding, and understandable pride, is clear in the following vision statements generated by this project for Lexington–Fayette County: "Great City Life in a Productive Rural Paradise" and "Lexington will be one of the world's great mid-sized cities by striking and sustaining a brilliant balance of dynamic urban living and a matchless rural setting" (Lexington–Fayette County 2009, 2).

Even more to the point is this statement from Destination 2040:

> We will continue to place a high value on how close our rural and urban areas are to each other, and on how quickly we can move from one to the other. The unusual closeness between the city and the adjacent countryside, commonly referred to as the "rural/urban mix" helps make Lexington truly unique, and requires vigorous protection for that delicate co-existence of urban and agricultural land use. (Lexington–Fayette County 2009, 9)

With that vision, it seems safe to say that Lexington–Fayette County is in no danger of becoming the "Former Horse Capital of the World."

14

MARICOPA COUNTY, ARIZONA

Golf courses, retirement complexes, and rapid development are most commonly associated with Maricopa County, Arizona, and its burgeoning cities, including Scottsdale, Glendale, and Phoenix, now the fifth-largest city in the United States. But these communities have also been preserving an impressive amount of their fragile desert landscape, often using compelling plans implemented by voter-approved taxes.

Open space preservation in Maricopa County took off in 1924, when Senator Carl Hayden and President Coolidge helped Phoenix save two mountain ranges south of the city. Today, South Mountain Park/Preserve is the largest municipal park in the United States, protecting more than 16,000 acres, 51 miles of trails, and habitat for hundreds of desert species, including the saguaro cactus, desert tortoise, kit fox, and roadrunner (Phoenix 2009b).

Between 1950 and 1970, the population of Phoenix more than quadrupled. A group of citizens known as the Phoenix Mountains Preservation Council initiated the preparation of a groundbreaking plan, ultimately named An Open Space Plan for the Phoenix Mountains, which recommended the preservation of 9,711 acres of desert landscape. After presentations at numerous public meetings, the Phoenix City Council held a public hearing before a packed auditorium and adopted the plan in January 1972 (Gilbert 1981). The plan bluntly described the cross-roads Phoenix faced:

> We have been busily dividing, reshaping, and exploiting our vast resource at an unprecedented rate and with little awareness of its intrinsic value. The anguish of a

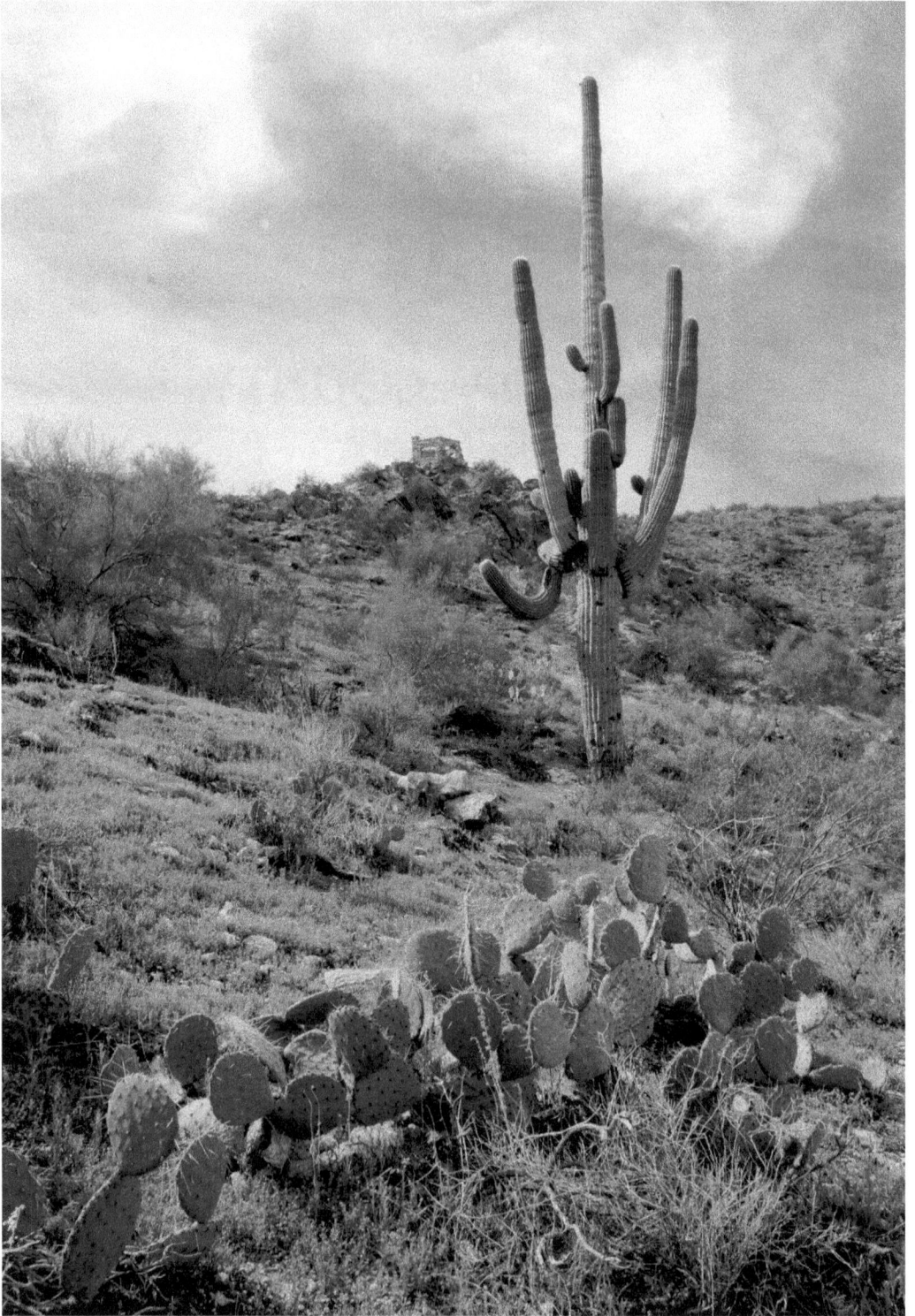

Figure 14-1.   Cacti thrive in the 16,000-acre South Mountain Park/Preserve, the largest municipal park in the United States.

few at bulldozer progress has gone largely unheeded by a local population and government exuberant in the intense activity of rapid growth. Arizona is so rich in scenery and land that we have given little thought to what our communities will be like when our major open spaces have disappeared. (Phoenix 1972, 1)

The significance of An Open Space Plan for the Phoenix Mountains was officially recognized in 2008 with a National Planning Landmark Award from the American Planning Association (APA). A more immediate impact came in May 1972, when Arizona's voters approved a constitutional amendment allowing cities to pass open space bonds. The following year, Phoenix voters approved the first of many open space bonds that funded most of the early land acquisitions, including Shaw Butte, North Mountain, and Dreamy Draw (APA 2007).

By 1998, the Phoenix Mountain Preserve protected 7,500 acres, and the city managed a total of 27,000 acres of open space. But the region was also growing at a breakneck pace. So Phoenix expanded its preservation vision and adopted its Sonoran Preserve Master Plan, which called for preservation of an additional 22,500 acres, including 16,800 acres owned by the Arizona State Land Department (Phoenix 1998). One year later, 80 percent of Phoenix voters approved the Phoenix Parks and Preserves Initiative, which established a 0.001 percent sales tax estimated to generate $256 million, mostly for the preservation of the Phoenix Sonoran Preserve and nine regional parks (Phoenix 2002a). Today, the Phoenix Mountain Preserve protects 37,000 acres, including the ever-expanding Phoenix Sonoran Preserve (Phoenix 2009a).

Just east of Phoenix, the City of Scottsdale has earned a reputation as an open space superstar in its own right. At the urging of the McDowell Sonoran Land Trust, Scottsdale adopted the ambitious goal of preserving more than 36,000 acres in the McDowell Mountains and the Sonoran Desert, roughly one-third of the city's total land area. To make this vision a reality, Scottsdale voters approved an 0.2 percent property tax increase in 1995, the use of sales tax for preserve expansion in 1998, and a 0.15 percent sales tax increase for open space acquisition in 2004 (Scottsdale 2010). The city has acquired roughly 17,000 acres so far, putting it almost halfway to its total preservation goal (Corbett 2010).

Maricopa County itself began preserving its mountainous terrain in 1954 and then accelerated its parkland acquisitions after a 1970 federal act allowed the county to buy land from the federal Bureau of Land Management for the extremely reasonable price of $2.50 per acre. Today, Maricopa County maintains 10 regional parks with more than 120,000 acres, giving it the largest county park system in the country (Maricopa County 2010). In 2004, the Maricopa County Board of Supervisors adopted the Maricopa County Regional Trail System Plan, which proposes a 1,521-mile regional trail system, including the 242-mile

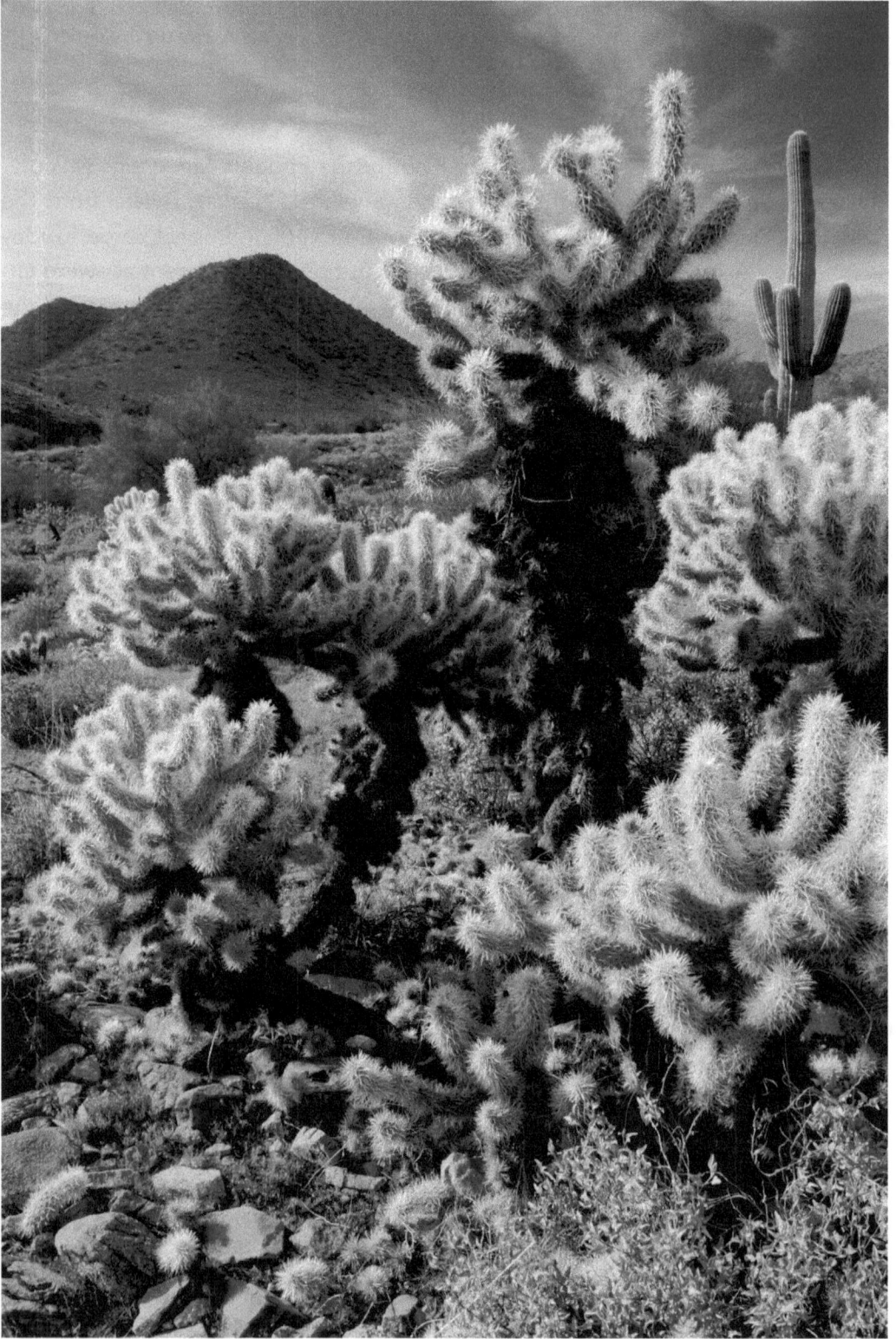

Figure 14-2. Cholla cacti line the trails of the McDowell Sonoran Preserve, in Scottsdale.

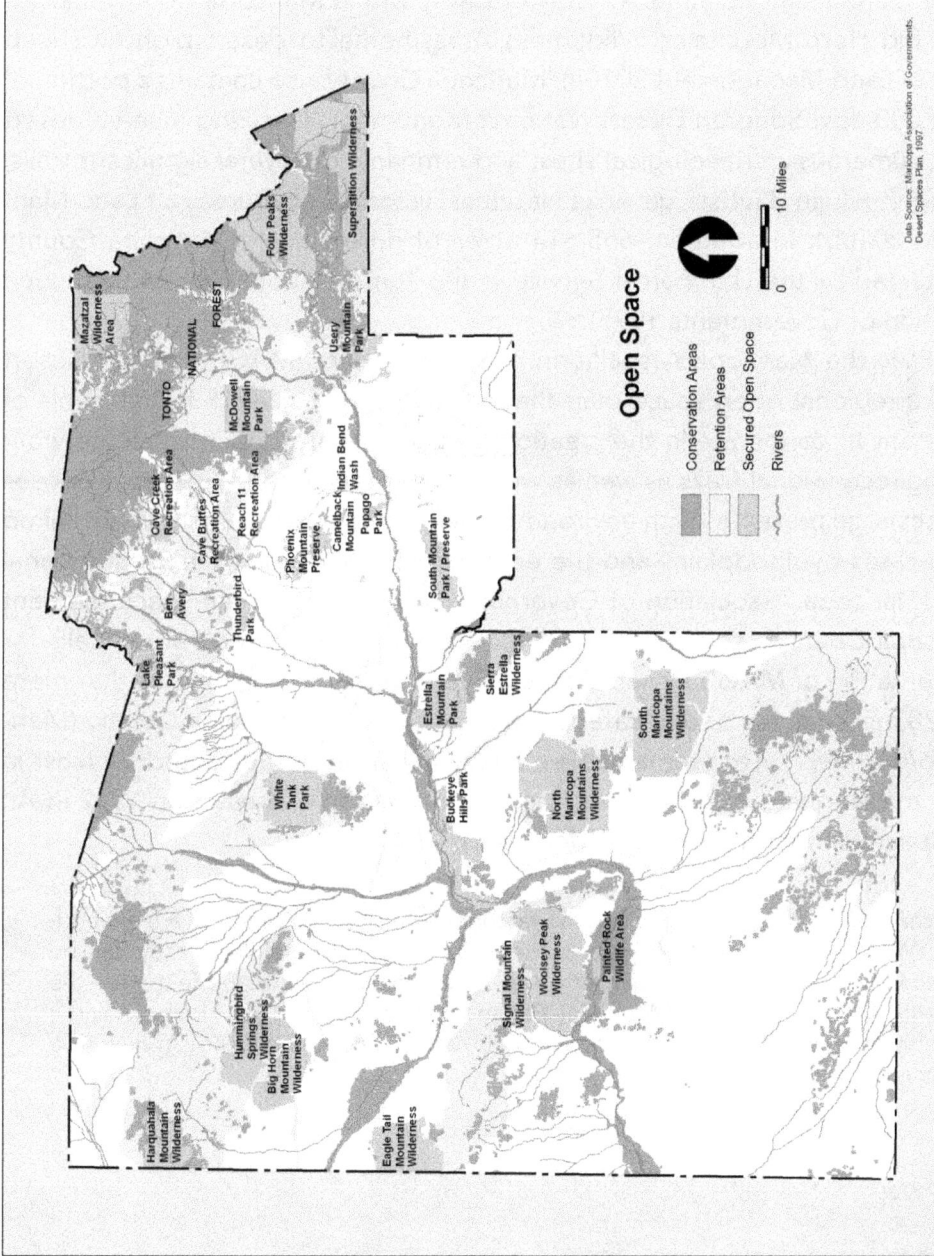

Figure 14-3.   The Maricopa Association of Governments' open space plan, Desert Spaces, links sensitive environmental areas, providing for recreational trails as well as wildlife movement. [Source: Maricopa Association of Governments]

Maricopa Trail connecting the regional parks with one another and with neighborhoods throughout the county (Maricopa County 2004).

In addition to the achievements of local government, federal land holdings contribute a vast amount of open space to Maricopa County. The Bureau of Land Management and the U.S. Forest Service protect almost a half million acres in nine wilderness areas that lie either entirely or partly within Maricopa County, including the Big Horn Mountains Wilderness Area, home to desert bighorn sheep (Bureau of Land Management 2010a). Maricopa County also contains a portion of the 487,000-acre Sonoran Desert National Monument, featuring diverse desert habitat, numerous archaeological sites, and remnants of several significant trails, including the Juan Bautista de Anza National Historic Trail (Bureau of Land Management 2010b). In addition, 655,614 acres of northeastern Maricopa County are protected by the U.S. Forest Service in the Tonto National Forest (Maricopa Association of Governments 1995).

In 1996, the Maricopa Association of Governments (MAG) adopted Desert Spaces, a regional open space plan that serves as a framework for all levels of government to cooperate in the creation of a coordinated open space network providing recreational trails as well as wildlife corridors. Desert Spaces proposes to protect large preserves with environmentally sensitive resources that are linked in many cases by floodplains and the easements of the region's extensive canal system (Maricopa Association of Governments 1995). The open space element in Maricopa County's comprehensive plan for 2020, Eye to the Future, calls for implementation of MAG's Desert Spaces. Eye to the Future estimates that more than 1.28 million acres of dedicated open space exist in Maricopa County (Maricopa County 1997). That remarkable achievement can be attributed, at least in part, to the eloquent plea for open space preservation expressed in 1972 in An Open Space Plan for the Phoenix Mountains:

> The cars, the homes, the offices and the factories we value so highly—all are expendable. When they outlast their personal value or economic usefulness they can be replaced with newer models. Similarly, the Valley's natural landscape features—the Phoenix Mountains, South Mountain, Papago Buttes, the McDowell Mountains— are also expendable. But, once altered, their natural scenic character can never be replaced. (Phoenix 1972, 2)

15

MARIN COUNTY, CALIFORNIA

Marin County lies on the other side of the Golden Gate Bridge from San Francisco. Despite being an obvious target for suburban sprawl, Marin County has defied the odds and retained much of its farmland, natural beauty, and community character. Community leaders there understand the importance of permanent preservation. One conservation group funded the county's first open space plan, which became the road map for early parkland protection. Another group, the Marin Agricultural Land Trust (MALT), the first conservancy in the nation devoted exclusively to saving farmland, now holds easements on 41,600 acres. Through private and public action, almost 160,000 acres of land, or roughly half of Marin County's total land area, has been permanently preserved.

The Golden Gate Bridge opened in 1937, putting Marin County within easy commuting distance of downtown San Francisco. Fearing that the county's natural heritage would be swept away in the coming land rush, Caroline Livermore and three other members of the Marin Garden Club formed a new group, ultimately called the Marin Conservation League, which raised $2,500 to pay for Marin County's first park and open space plan. This 1943 plan called for preservation action "before it was too late" and served as the county's guide to open space protection until a new plan was adopted in 1965 (Marin Conservation League 2010a).

Over time, the Marin Conservation League, the Tamalpais Conservation Club, and others worked to expand a small park on the slopes of 2,571-foot Mount Tamalpais, donated by philanthropists William and Elizabeth Kent. Today, 6,300-acre Mount Tamalpais State Park offers more than 50 miles of trails, including

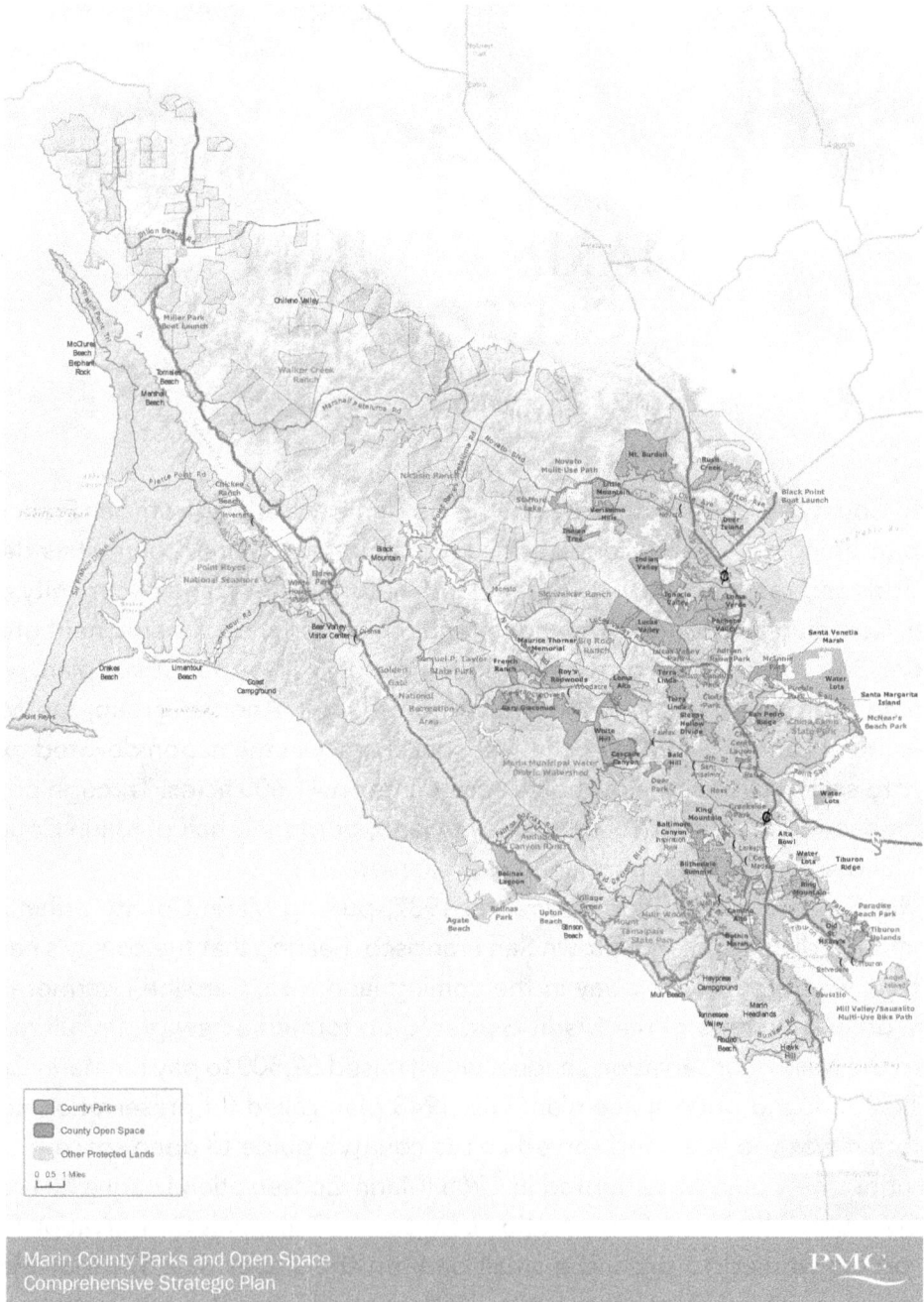

County Parks
County Open Space
Other Protected Lands

0 0.5 1 Miles

Figure 15-1.   Preservation in Marin County has been accomplished through the
combined efforts of all levels of government plus private nonprofit
conservation organizations. [Source: Marin County]

routes with spectacular views of the entire San Francisco Bay region, fog will-ing (California State Parks 2007). The Kents also gave the federal government a 295-acre canyon filled with ancient, uncut redwoods in the foothills of Mount Tamalpais. This gift became Muir Woods National Monument, which Sierra Club founder John Muir called "the best tree-lover's monument that could possibly be found in all the forests of the world" (National Park Service 2008, 1).

In 1956, construction was started on a 400-unit housing development near Limantour Beach, on Point Reyes, an area that the Nature Conservancy identifies as part of a "global biodiversity hotspot" due to its concentration of diverse spe-cies (National Park Service 2010). Legislation to create the Point Reyes National Seashore was introduced in the late 1950s. In 1962, the Sierra Club published Harold Gilliam's book about Point Reyes, *Island in Time*, and gave a copy to every member of the 87th U.S. Congress. That year, the legislation passed, and Presi-dent Kennedy signed an act creating the 71,000-acre Point Reyes National Sea-shore, which includes 32,000 acres of wilderness and 80 miles of natural coastlines. Point Reyes provides a welcome refuge for birders, bicyclists, and other belea-guered humans, as well as elephant seals, sea lions, and tule elk. The National Park Service bought 13 ranches there and leased them back for farming, thereby creating a working landscape that also protects natural and cultural resources. The Point Reyes National Seashore is now included in the Golden Gate Biosphere Reserve, which is considered unique because it combines marine, coastal, and upland habitats at the doorstep of a major metropolitan area (UNESCO 2002).

In 1965, Marin County replaced the 1943 plan with its Parks and Recreation Plan 1990, which created the template for the current park system (Marin County 2008). Throughout the 1960s, pro-growth elected officials were increasingly chal-lenged by growth-control advocates, who ultimately took charge by the end of the decade. During this period, the Marin Conservation League joined with the Nature Conservancy to prevent dredging of the Bolinas Lagoon to create a marina and related development. Strategic land acquisitions also created a speed bump for plans to make roadway improvements that would have essentially created a free-way between West Marin and San Francisco (Marin Conservation League 2010a).

In the late 1960s, the federal government was looking for someone to buy Alcatraz Island, home of the notorious penitentiary in San Francisco Bay, as well as several decommissioned military installations throughout the San Francisco Bay area. One developer proposed Marincello, a city for more than 30,000 people on the Marin Headlands, at the northern end of the Golden Gate Bridge. This sparked more than 60 organizations to form a coalition called People for a Golden Gate National Recreation Area and enlist the help of Congressman Philip Burton. Fortunately, the National Park Service was also looking to expand its outdoor rec-reational opportunities to city residents who might not have the time or money to travel long distances to traditional national parks. Finally, Republicans as well as

Democrats were largely swept up in the environmental enthusiasm that followed the first Earth Day in 1970. The synergy of these events led President Richard Nixon to sign a bill in 1972 establishing the Golden Gate National Recreation Area, which has since grown to more than 75,000 acres (National Park Service 2009).

In 1971, an impassioned county report called *Can the Last Place Last?* proposed an environmental vision that guides land preservation in Marin County to this day. In 1972, the voters of Marin County overwhelmingly approved a proposition creating the Marin County Regional Park and Open Space District, which underwent a name change two years later to become the Marin County Open Space District (Marin County 2008). The district is primarily funded by an ad valorem property tax of slightly less than 1 percent, which generates about $4 million per year. This tax is supplemented by state funds, grants, and revenues from assessment districts and community facility districts. Currently, most of the property tax income is budgeted for operation and maintenance. But in the district's early years, the property tax was used primarily to buy land for greenbelts, community separators, and nature preserves. The Marin County Open Space District currently manages 34 preserves, with 15,230 acres owned in fee and another 3,500 acres protected by conservation easements (Raives 2010). The district maintains more than 190 miles of trails on these preserves for hiking, biking, horseback riding, and the treatment of "nature deficit disorder" (Marin County 2007). In addition to managing the Marin County Open Space District, the Marin County Department of Parks and Open Space maintains more than 800 acres in 24 county parks and trails (Marin County 2008).

As of 2000, a total of 159,744 acres, or 48 percent of Marin County's total land area, had been preserved as open space, watershed, parkland, and permanently preserved farmland (Marin County 2008). Despite this remarkable achievement, the Marin Countywide Plan calls for preservation of an additional 23,296 acres by 2015 (Marin County 2007).

The Marin Countywide Plan confines most development to the eastern quarter of the county, generally following a 25-mile-long stretch of U.S. Route 101 as it leaves the Golden Gate Bridge at the City of Sausalito, bisects the City of San Rafael, and enters Sonoma County north of the City of Novato. The plan calls for most of the western three-quarters of the county to remain undeveloped. Much of this goal has already been accomplished through the establishment of the parks and preserves discussed above , particularly the Golden Gate National Recreation Area, the Point Reyes National Seashore, and the preserves of the Marin County Open Space District. But roughly 169,000 acres in western Marin County are currently in agriculture, and the countywide plan aims to keeps it that way.

Marin County farms generated $57 million in sales in 2007, with dairy and cattle operations producing more than 80 percent of that value (USDA 2007). Some farmers have reinvented themselves by converting their farms to the production of

Figure 15-2.   Roughly half of Marin County's total land area has been permanently
preserved, including Stinson Beach, part of the Golden Gate National
Recreation Area.

more-valuable commodities such as grass-fed beef and organic foods. In fact, the Marin County agriculture commissioner's office established the first local organic certification agency in the nation (Marin County 2007). Despite the high cost of land there, farmland preservation has been remarkably successful. Of the 169,000 acres in agricultural use, 32,000 acres are publicly owned and leased to farmers by the federal government within the Golden Gate National Recreation Area and the Point Reyes National Seashore. That leaves 137,000 acres of privately owned farmland that Marin County would like to keep in agriculture (Marin County 2007).

To understand Marin's farmland preservation story, it helps to backtrack to the growth battles raging there during the 1960s. Marin County's population had mushroomed by 70 percent in the 1950s, and a study by the U.S. Army Corps of Engineers projected the county's population would quadruple between 1960 and 2020. A second bridge between San Francisco and Marin County was proposed as a way of relieving growing congestion on the Golden Gate Bridge. Highway engineers were preparing plans for a freeway to West Marin and a freeway-style Shoreline Highway on the Pacific coast (Dyble 2007). A city of 125,000 people was planned near the shores of Tomales Bay. Not surprisingly, many farmers were resigned to raising the white flag and selling to developers (Hattam 2002).

However, an expanding coalition of environmentalists fought back, defeating proposals for the Shoreline Highway as well as the sequel to the Golden Gate Bridge. In 1966, the proposed freeway to West Marin was also buried by angry opposition from a wide spectrum of citizens, including many who simply wanted to protect West Marin. With the 1968 elections, the new county board had an anti-sprawl mandate, and the planning department prepared plans reflecting this agenda. The report *Can the Last Place Last?* made the following observation: "It is common knowledge that a home in Marin commands more money than similar homes elsewhere and commuters go on paying this premium on environment through a costly and inconvenient transportation system all because they largely believe that living here is worth the extra effort and cost" (Dyble 2007, 39).

Marin County's first countywide plan, adopted in 1973, designated the central and northwestern portion of the county primarily for agriculture (Marin County 2007). The county rezoned most of this area to prevent farmland from being carved into parcels of fewer than 60 acres. The California Coastal Act of 1972 further limited the conversion of farmland in coastal areas. And in 1976, the county voters rejected plans to construct a pipeline to import water from neighboring Sonoma County. This, plus the difficult access resulting from the death of the freeway proposals, eliminated the near-term likelihood that any cities would be built in West Marin. Nevertheless, commercial farms were still vulnerable to being carved into 60-acre hobby farms, a possibility that particularly threatened the viability of the county's dairy industry (Faber 1999). Preserving these farms was

Figure 15-3.   The Marin Agricultural Land Trust, the nation's first land trust devoted exclusively to farmland, has preserved more than 41,000 acres to date.

critical to the countywide plan's rural preservation goals for West Marin as well as the survival of those dairy farmers who wanted to stay in business.

A novel solution appeared in 1980, when MALT was formed by Ellen Straus, who owned a dairy farm on the shores of Tomales Bay with her husband; Phyllis Faber, a onetime member of the California Coastal Commission; and Ralph Grossi, who later served as president of the American Farmland Trust for 23 years. The trust became the nation's first private nonprofit organization established exclusively to preserve farmland. The Strauses were also among the first farmers to place a MALT conservation easement on their land (Hattam 2002). Early funding to buy perpetual conservation easements on farmland was provided in 1984 by a $1 million grant from the California Coastal Conservancy, which was matched by a grant from the Leonard and Beryl Buck Trust Fund (Faber 1999). In 1988, California voters approved Proposition 70, which provided a total of $63 million for farmland preservation in eight counties, including Marin County (Vink 1998). The Marin County Board of Supervisors granted MALT the entire $15 million in that bond, earmarked for Marin County farmland preservation (Dyble 2007). Today, with the Proposition 70 money spent years ago, MALT continues to preserve farmland through private contributions, grants, and an annual infusion of roughly $35,000 from the Marin County Open Space District (Marin County 2007).

As of 2010, Marin County had preserved 44,350 acres of farmland, with 41,892 acres conserved by MALT alone. Based on this record, *Farmland Preservation Report* ranked Marin County's farmland preservation program as number 11 in its annual survey of the most successful ones in the nation (*Farmland Preservation Report* 2010). In total, Marin County has preserved roughly half of its total land area, an extraordinary accomplishment for a jurisdiction located just one bridge away from the heart of one of the most prosperous metropolitan areas on Earth.

16

MINNEAPOLIS AND THE TWIN CITIES REGION, MINNESOTA

Minneapolis arguably has the best park system in the nation. Its 6,400 acres are anchored by the Grand Rounds, a 50-mile loop of interconnected green space that has won awards as a model of urban design and landscape architecture and acclaim for its provision of recreational opportunities. In addition, the Grand Rounds offers a textbook example of how to succeed in open space preservation: Start with an inspiring plan, and never stop perfecting and implementing it, even if it takes more than 125 years.

It helps that nature blessed the area that eventually became Minneapolis with a 15-mile stretch of the Mississippi River, a chain of lakes, and Minnehaha Falls, the cascade immortalized by Longfellow's beloved poem "The Song of Hiawatha." Outdoor enthusiasts began using the area for recreation long before the city incorporated in 1867. Rapid urban growth soon followed, thanks to the city's location at St. Anthony Falls, where a water-powered industrial complex on the banks of the Mississippi made Minneapolis the nation's leading producer of flour between 1880 and 1930. The population also exploded, tripling in size between 1880 and 1885. Fortunately, city leaders as well as the general public grasped the need to secure their natural heritage before it was subdivided.

Through the efforts of the Minneapolis Board of Trade, a civic group that included prominent businessmen such as George A. Pillsbury, city voters approved a referendum in 1883 creating a park board independent of city government, with the power to acquire land, issue bonds, and levy taxes. The board promptly started work on a park plan by hiring Horace Cleveland, a pioneer landscape architect who was critical of monotonous street patterns and urban designs that ignore natural features. Instead, Cleveland believed that towns, like individual people, should develop a character of their own (Roise 2000). In the same spirit as Daniel Burnham's famous exhortation to "make no little plans," Cleveland made the following proclamation about his design approach in Minneapolis:

> I would have the city itself a work of art as may be the fitting abode of a race of men and women whose lives are devoted to a nobler end than money-getting, and whose efforts shall be inspired and sustained by the grandeur and the beauty of the scenes in which their lives are passed. (Cleveland 1888)

With that can-do spirit, Cleveland proposed a park system that combined parkways with rivers, streams, and lakes for multiple benefits, including aesthetics and public heath as well as protection from wildfires like the one that had destroyed much of Chicago in 1871. Cleveland pointed out how parks enhance private property value and argued that acquisition costs would be reasonable if Minneapolis acted quickly, while land values were relatively low. He wrote,

> Look forward for a century, to the time when the city has a population of a million, and think what will be their wants. They will have wealth enough to purchase all that money can buy, but all their wealth cannot purchase a lost opportunity, or restore natural features of grandeur and beauty, which would then possess priceless value. (Cleveland 1883)

Minneapolis land prices rose so fast in the 1880s that plans for some boulevards had to be abandoned. But the park board was determined to protect the riverfront and bluffs of the Mississippi River gorge. Cleveland used the infamous Twin Cities rivalry to spur acquisition efforts. Noting that St. Paul had already secured parkland on its side of the river, Cleveland added that failure to preserve the Minneapolis side of the river "would be a standing and conspicuous reproach and stigma upon Minneapolis and one with which St. Paul might justly taunt her from its contrast with the superb development of her own side of the river" (Cleveland 1890). By 1905, the park board had acquired the riverfront, allowing construction of parkways that are now part of the Great River Road, the 3,000-mile-long route that follows the Mississippi River through 10 states.

In 1891, the park board approved Cleveland's recommendation to expand the original vision to include a "great parkway, which shall practically encircle the solid parts of the city . . . forming the main framework of the park system" (Cleveland 1890). The board dubbed this design the Grand Rounds, a name that evokes the image of an integrated network of parks connecting all parts of the city.

By 1902, roughly half of the land needed to complete the Grand Rounds had been purchased. Theodore Wirth, park superintendent from 1905 to 1935,

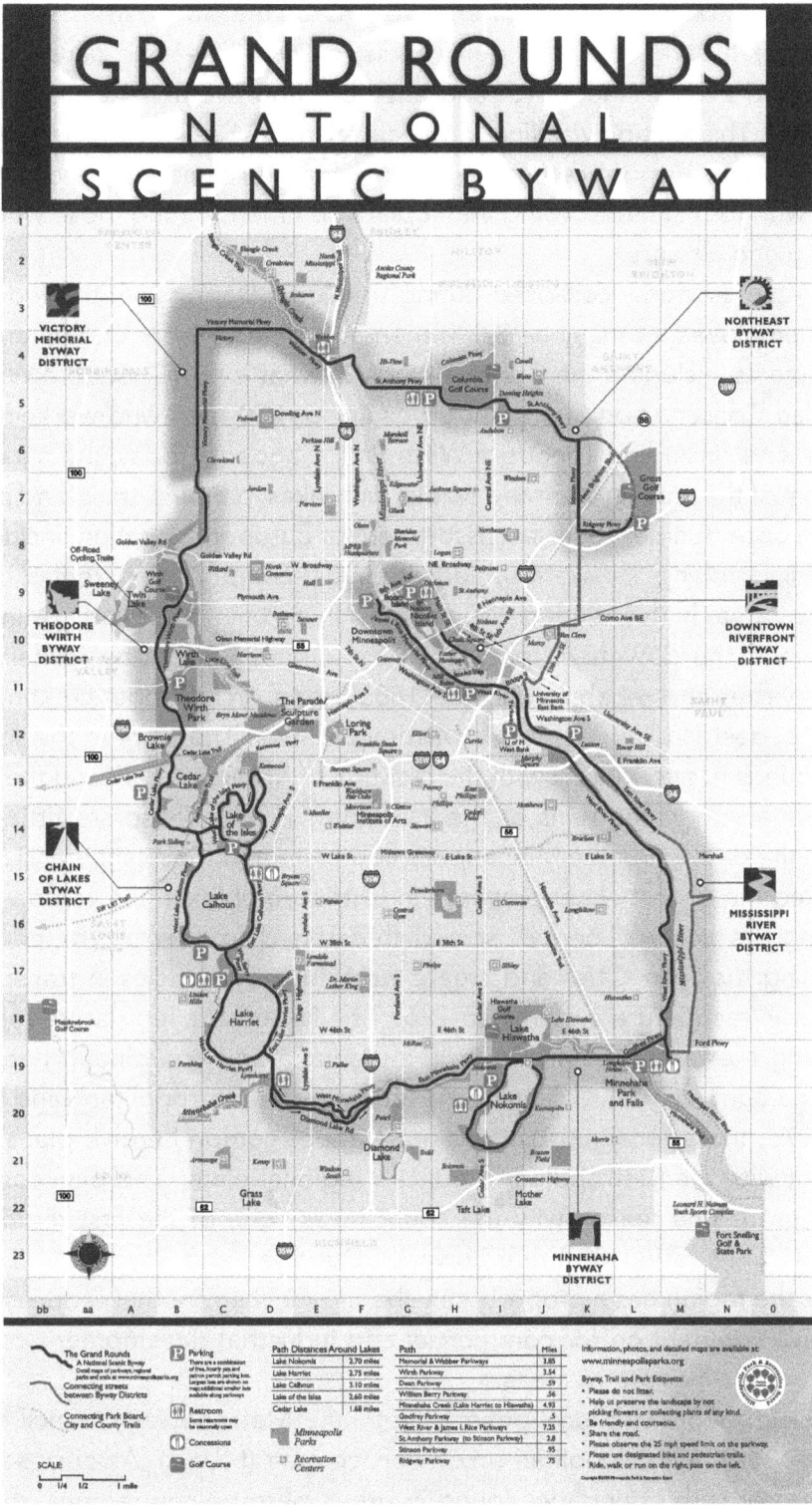

Figure 16-1. The Grand Rounds, a 50-mile loop of parks and parkways, began as a visionary plan adopted in 1883. [Source: Minneapolis Park and Recreation Board]

oversaw the expansion of the Grand Rounds to the north, in a segment that now includes a park, lake, and golf course, which all bear his name. Land was also acquired even farther north and east, but improvements were delayed by World War I. This section was finally dedicated in 1921 as Victory Memorial Drive and incorporates a more ceremonial design than other segments of the Grand Rounds, with formal landscaping and a plaza commemorating those who died in the war to end all wars.

When the economy collapsed during the Great Depression, the federal government employed as many as 3,000 men at a time to work on numerous park board projects, including the Grand Rounds. In what is now Theodore Wirth Park, the Civilian Conservation Corps set up camp for 200 men who worked on park improvements, including Theodore Wirth Park's lagoons. Today, the park offers a microcosm of the parks system as a whole, with lakes, gardens, trails, and playfields providing opportunities for a vast assortment of outdoor recreation, including hiking, bicycling, fishing, ice-skating, sledding, cross-country skiing, tennis, and golf.

Following a hiatus during World War II and its aftermath, Minneapolis strengthened the downtown portion of the Grand Rounds by revitalizing historic properties and rehabilitating the 1883 Stone Arch Bridge, creating a bicyclist and pedestrian link across the Mississippi River. The work in this leg of the Grand Rounds has continued with the creation of Mill Ruins Park and the Mill City Museum, housed in the ruins of the Washburn A Mill. These are fitting monuments to the days when the Minneapolis flour mills and their canals and raceways constituted the largest water-powered industrial complex in the world.

During the postwar period, sprawl threatened to overrun the countryside surrounding the Twin Cities and create wasteful inefficiencies in transportation and other infrastructure systems. In 1967, the Minnesota legislature responded by creating the Metropolitan Council, a planning and coordinating agency for the seven-county region. Following adoption of the Metropolitan Land Planning Act in 1976, these local jurisdictions must adopt comprehensive plans that are consistent with the Metropolitan Council's regional plans. This plan consistency requirement is one reason why the council was "one of the first regional governments in the nation with real powers" (Duerksen and Snyder 2005, 317). In addition, the region has a property-tax-sharing mechanism that reduces the self-destructive competition for commercial and industrial development commonly found in most other metro areas.

In collaboration with local governments, the Metropolitan Council develops and administers a metropolitan urban service area (MUSA). As opposed to the rigid urban growth boundaries found in other metropolitan regions, the MUSA is a flexible boundary that expands as needed to accommodate responsible growth (Metropolitan Council 2006). The MUSA determines the location of major regional investments, such as sewers and highways, thereby creating efficiencies in infrastructure funding and facilitating implementation of the council's comprehensive plans, including its regional parks plan.

The Twin Cities regional parks system was born in 1974, when the Minnesota legislature re-designated 31,000 acres of existing city and county parkland as regional parks and authorized the Metropolitan Council to acquire land for 10 additional parks. Between 1974 and 2004, the council spent $367 million helping

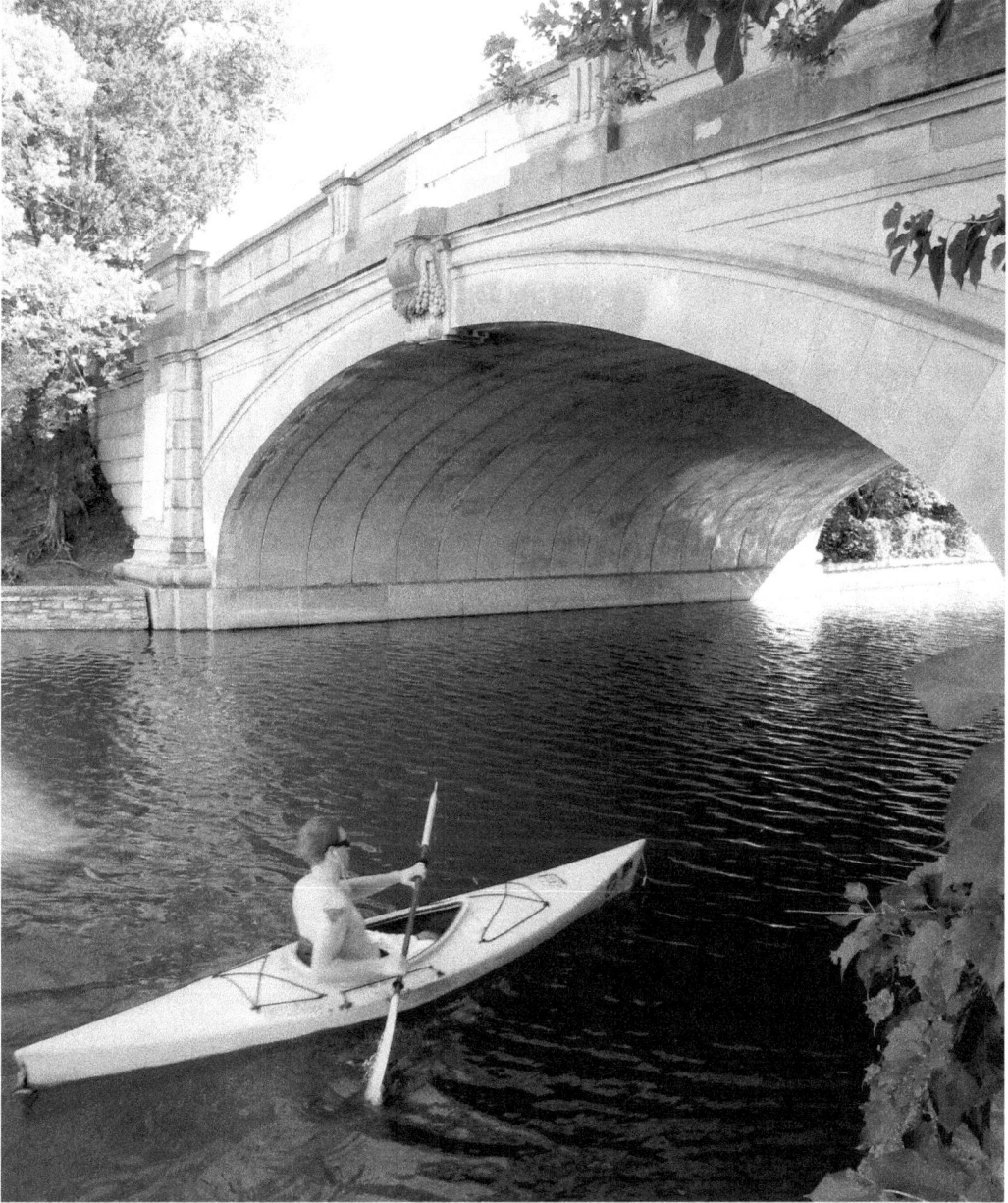

Figure 16-2.   A chain of lakes lets paddlers travel portions of the Grand Rounds by canoe or kayak.

local park districts build the regional park system, which now has 53,000 acres in 49 regional parks and 177 miles of regional trails (Metropolitan Council 2005).

The council plans the development of the regional parks system with the multiple objectives of permanently protecting natural resources while providing a wide assortment of recreational opportunities. These multiple goals are often achieved within individual parks. For example, at Carver Park Reserve, outdoor recreation opportunities (including ice golf) are provided, habitat for trumpeter swans is preserved, and the Grimm family farmstead has been restored (Three Rivers Park District 2010).

The U.S. Fish and Wildlife Service protects 14,000 acres within the Minnesota Valley National Wildlife Refuge, which follows a 99-mile stretch of the Minnesota River. The Minnesota Department of Natural Resources (DNR) adds another 68,000 acres of protected open space to the metro area, including four state parks (Duerksen and Snyder 2005). In the 1990s, the DNR also led a planning effort in conjunction with the Greenways and Natural Areas Collaborative, a group of leaders from the private and public sectors. In 1997, the collaborative released *Metro Greenprint: Planning for Nature in the Face of Urban Growth*, which recommended the creation of a metropolitan greenways and natural area program designed to conserve and restore native ecosystems and connect them with other natural and cultural features throughout the seven-county region (Minnesota DNR 1997). In 1998, the Minnesota legislature began funding the Metro Greenways Program, which offers 50-50 matching grants for projects that "protect, connect and restore a metro-wide area network of significant natural areas and open space" (Minnesota State Lottery 2009).

Metro Greenprint credits the Grand Rounds for demonstrating the wisdom of connecting as well as preserving open space when designing and building a park system at the regional or city level. In 1998, the Grand Rounds was designated as a National Scenic Byway, the only one located entirely within a major metropolitan area. The Grand Rounds is the longest continuous system of public urban parkways in the country, and the National Scenic Byways Program of the U.S. Department of Transportation calls it "the preeminent urban parkway system for more than a century" (National Scenic Byways 2009).

Well-deserved recognition has given Minneapolis residents ample reason to support their park system. Alexander Garvin in *The American City: What Works, What Doesn't* begins a section entitled "Minneapolis: America's Outstanding Park System" with the following emphatic statement: "The best-located, best-financed, best-designed, best-maintained park system in America is the Minneapolis park system" (Garvin 2002, 67). The Minneapolis Park and Recreation Board (MPRB) is not shy about admitting that they believe it to be "the best park system in the galaxy." The MPRB website adds that it was described by the Trust for Public Land in 2000 as the "closest thing to park nirvana" (MPRB 2006).

Figure 16-3. The 1883 Stone Arch Bridge was restored and reopened to bikes and pedestrians, creating a crossing of the Mississippi River for the Grand Rounds.

In 2009, the American Planning Association (APA) recognized the Grand Rounds as one of its Great Places in America.

More than 125 years after Horace Cleveland first presented his vision, the Grand Rounds forms a complete loop around Minneapolis with the exception of "the missing link," a three-mile gap, which the MPRB pledged to close in its 2007 comprehensive plan. One year later, the board selected a route for closing the gap. Even though the project is eligible for local, state, and federal funding, making the Grand Rounds completely round will take several more years (MPRB 2010). Luckily, Minneapolis understands that patience and persistence work, particularly when guided by an inspirational plan.

17

MONTGOMERY COUNTY, MARYLAND

With a total of 132,603 acres in preserved farmland and parks, Montgomery County, Maryland, has protected more than 41 percent of its total land area. That accomplishment is particularly remarkable considering that Montgomery County is immediately adjacent to Washington, D.C., and encompasses growth magnets such as Bethesda, Silver Spring, and Rockville. By preserving this much land within a booming metropolitan region, Montgomery County has validated the time-tested approach of adopting a strong plan and following through with effective implementation. In this case, Montgomery County took some risks with the then fledgling tool of transfer of development rights (TDR) and managed to create a model program now emulated by scores of communities throughout the nation.

Montgomery County's borders are formed by the Potomac River on the west and the Patuxent River on the east. The county's 1969 general plan called for a concentration of urban development in a spoke radiating north through the center of the county from the regional hub, Washington, D.C. The general plan is titled On Wedges and Corridors, which alone gives residents a clear idea of the county's goals, regardless of whether or not they ever open the cover. The *corridor* flanking Interstate 270 provides for urban development served by efficient infrastructure. The *wedges* surrounding this corridor are to remain in farmland, natural areas, and rural open space.

On Wedges and Corridors was a conceptual triumph. But it could not independently correct past regulatory mistakes, such as the preexisting zoning that allowed one- and two-acre lots. In 1974, the Montgomery County Council

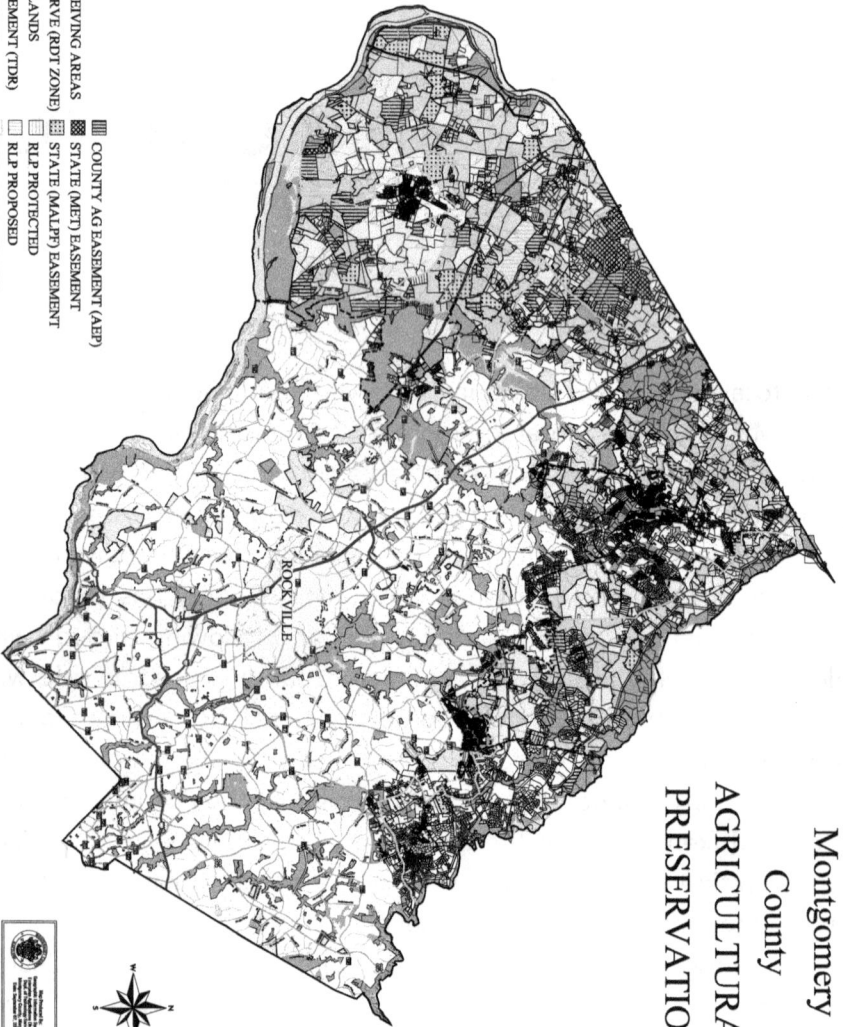

Figure 17-1. Montgomery County has preserved more than 71,000 acres of farm land to date.
[*Source: Montgomery County*]

Montgomery
County
AGRICULTURAL
PRESERVATION

WATER
TDR RECEIVING AREAS
AG RESERVE (RDT ZONE)
PUBLIC LANDS
TDR EASEMENT (TDR)
AEP PROPOSED

COUNTY AG EASEMENT (AEP)
STATE (MET) EASEMENT
STATE (MALPF) EASEMENT
RLP PROTECTED
RLP PROPOSED
RURAL LEGACY AREA

ROCKVILLE

downzoned much of the wedge area to a maximum density of one unit per five acres. But this only led to a spate of five-acre-lot subdivisions.

In the next five years, the county lost almost 12,000 acres of farmland to development, leading to a condition that the Maryland–National Capital Park and Planning Commission (M–NCPPC) termed "Impermanence Syndrome—the feeling by farmers that farming is doomed in their area" (M–NCPPC 1980, 11). This psychology was considered as harmful to the long-term viability of farming as tangible symptoms such as encroaching development, rising taxes, the loss of agricultural support services, reduced political clout, laws that restrain agricultural operations, and land-use conflicts with nonagricultural neighbors. The M–NCPPC continued: "The Syndrome is manifested in an agricultural community that sees no future for itself and its children; that regards eventual over-running by the suburbs as inevitable. Soon, the critical mass of farms and services necessary to sustain a viable agricultural community crumbles" (M–NCPPC 1980, 11).

In 1980, Montgomery County adopted its Functional Master Plan for the Preservation of Agriculture & Rural Open Space. The preservation plan demonstrated that Montgomery County was as serious about preserving the wedges as it was about confining urban growth to the corridors. In laying a foundation for its ambitious goals, the preservation plan goes beyond the usual statistics about farm income and employment. It explains how preservation helps to accomplish the goals of the general plan, including the creation of livable communities served by efficient public services. In addition, the preservation plan details the benefits derived directly from saving the wedges, including environmental protection and outdoor recreation, as well as the multiple rewards of farmland preservation itself, such as the security of locally grown food and the retention of a significant agricultural economy. The preservation plan even likens the wedges to museums showcasing remnants of the cultural heritage of the 18th-century English planters and the 19th-century German and Quaker settlers.

The preservation plan established the Agricultural Reserve, with 93,000 contiguous acres of land that include wooded areas, stream corridors, wildlife habitat, and parkland, as well as the best remaining farmland in the county. Most of the Agricultural Reserve was downzoned from a maximum density of one unit per five acres to one unit per 25 acres, based on an agricultural economist's determination that at least 25 acres of land is needed to support a farm family in Montgomery County. John Zawitoski, director of planning for the Montgomery County Department of Economic Development, stresses that the 93,000 acres is called a reserve because zoning is not permanent: "Zoning buys you time but it only lasts as long as there is political will. Farmland is reserved through zoning but it is permanently protected only by preservation easements" (Zawitoski 2011).

With the goal of permanently protecting the Agricultural Reserve, the 1980 preservation plan launched what was to become the most famous TDR program in the nation. Transfer of development rights uses private market forces to steer growth away from places that a community wants to save, called sending areas, into places that the community wants to grow, called receiving areas. In this case, the sending area is the Agricultural Reserve. Montgomery County wants landowners in the Agricultural Reserve to record easements that permanently restrict development to the density limit of one unit per 25 acres that was imposed by the rural density transfer (RDT) zoning adopted for the reserve. The owners of farmland who choose to record such easements are granted transferable development rights at a ratio of one right per five acres of restricted land. In keeping with the preservation plan's goal of preserving the Agricultural Reserve as an integrated whole, all RDT properties in their entirety qualify for the same TDR allocation ratio regardless of their agricultural characteristics or suitability for development.

The Montgomery County TDR program is so successful that it has become a national model. Farmland owners are compensated for recording agricultural easements while continuing to own their land and use it for farming and other activities consistent with the goals of the preservation plan. Developers have demonstrated their acceptance by buying thousands of transferable development rights in order to build at higher densities in the receiving areas. And Montgomery County itself accomplishes land preservation as well as the growth goals of its general plan by harnessing development proceeds rather than relying on tax dollars. As of June 2009, the Montgomery County TDR program had protected 52,052 acres, more land than any other TDR program in the nation had protected, with the exception of King County, Washington, and the New Jersey Pinelands (Pruetz and Standridge 2009).

In addition to TDR, Montgomery County uses the following four supplemental preservation programs (Montgomery County Department of Economic Development 2009):

- The Montgomery County Agricultural Easement Program buys easements from exceptional properties regardless of the availability of state funding.
- The Maryland Agricultural Land Preservation Foundation uses state money to buy easements offered by landowners at an average 15 percent discount.
- The Maryland Rural Legacy Program offers competitive grants for the acquisition of easements on land with significant farm, forest, cultural, or natural resources.
- The Maryland Environmental Trust provides specified income, estate, gift, and property tax benefits to owners who donate conservation easements on land with scenic open space and natural resources.

Figure 17-2.   Montgomery County has the second-most successful locally operated farmland preservation program in the United States.

All of Montgomery County's strategies combined preserved a total of 71,662 acres of farmland as of September 2010, putting Montgomery County in second place for successful locally operated farmland preservation programs, surpassed only by Lancaster County, Pennsylvania (*Farmland Preservation Report* 2010).

The preservation plan recognized the importance not only of preserving land but of all factors that contribute to impermanence syndrome. Consequently, the county's Agricultural Services Division combines the coordination of all land preservation efforts with other programs that support the county's agricultural industry, including buy-local campaigns, farmers markets, farm tours, and the promotion of farms that allow urbanites the opportunity to pick their own apples and pumpkins, chop their own Christmas trees, take hayrides, and wander in corn mazes. The division assists the farming community with technical and regulatory issues, such as deer management and tax relief. Occasionally, the division also acts as an advocate for its farmers when dealing with other branches of government (Benfield 2001). This effort has paid off, as demonstrated by Montgomery County's vigorous agricultural sector with 577 farms and 350 horticultural businesses generating more than $251 million in revenue and 10,000 jobs for the local economy (Montgomery County Department of Economic Development 2010).

In addition to preserved farmland, 61,250 acres in Montgomery County are protected in federal, state, and county parks (Montgomery County Department

Figure 17-3.   Montgomery County's TDR program alone has preserved more than 52,000 acres.

of Parks 2010). The Chesapeake and Ohio Canal National Historical Park saves a linear strip of open space along the Potomac River, incorporating a segment of the 335-mile multiuse trail connecting Washington, D.C., with Pittsburgh, currently the longest multipurpose recreational trail in the United States. Montgomery County alone manages 33,000 acres of parkland and more than 100 miles of trails. Roughly 12,000 acres of the county's parklands are in stream-valley parks that serve as greenways, connecting urban areas with the surrounding countryside. The paths and water trails within these greenways offer county residents an enjoyable way to travel from the corridors to the wedges. In fact, the Agricultural Reserve contains more than 10,000 acres of parkland, demonstrating how the preservation plan nimbly combines many protection strategies to preserve the natural, cultural, and agricultural resources that together form a cohesive and viable countryside.

By promoting agritourism and outdoor recreation in the wedges, Montgomery County has retained and strengthened the public's love of the Agricultural Reserve. One indication of the level of support is the Montgomery Countryside Alliance, a coalition of nonprofit organizations and businesses that originally formed to defeat the proposed building of a bridge and roadway that would have linked Washington Dulles International Airport, in Virginia, with the I-270 corridor in Montgomery County, by way of the Agricultural Reserve. The coalition still fights threats to the reserve but now also supports local farmers, promotes rural activities, and enthusiastically celebrates the reserve. Every year, the alliance presents an award recognizing outstanding commitment to the reserve's protection. The award is named after Royce Hanson, the former chair of the Montgomery County Planning Board, who is widely recognized as the architect of the Agricultural Reserve. Dr. Hanson, who was also the first recipient of the award that bears his name, made the following observations about Montgomery County's Agricultural Reserve:

> Value is added to every home and household in the area when we know future generations can see Sugarloaf rise from fields instead of roofs; bike a country road on the weekend without having to drive to West Virginia; and learn that it is both possible and practical to grow smart. And, if we remain constant in purpose and inventive in spirit and policy, this broad wedge of piedmont will forever interrupt an unremitting urban advance. (Hanson 2004)

18

PALM BEACH COUNTY, FLORIDA

Palm Beach County, Florida, identified the best remaining ecosystems in its comprehensive plan and then proceeded to acquire these sites with a voter-approved bond. Using its innovative transfer of development rights (TDR) program, the county now sells the development rights from these preserved lands and applies the proceeds to maintaining and extending its Natural Areas Program. Remarkably, Palm Beach County continues this and other conservation efforts despite the fact that governments at the federal, state, and local levels have already preserved more than one-quarter of Palm Beach County's total land area.

Palm Beach County extends from the Atlantic Ocean to the center of the Florida peninsula, about 40 miles north of Miami. Today, the county's population stands at 1.35 million, mostly living in coastal communities, such as Jupiter, Boca Raton, and West Palm Beach. But the preservation story started back in 1947, when roughly 100,000 people lived there. In that year, the state acquired the first of four state wildlife refuges that now protect more than 136,000 acres of land in Palm Beach County.

- The 60,288-acre J. W. Corbett Wildlife Management Area, once used for timber harvesting and cattle grazing, is now home to the popular Hungryland Boardwalk and a segment of the 1,400-mile-long Florida Trail, one of only 11 congressionally designated National Scenic Trails in the United States (Florida Fish and Wildlife Conservation Commission 2010a).

- The 35,350-acre Holey Land Wildlife Management Area gets its name from the holes left there after the area was used as a practice bombing range during World War II (Florida Fish and Wildlife Conservation Commission 2010b).
- The 29,297-acre Rotenberger Wildlife Management Area offers habitat for migratory birds, wood storks, ibises, and occasionally, Florida panthers (Florida Fish and Wildlife Conservation Commission 2010c).
- The State of Florida acquired the John C. and Mariana Jones/Hungryland Wildlife and Environmental Area following a failed real estate venture that ended after canals were carved into the land in an attempt to drain the area for development (Florida Fish and Conservation Wildlife Commission 2010d).

John D. MacArthur Beach State Park also contributes 325 acres to Palm Beach County's open space inventory, with a stunning natural setting that includes a mangrove-bordered estuary and a beach with prime nesting sites for loggerhead, leatherback, and green turtles (Florida State Parks 2011).

Federal open space preservation in Palm Beach County took a giant step forward in 1951 with the establishment of the 143,328-acre Arthur R. Marshall Loxahatchee National Wildlife Refuge, home to at least 63 threatened, endangered, or special-concern species (U.S. Fish and Wildlife Service 2002). Unfortunately, an ill-conceived "improvement project" was launched in 1948 that created ecological problems for the Loxahatchee refuge and other environmentally sensitive areas. In that year, Congress authorized the U.S. Army Corps of Engineers and the South Florida Water Management District to build the Central & Southern Florida Project (CSFP), considered the most ambitious water management system in the world. The CSFP succeeded in protecting vast stretches of Florida's interior from floodwater, thereby facilitating urban development. But it also degraded the natural ecosystem of the Everglades. Consequently, 50 years after approving the CSFP, Congress approved the Comprehensive Everglades Restoration Plan (CERP). Ironically, it is considered one of the most ambitious ecological restoration plans in the world. This $12 billion plan, prepared by the U.S. Army Corps of Engineers and numerous partner agencies, is designed to repair environmental damage primarily by retaining water in the Everglades. The CERP will take 30 years to implement. In 2010, the CERP team broke ground on a project in Palm Beach County that will reduce urban water demands on the Loxahatchee refuge, leaving more freshwater there in order to help in the revival of the original Everglades ecology (CERP 2010a; CERP 2010b).

Palm Beach County's 1980 comprehensive plan focused on confining urban development to areas that could be served by infrastructure and reducing densities in areas that were planned to remain rural (Palm Beach County 1989).

Nevertheless, environmentalists became increasingly alarmed at the rapid loss of native vegetation in Palm Beach County and formed the Coalition for Wilderness Islands in 1984. In 1988, the county completed an inventory of native communities, recommending the preservation of 38 sites with the best remaining examples of natural ecosystems in the county (Palm Beach County 2010a).

In 1989, the county adopted a new comprehensive plan with a conservation element that emphasized the acquisition of the natural ecosystems identified in

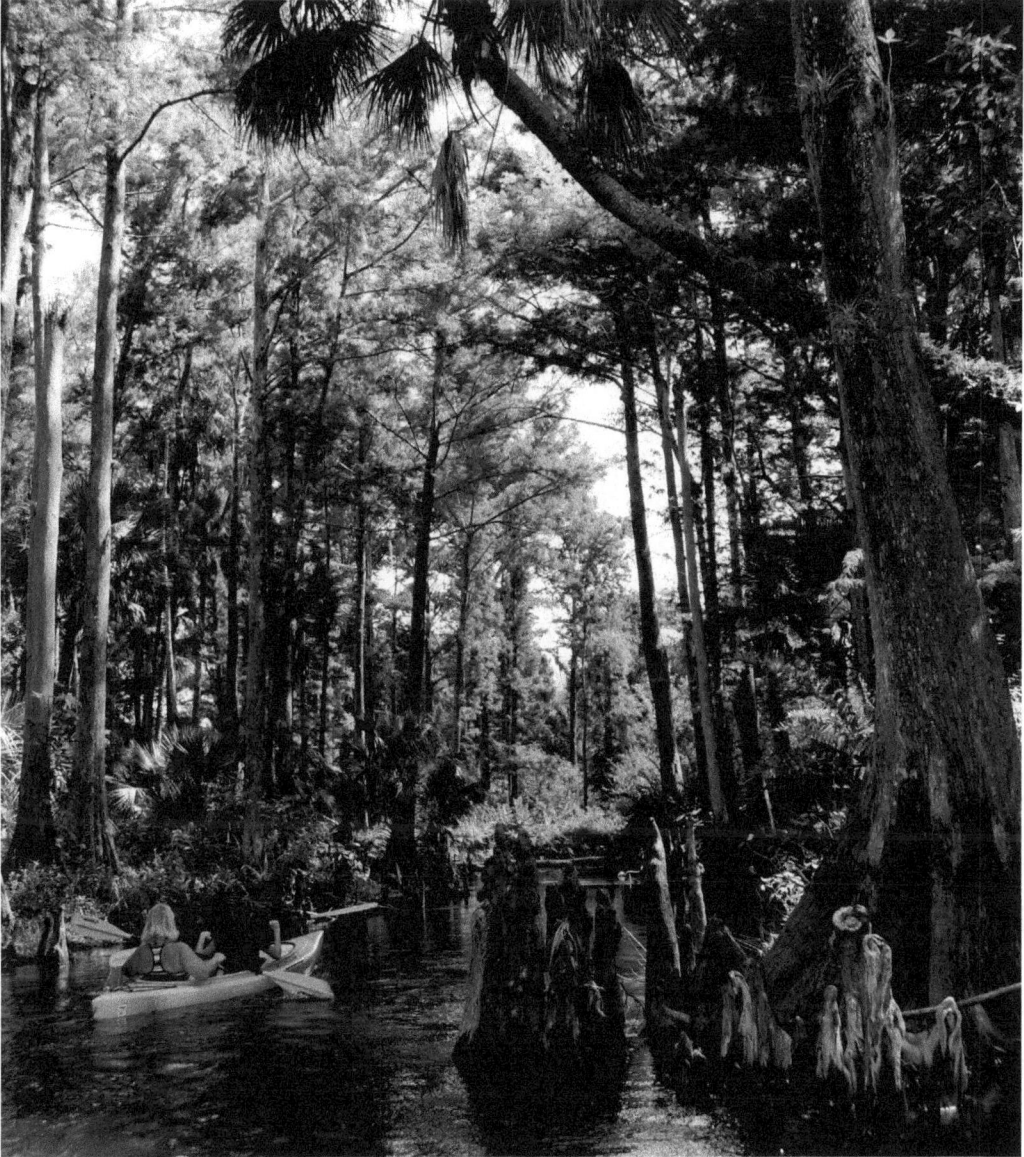

Figure 18-1.   Palm Beach County's Riverbend Park gives paddlers access to the largely pristine Loxahatchee River, one of only two federally designated Wild and Scenic Rivers in Florida.

the inventory. Following an extensive public education campaign, county voters approved a $100 million bond in 1991 to begin buying these sites. The county matched this money with funding from state sources and succeeded in preserving such an impressive amount of land that the voters approved another open space bond in 1999 for $150 million, with $50 million earmarked for the purchase of conservation land (Palm Beach County 2010a).

Figure 18-2.   John D. MacArthur Beach State Park offers refuge for snakes as well as prime nesting sites for loggerhead, leatherback, and green turtles.

Today, Palm Beach County manages more than 31,000 acres of environmentally sensitive land within 31 preserves. Although these natural areas are primarily intended for the preservation and restoration of ecosystems and habitat, they are also open for nature study, birding, photography, hiking, and other passive recreation. Loxahatchee Slough is the largest of the Palm Beach County natural areas, protecting almost 13,000 acres at the headwaters of the Wild and Scenic Loxahatchee River and preserving habitat for sandhill cranes. In addition to preserving several remnants of the Everglades ecosystem, the Natural Area Program has preserved properties in coastal areas, including Juno Dunes Natural Area, with beaches that provide nesting sites for three protected species of sea turtles (Palm Beach County 2010b).

Palm Beach County should be recognized not just for its preservation accomplishments but also for its innovative method of combining traditional bond funding with TDR. The land that Palm Beach County acquired for its Natural Areas Program generated 9,000 units of transferable development potential under the county's TDR ordinance. The county deposited these 9,000 units in its TDR bank and sells them to developers who want additional residential density in the county's designated growth areas. In fiscal year 2004–2005 alone, the county sold 435 units for $25,000 each, generating more than $10 million in revenue that it would not have received without using its TDR ordinance. The county uses the revenue from the sale of these units for expansion and maintenance of its Natural Area System (Palm Beach County 2005).

In addition to its Natural Area System, Palm Beach County maintains 8,550 acres of county parkland, including the 680-acre Riverbend Park, which offers canoe and kayak access to the Loxahatchee River, federally designated as a National Wild and Scenic River. The Loxahatchee threads its way through a largely pristine bald cypress swamp beneath a closed canopy of trees that are up to 500 years old. Hearty paddlers can continue to the Loxahatchee River–Lake Worth Creek Aquatic Preserve, home to 27 rare or endangered species, including butterfly orchid, tricolored heron, and the 3,500-pound Florida manatee (Florida Department of Environmental Protection 2005).

The cities in Palm Beach County have also contributed significantly to the total open space preservation effort. Most notably, the City of West Palm Beach established Grassy Waters Preserve, which protects 12,800 acres of Everglades environment. Grassy Waters safeguards the drinking water used by 130,000 people. It also serves as an open-air classroom where people can learn about sustainability, hike through marshes, and explore wilderness areas by pole boat (West Palm Beach 2008).

In addition to preserving land, Palm Beach County has joined forces with other resource agencies to coordinate the planning and management of more than 165,000 acres of publicly owned conservation lands in northern Palm Beach

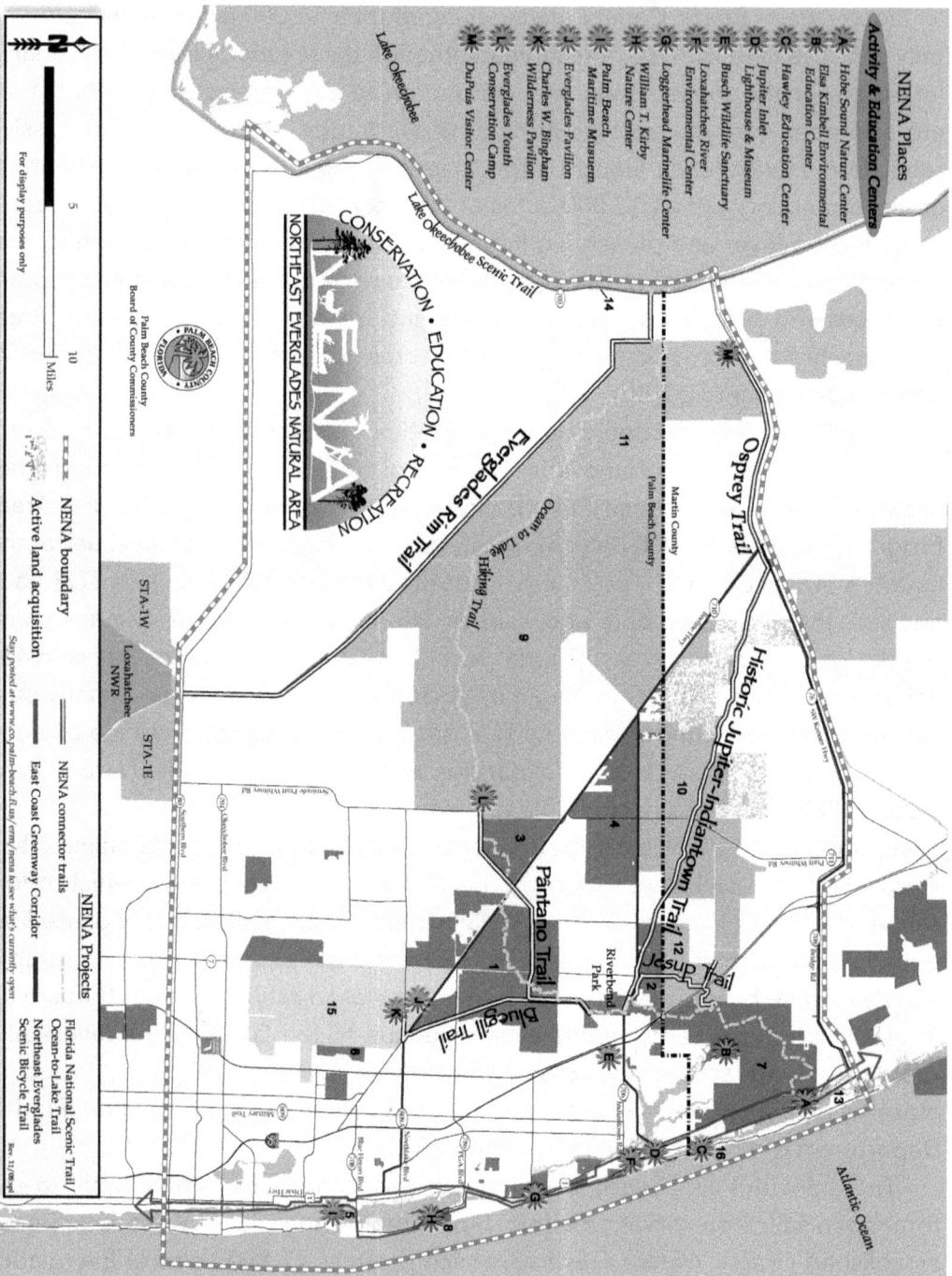

NENA Places

Activity & Education Centers

- A Hobe Sound Nature Center
- B Elsa Kimbell Environmental Education Center
- C Hawley Education Center
- D Jupiter Inlet Lighthouse & Museum
- E Busch Wildlife Sanctuary
- F Loxahatchee River Environmental Center
- G Loggerhead Marinelife Center
- H William T. Kirby Nature Center
- I Palm Beach Maritime Museum
- J Everglades Pavilion
- K Charles W. Bingham Everglades Pavilion
- L Everglades Youth Conservation Camp
- M DuPuis Visitor Center

NENA Places

County Park or Natural Area (NA)
1. Loxahatchee Slough NA
2. Cypress Creek NA
3. Hungryland Slough NA
4. Pine Glades NA
5. Peanut Island Park
6. Solid Waste Authority

State Park (SP)
7. Jonathan Dickinson SP
8. John D. MacArthur Beach SP

Wildlife Management Area (WMA)/ Environmental Area (WEA)
9. J.W. Corbett WMA
10. Jones/Hungryland WEA

South Florida Water Management District
11. DuPuis Management Area/ DuPuis WEA
12. Cypress Creek Management Area

Federal Refuge (NWR) or Trail
13. Hobe Sound NWR
14. Lake Okeechobee Scenic Trail

Preserve or City Park
15. Grassy Waters Preserve
16. Blowing Rocks Preserve

See table on reverse side for contact info

Legend

NENA boundary
Active land acquisition
NENA connector trails
East Coast Greenway Corridor
Northeast Everglades Scenic Bicycle Trail

NENA Projects
Florida National Scenic Trail/ Ocean-to-Lake Trail

For display purposes only

0 5 10 Miles

N

Stay posted at www.co.palm-beach.fl.us/erm/nena to see what's currently open

Rev 11/08(jqd)

Map labels:
Lake Okeechobee · Lake Okeechobee Scenic Trail · Everglades Rim Trail · Ocean to Lake Hiking Trail · Osprey Trail · Historic Jupiter-Indiantown Trail · Jessup Trail · Pantano Trail · Bluegill Trail · Riverbend Park · Martin County · Palm Beach County · Atlantic Ocean · STA-1W · STA-1E · Loxahatchee NWR

County and southern Martin County. In 2002, Palm Beach County sponsored a plan for this area—the Northeast Everglades Natural Area (NENA) plan—which treats these preserves as a world-class destination comparable to a national park. That comparison is apt considering that NENA offers more than 300 miles of trails, 25 natural areas, 14 miles of Atlantic Ocean shoreline, two state parks, four wildlife refuges, and a National Wild and Scenic River. The NENA plan aims to strengthen these interconnections by using a coordinated acquisition strategy and linking the various components with an extensive trail system (Palm Beach County 2010c).

In March 2011, Palm Beach County and its NENA partners completed Phase 1 of the Bluegill Trail, connecting Riverbend Park with the City of West Palm Beach's Grassy Waters Preserve. This multiuse trail forms part of the 70-mile Ocean-to-Lake Greenway, which will ultimately connect Hobe Sound on the Atlantic Ocean with Port Mayaca on Lake Okeechobee through a contiguous 140,000-acre corridor of preserved open space. For years, communities from around the country have studied Palm Beach County's creative combination of TDR and traditional open space funding. In the future, they will also be closely watching Palm Beach County's collaborative approach to achieving economic development as well as watershed management, habitat protection, outdoor recreation, and open space preservation goals through the NENA plan.

OPPOSITE PAGE

Figure 18-3.   In the Northeast Everglades Natural Area (NENA), Palm Beach County and its partners plan and promote 165,000 acres within various nature preserves and parks as a coordinated, world-class destination comparable to a national park. *[Source: Map courtesy of Palm Beach County Board of County Commissioners, Department of Environmental Resources Management]*

Note: This data is provided "as is" without warranty or any representation of accuracy, timeliness or completeness. The burden for determining accuracy, completeness, timeliness, merchantability and fitness for or the appropriateness for use rests solely on the requester. The County makes no warranties, express or implied, as to the use of the data. There are no implied warranties of merchantability or fitness for a particular purpose. The requester acknowledges and accepts the limitations of the data, including the fact that the data is dynamic and is in a constant state of maintenance, correction and update.

19

PIMA COUNTY, ARIZONA

Pima County, Arizona, aims to go beyond the mere peaceful coexistence of nature and humankind. It wants to nurture something that almost sounds like a good marriage: "an interdependent relationship, where one enhances the other" (Pima County 2000a, 8). With that goal in mind, Pima County launched its award-winning Sonoran Desert Conservation Plan, which strives to balance the built environment with the ecosystems, landscapes, and cultural treasures that are partly responsible for the county's phenomenal rate of growth. In pursuit of this balance, public agencies and private organizations have already protected more than 1.6 million acres of Pima County's fragile environment.

Pima County surrounds the City of Tucson, in south-central Arizona, and shares a 125-mile-long border with Mexico. It is bigger than the state of New Jersey, but more than 40 percent of its land area is within Native American nations. For decades, northerners have fled there for the warmth and wide open spaces. This attraction takes its toll on the environment, with 10 square miles of desert land being converted to subdivisions every year.

Fortunately, conservation efforts preceded the steepest part of the growth curve, producing outstanding land preservation successes in Pima County since the start of the 20th century. Many of these pioneering conservation efforts involved the preservation of federally owned land. But in 1974, Pima County voters demonstrated a growing commitment to conservation by approving a $4.5 million open space bond to acquire what is now Catalina State Park. In the 1980s,when county population grew by more than 25 percent, Tucson adopted a comprehensive plan calling for the preservation of primary riparian corridors connecting major public open spaces. In 1986, Pima County voters again stepped up to the plate and approved a $17 million open space bond that jump-started the acquisition of Tortolita Mountain Park. In the 1990s, as the growth rate went even higher, the voters gave a thumbs-up to a $30 million bond that purchased 7,200 acres, expanding three existing parks, conserving the Clyne Ranch, and establishing the Raul M. Grijalva Canoa Conservation Park (Pima County 2011).

But the catalyst for coordinated conservation in Pima County is often attributed to the 1997 listing of the cactus ferruginous pygmy-owl as an endangered species under the federal Endangered Species Act. The dwindling habitat of this fist-sized bird is directly in the path of the development wave radiating from Tucson. In order to maintain reasonable opportunity for future development and a reasonably healthy economy, Pima County proposed to prepare a multispecies conservation plan (MSCP) that would demonstrate how a limited portion of critical habitat could be sacrificed as long as enough habitat was preserved to ensure the survival of the pygmy-owl and several other species that were either listed or likely to be listed.

However, the board of supervisors was ultimately persuaded to take a broader and more holistic approach. What evolved was the Sonoran Desert Conservation Plan (SDCP), which creates a strategy for conserving cultural landmarks, riparian corridors, mountain parks, and ranchlands, as well as critical habitat. In 1998, the SDCP concept document added the following: "If fully implemented, the proposed plan will dramatically effect [sic] regional urban form, arrest urban sprawl, and protect those lands that contain the highest quantity and quality of regional resources" (Pima County 1998, 1).

SDCP Historical and Cultural Resources Element

Outstanding historic and archaeological sites were protected in Pima County prior to the SDCP. In Catalina State Park, dedicated in 1983, visitors can hike through the ruins of a 1,000-year-old village built by the Hohokam, or "those who came before," and imagine the games played within its prehistoric ball courts. Remnants of the Hohokam civilization can also be found in the Rincon Mountain Foothills National Archeological District in Saguaro National Park. Similarly, three historically significant ranches were already protected when the SDCP was still in its concept phase (Pima County 1998).

This element of the SDCP calls for additional protection of Pima County's archaeological sites, landmark structures, historic communities, ghost towns, and historic trails using a wide range of preservation tools (Pima County 2009b). In many cases, the preservation of historic sites can hit multiple targets. For example,

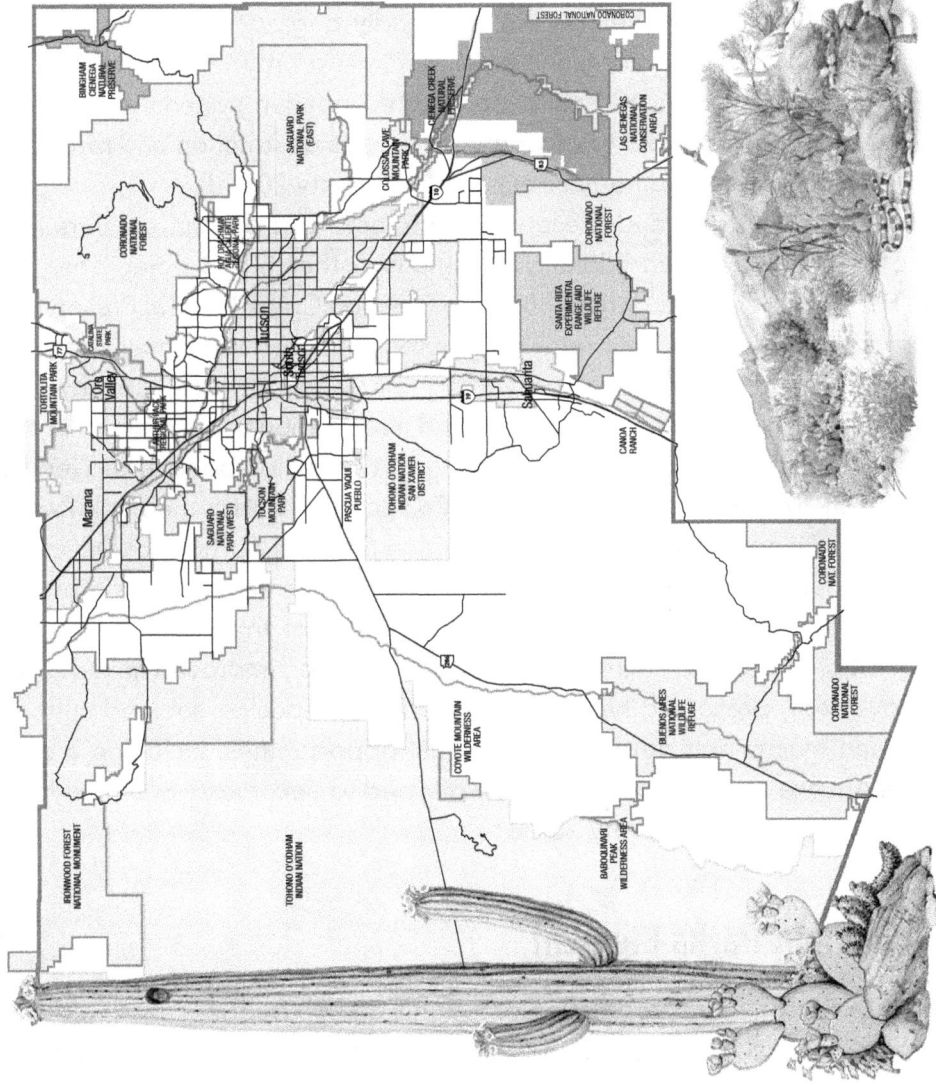

SONORAN DESERT CONSERVATION PLAN

MOUNTAIN PARKS AND NATURAL PRESERVES

Pima County's establishment of Tucson Mountain Park in 1929 marked the beginning of an unparalleled conservation ethic. Two other parks and a natural preserve followed. Ironwood Forest National Monument and Las Cienegas National Conservation Area were established in 2000. Even so, we have not yet assembled a system that protects groups of plants and animals. We must expand our efforts at creating mountain parks to sustain biological diversity in the Sonoran Desert and provide recreation for our citizens.

LEGEND

Proposed Mountain Park Expansion

Proposed Natural Preserve

Proposed New Mountain Park

Las Cienegas Planning District

Existing Preserves

PIMA COUNTY BOARD OF SUPERVISORS
Sharon Bronson, Chair • District 3
Ann Day • District 1
Ramón Valadez • District 2
Raymond J. Carroll • District 4
Richard Elías • District 5

Chuck Huckelberry • Pima County Administrator

Visit the Sonoran Desert Conservation Plan Web site
www.pima.gov/sdcp

Sonoran Desert Conservation Plan
County Administrator's Office
130 West Congress, 10th Floor
Tucson, AZ 85701
520-740-8162

Figure 19-1.   Pima County's Sonoran Desert Conservation Plan creates a strategy for conserving cultural landmarks, riparian corridors, mountain parks, and ranchlands, as well as critical habitat. [Source: Pima County]

Pima County bought 4,800 acres of the Canoa Ranch on the banks of the Santa Cruz River and began developing it as Raul M. Grijalva Canoa Conservation Park. The plans for this park combine habitat preservation, riparian restoration, a segment of the Anza Trail, controlled access to Native American cultural sites, and a heritage center that tells the Canoa story from prehistory to its recent past as a working ranch (Pima County 2007).

SDCP Riparian Restoration Element

The Santa Cruz River and its tributaries once flowed year round through what is now Tucson, supporting streamside forests of mesquite, cottonwood, and willow trees. Many of these desert lifelines are now badly degraded by groundwater pumping, floodplain development, and erosion (Pima County 1998). The riparian restoration element of the SDCP calls for selected riparian systems to be preserved, restored, and managed to compensate for this destruction and re-create these streams for wildlife and humans alike (Pima County 2009d).

This element proposes land preservation projects that protect aquifers and reduce flood damage but additionally accomplish other SDCP objectives. For example, Pima County created the 3,886-acre Cienega Creek Natural Preserve in 1986 to safeguard one of the few remaining perennial streams in Pima County. In addition to recharging the aquifer and adding floodwater storage capacity, this preserve provides excellent riparian habitat and a recreational trail system. In the implementation phase of SDCP, a portion of the $174 million bond approved by county voters in 2004 was used to protect 13,763 acres of land in the Bar V Ranch adjacent to the Cienega preserve. This acquisition protects portions of Davidson Canyon, which features a popular recreational trail and a stream that is a tributary of Cienega Creek. In keeping with the multiple goals of the SDCP, this single ranch acquisition protected an important riparian corridor, improved linkages for wildlife movement, preserved habitat for endangered species, secured cultural resources, and maintained outdoor recreational opportunities, including a segment of the Arizona Trail, which is ultimately planned to become an 800-mile-long National Scenic Trail (Pima County 2004).

SDCP Mountain Parks Element

In 1928, when Tucson had a population of roughly 30,000 people, farsighted citizens and public officials realized that their beloved desert setting would be permanently scarred unless key federal holdings surrounding the city were permanently protected from homesteading and mining. Working with Congress, they established the 20,000-acre Tucson Mountain Park, one of the largest natural resource areas in the United States owned and managed by a local government. Today this park creates an enormous playground for hikers and mountain bikers as well as a home for wildlife, including mountain lions and bobcats. The county added Tortolita Mountain Park to its mountain park system when the voters approved

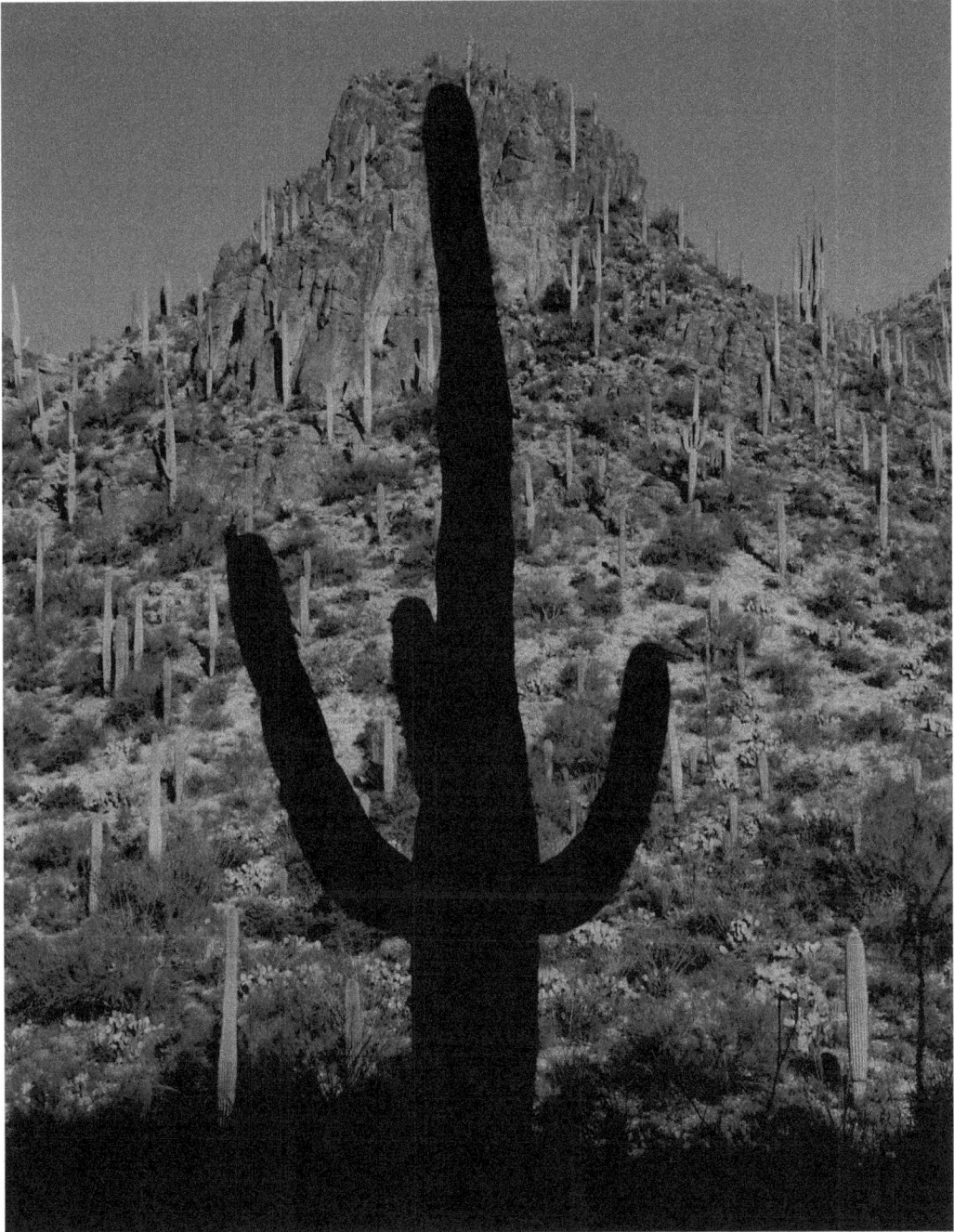

Figure 19-2.   More than 1.6 million acres of Pima County's fragile environment are already preserved, including 20,000-acre Tucson Mountain Park.

an open space bond in 1986. And in 1992, the county established Colossal Cave Mountain Park, which is home to a remarkably diverse assortment of wildlife, including at least a dozen bat species.

Pima County's mountain park system has been significantly supplemented by national forests, parks, and monuments. In the early 1900s, the federal government protected 337,254 acres of land within Pima County in what is now Coronado National Forest (Pima County 2000b). This national forest features sky islands, mountain ranges sculpted by millions of years of volcanic upheaval and erosion. The sky islands contain astonishing biodiversity, with natural communities ranging from cacti to spruce trees according to elevation (USDA Forest Service 2010).

In 1933, President Hoover designated a huge portion of federal land east of Tucson as Saguaro National Monument, named for the 50-foot-tall, candelabra-shaped cactus that is now a world-famous icon of the American West. In 1961, President Kennedy protected a similar area west of Tucson, adjacent to Tucson Mountain Park. Then, in 1994, President Clinton signed a bill that enlarged these preserves to more than 91,000 acres and reestablished them as our 52nd national park (National Park Service 2010). In 1937, President Roosevelt protected 331,272 acres of western Pima County as Organ Pipe Cactus National Monument, which has been named as a United Nations Biosphere Reserve, one of only 47 such reserves in the United States.

In 2000, when the SDCP was still being drafted, President Clinton established 129,000 acres of federal land northwest of Tucson as Ironwood Forest National Monument. The monument is home to the Silver Bell Mountains and more than 674 species ranging from endangered cacti and bats to a population of desert bighorn sheep (Clinton 2000). Later in 2000, President Clinton approved the creation of the Las Cienegas National Conservation Area (Las Cienegas NCA), 50 miles southeast of Tucson. The Las Cienegas NCA and its adjacent acquisition planning area total 142,800 acres, adding to an informal greenbelt that surrounds portions of the greater Tucson region (Bureau of Land Management 2000).

Despite the amount of land that had already been preserved by the end of 2000, the scientists working on the SDCP reported that this parkland did not protect enough of the habitat and wildlife corridors needed to maintain and restore native species. Consequently, the mountain parks element proposes to add 30,000 more acres to existing parks and create two new natural preserves and a new mountain park (Pima County 2000a; Pima County 2009a).

SDCP Ranch Conservation Element

More than half of eastern Pima County's 2.4 million acres are dedicated to ranching, a land use that is well suited to preserving natural habitat, open space, and cultural resources as well as promoting a compact, efficient urban form for the region. Unfortunately, ranching is a precarious enterprise, which makes ranchland a prime target for development. All of the larger ranches in eastern Pima County are a combination of land owned in fee and land leased from the Bureau of Land Management and/or the State Land Trust (Pima County 2009c). Leases with the State Land Trust can be terminated when developers offer to buy the land in fee, greatly increasing the risk that these large ranches will be fragmented.

In 1987, Pima County used an increase in its flood control district tax levy to preserve the Empire and Cienega ranches, where up to 100,000 homes were proposed for development within a regionally important watershed (Huckelberry 1999). Shortly thereafter, the county preserved two other ranches in a gap between two districts of the Coronado National Forest, partially blocking the path of sprawl spreading southwest from Tucson along Interstate 10.

The SDCP reconfirmed that ranchland preservation is uniquely suited to protecting habitat, preserving large expanses of open space, and conserving the heritage and culture of the Southwest (Pima County 2009c). By 2011, the county had acquired 16 large ranches (Pima County 2011), purchasing more than 40,000 acres in fee and protecting more than 127,000 additional acres with limited-term leases. With one exception, the county entered into agreements allowing ranchers to graze livestock on some portions of these properties while managing other portions for the protection of ecological, riparian, and cultural resources (Pima County 2009c).

Rather than using acquisition in fee, Pima County would prefer to preserve ranchlands using purchase or donation of development rights, since these methods allow ranchers to retain fee ownership and remain on their own property, where they can maintain it as a working landscape. The ranch conservation element of the SDCP targets five valleys where ranching has the greatest long-term viability and where preservation would have the best chance of defining urban boundaries (Pima County 2009c).

SDCP Critical Habitat and Biological Corridor Elements

In addition to fostering the recovery of federally listed species, the critical habitat and biological corridor elements of the SDCP aim to reintroduce species that were once indigenous to Pima County and promote overall environmental health. If natural preserves are fragmented and isolated, native species will struggle for long-term survival, and entire ecosystems will suffer. Consequently, these two elements of the SDCP plan to link Pima County's reserves and refuges, including the 42,000-acre Santa Rita Experimental Range, the 399,2190-acre Cabeza Prieta National Wildlife Refuge, and the 118,000-acre Buenos Aires National Wildlife Refuge.

The biological corridor element of the SDCP calls for connections between these and other natural areas in Pima County, while the critical habitat element identifies preservation priorities based on an extensive understanding of desert ecology (Pima County 2009e). Between 1999 and 2009, Pima County purchased 71,000 acres in fee and acquired 30-year leases on 130,000 acres of State Trust

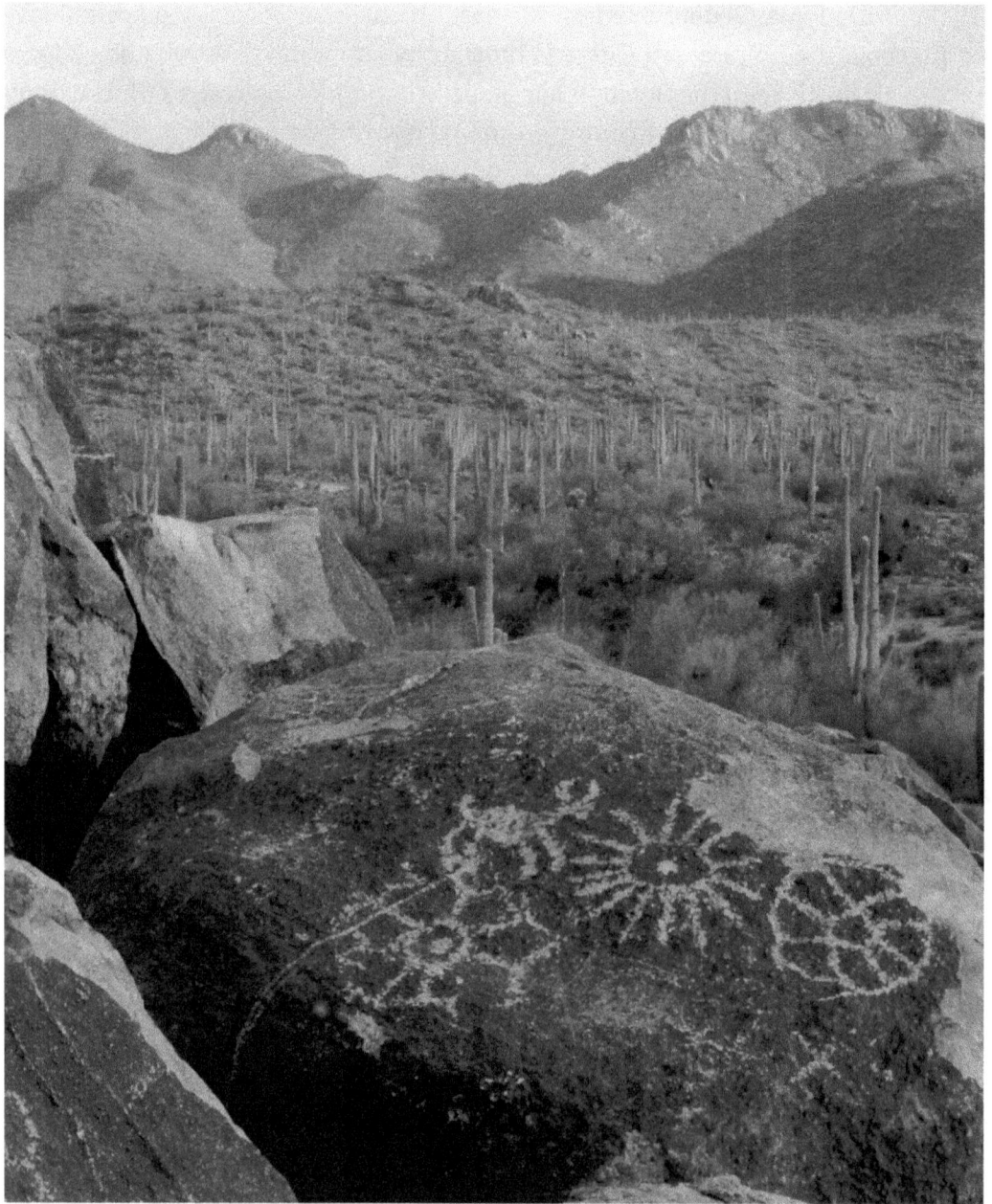

Figure 19-3.   With more than 90,000 acres, Saguaro National Park preserves cultural treasures as well as environmental resources.

Lands, which it proposes as the equivalent of purchasing 32,500 acres in fee. Consequently, according to current projections of mitigation needs, Pima County is well on its way to meeting its projected preservation requirements assuming the U.S. Fish and Wildlife Service approves the MSCP in 2011 as planned (Pima County 2010).

Is Pima County achieving its goal of building a mutually rewarding relationship between nature and humankind? Public agencies and private conservation organizations have together permanently protected more than 1.6 million acres, which is an admirable 49 percent of the total land area of Pima County excluding land within Native American nations (Pima County 2000b). Pima County alone now manages 230,000 acres for conservation, including 100,000 acres owned in fee (Pima County 2011). The SDCP in particular has gained well-deserved recognition, winning many awards, including the national Outstanding Planning Award for a Plan from the American Planning Association as well as the County Leadership in Conservation Award from the Trust for Public Land and the National Association of Counties. But perhaps most importantly, Pima County itself is pleased with the results, as demonstrated in the following quote on the SDCP website:

> Great communities are no accident. They are born out of natural strength and beauty and have a deep respect for ecology, history, culture and diversity. They are inspired by the vision of residents drawn to them. They are brought to maturity through hard work and investment. And they survive because of compromise and consensus. In a sense they achieve balance. Such balance is at the heart of the Sonoran Desert Conservation Plan. (Pima County 2009f, 1)

20

SANTA CLARA COUNTY, CALIFORNIA

In the 1960s, Santa Clara County, California, planned a "necklace of parks" with the "pearls" consisting of mountain and valley regional parks strung on scenic roads and recreational trails. Much of that vision has become a reality through the combined work of the county park system, two regional open space districts, California State Parks, the U.S. Fish and Wildlife Service, and countless other partners. Today more than 160,000 acres in Santa Clara County are permanently preserved, a particularly significant accomplishment considering the county's location within the booming San Francisco Bay region.

Santa Clara County is home to Stanford University and the City of San Jose, the self-proclaimed capital of Silicon Valley. It has one of the highest concentrations of computer, communication, and other high-tech industries in the world. The county's growth reflects that success; it has swollen by more than 600 percent since 1950 to its current population of 1.8 million.

The county acquired its first parkland in 1924, when it bought the site that eventually became Stevens Creek County Park. In 1956, the Department of Parks and Recreation was formed, and the park system now offers 28 regional parks with almost 46,000 acres of open space (Santa Clara County 2010a). The largest is the 4,147-acre Almaden Quicksilver County Park, which was once the site of the most productive mercury mine on the continent (Santa Clara County 2007).

In 1969, a study for the City of Palo Alto concluded that it would be cheaper to acquire and preserve land in the Santa Cruz Mountains than build roads and other infrastructure there. The environmental organization Committee for Green

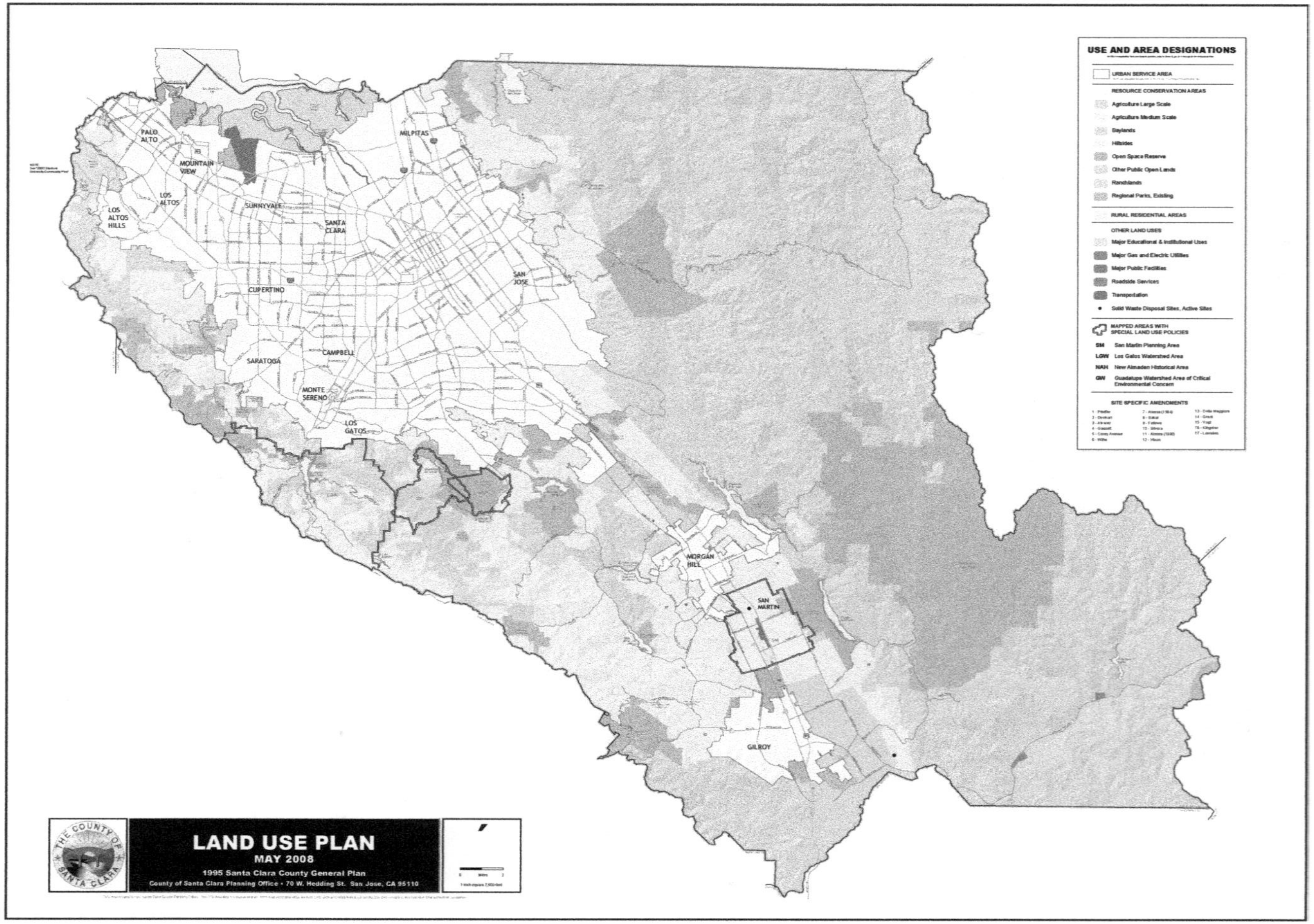

Figure 20-1. Much of the land outside Santa Clara County's urban service areas is protected as parks and permanently preserved open space. [*Source: Santa Clara County*]

Foothills used this report to promote the creation of a special park district with its own elected officials and taxing authority in order to preserve the Palo Alto hillsides as well as other undeveloped lands (Committee for Green Foothills 2005; Press 2002). In 1972, the voters of northwestern Santa Clara County demonstrated their agreement by approving the formation of the Midpeninsula Regional Park District by more than a two-thirds majority. Four years later, voters extended the district into eastern San Mateo County. Following a minor name change, the Midpeninsula Regional Open Space District (MROSD) then expanded into part of Santa Cruz County in 1992, becoming the first regional park district in California to operate in three counties (Weintraub 2004). The MROSD generates more than $20 million annually from a portion of property tax revenues and has used that funding to acquire 26 preserves with more than 58,000 acres to date (MROSD 2010a).

Of the MROSD's total holdings, roughly 30,000 acres of land and more than 100 miles of trails are located within 11 preserves in Santa Clara County. The largest of these preserves protects more than 17,000 acres of rugged wilderness in the Sierra Azul ("Blue Range") mountains, only 15 miles south of downtown San Jose (MROSD 2010b).

In 1973, an urban development/open space (UD/OS) plan was adopted by the county, its cities, and the Santa Clara County Local Agency Formation Commission (LAFCO), the body that regulates annexations and promotes orderly urban expansion. Following the adoption of the UD/OS plan, urban development is confined to urban service areas within the cities and any proposed urban service area boundary changes are subject to LAFCO approval. Permanently preserved open space is one of the key factors used to plan for any future changes to these urban service areas (Santa Clara County 1994).

In 1993, the Santa Clara County Open Space Authority (OSA) was formed to serve portions of the county outside the MROSD boundaries (OSA 2010a). As of 2010, OSA had spent more than $50 million preserving 15,304 acres of open space. The largest of OSA's preserves is the 4,334-acre Rancho Canada del Oro, adjacent to county parkland and home to golden eagles, the endangered California red-legged frog, and the occasional mountain lion (OSA 2010b).

The 1995–2010 general plan documented that Santa Clara County was home to 16 threatened or endangered species and called for the development of a habitat conservation plan (Santa Clara County 1994). In 2005, Santa Clara County and its partners started work on a habitat conservation plan/natural community conservation plan (HCP/NCCP) designed to allow future development at appropriate locations within a 520,000-acre area while assuring the survival of 21 species of concern. The draft plan, released in 2010, calls for the creation of a 58,000-acre preserve, to be funded by various revenue sources, including development fees. After adoption by Santa Clara County and its local partners, the plan will need approval from the California Department of Fish and Game and the U.S. Fish and Wildlife Service before going into effect (Santa Clara County 2011).

Portions of Castle Rock, Henry W. Coe, and Pacheco state parks protect more than 50,000 additional acres of open space in Santa Clara County. The Martial Cottle Park is a new cooperative effort of California State Parks and the

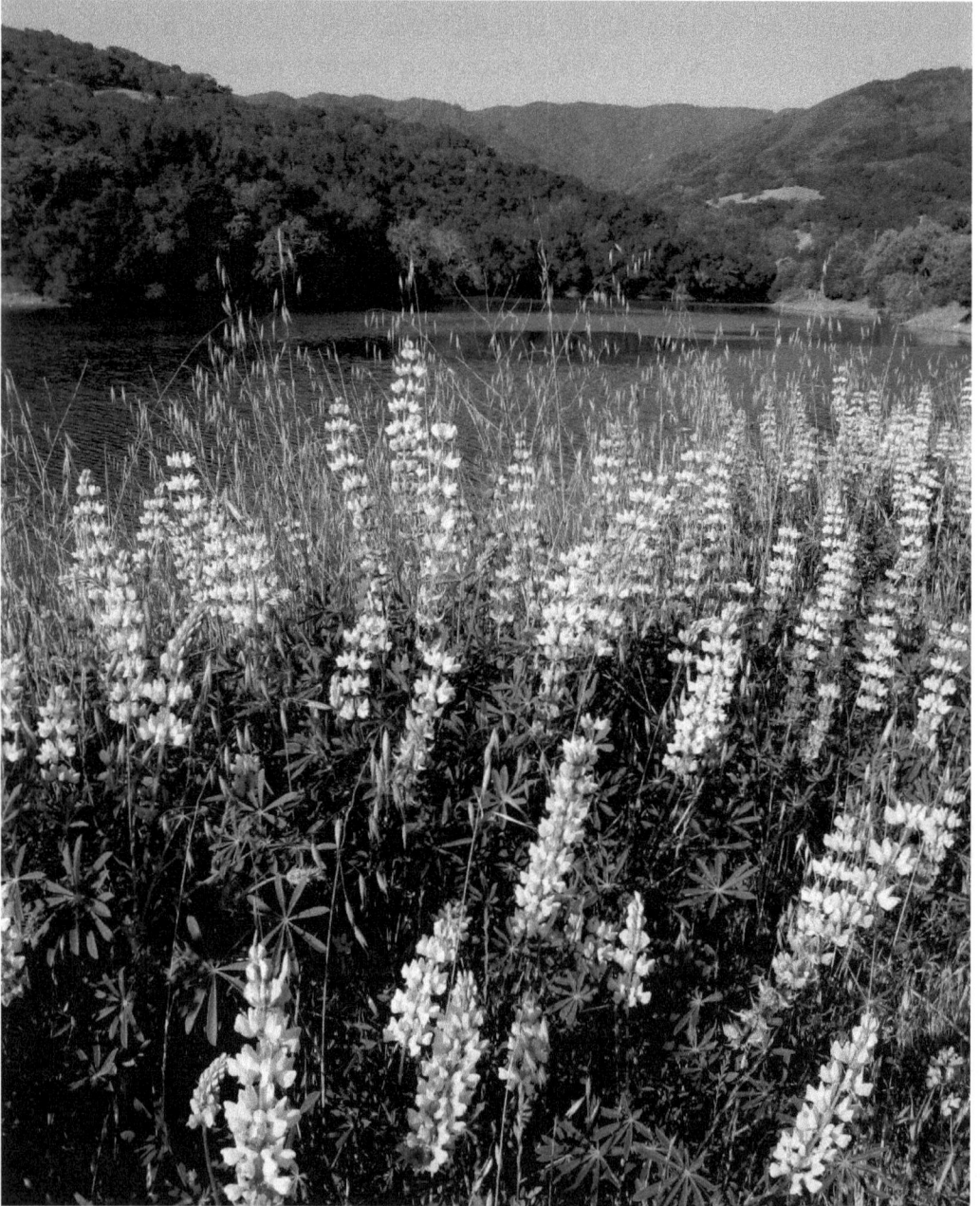

Figure 20-2.   The Sierra Azul Open Space Preserve protects 17,000 acres of mountainous terrain only 15 miles south of downtown San Jose.

Santa Clara County Department of Parks and Recreation to create an educational park focused on the county's agricultural heritage (California State Parks 2010). Adjoining Henry W. Coe State Park is Cañada de los Osos Ecological Reserve, a 4,400-acre property protected by the Nature Conservancy and transferred to the California Department of Fish and Game for the protection of rare plants and animals (California Department of Fish and Game 2005).

The U.S. Fish and Wildlife Service protects more than 6,000 acres of wetlands in the Don Edwards San Francisco Bay National Wildlife Refuge, the country's first urban national wildlife refuge (U.S. Fish and Wildlife Service 2010). In addition, the City of Palo Alto created its own 1,940-acre Baylands Preserve, on San Francisco Bay, with 15 miles of hiking trails meandering through both tidal and freshwater habitats that shelter waterfowl and wading birds, including the endangered California clapper rail (Palo Alto 2010).

In 2003, the Santa Clara County Department of Parks and Recreation's strategic plan recognized that the necklace of parks was evolving into an "Emerald Web" featuring multiple strands of traditional parks and preserved open space with linkages for wildlife movement as well as recreational trails (Santa Clara

Figure 20-3.   Part of the Picchetti Ranch Open Space Preserve is leased to a winery, where visitors can enjoy a wine tasting after sampling the trails.

County 2003). With more than 160,000 acres of preserved open space, Santa Clara County demonstrates that success is possible when a compelling plan is implemented through intergovernmental cooperation and strong public support. It also helps to have farsighted individuals who are willing and able to nurture that public support. When the Committee for Green Foothills formed in 1963, its first president was Wallace Stegner, the Pulitzer Prize–winning author who headed Stanford's creative writing program in the 1960s. Stegner penned the following thoughts about open space in his now famous "Wilderness Letter":

> We need wilderness preserved—as much of it as is still left, and as many kinds— because it was the challenge against which our character as a people was formed. The reminder and the reassurance that it is still there is good for our spiritual health even if we never once in ten years set foot in it. It is good for us when we are young, because of the incomparable sanity it can bring briefly, as vacation and rest, into our insane lives. It is important to us when we are old simply because it is there. (Stegner 1960)

21

SANTA CRUZ AND SANTA CRUZ COUNTY, CALIFORNIA

Santa Cruz, California, 60 miles down the coast from San Francisco, is famous for surfing and a counterculture personality perhaps best symbolized by the official mascot of the University of California, Santa Cruz: the Banana Slug. But Santa Cruz County and its cities are also getting attention for their smart approach to preservation: saving land that not only protects nature and agriculture but also forms greenbelts to confine and define urban areas.

Santa Cruz County adopted its first comprehensive general plan in 1961, at the start of a two-decade period in which its population more than doubled, due largely to the success of nearby Silicon Valley; the growth of the University of California, Santa Cruz; and Americans' love affair with coastal living. The county's 1980 general plan integrated and consolidated the various area plans and growth management policies that had been approved individually during those two decades, including the California Coastal Act of 1976 and Measure J, which was adopted by county voters in 1978 (Santa Cruz County 1994).

As required by Measure J, the 1980 general plan created strict distinctions between urban and rural land, which remain intact today. The county's Urban Services Line encircles four incorporated cities and four unincorporated but urbanized areas. Santa Cruz County also has a rural equivalent of the Urban Services Line, the Rural Services Line, which defines the limits of 15 smaller communities that receive some but not necessarily all urban services. In addition to creation of urban and rural limit lines, Measure J instituted a growth management system with annual population growth goals designed to accommodate the county's fair

Figure 21-1.   A banana slug, mascot of the University of California, Santa Cruz,
races up a redwood in the Santa Cruz Mountains.

share of statewide population within environmental and economic constraints
(Santa Cruz County 1994).

In 1990, just as Santa Cruz County began updating the 1980 general plan, the
voters passed Measure C, declaring the 1990s the "Decade of the Environment"
and establishing policies to address global climate change, develop a sustainable
local economy, and deal with a host of other concerns, including the protection
and restoration of forests and greenbelts. This demonstration of public support
created a solid foundation for the strong environmental goals adopted in the
1994 Santa Cruz general plan, including the preservation of forests, coastal areas,
agricultural land, and other vital resource lands (Santa Cruz County 1994).

In addition to creating the Urban Services Line, the City of Santa Cruz has
largely encircled itself with greenbelts, an action that was initiated by the voters
when they approved Measure O in 1979 (Santa Cruz 1992). Measure O placed a
moratorium on development for key properties designated as greenbelt overlays.

Figure 21-2.   Tide pools are home to giant green sea anemones at Natural Bridges State Beach.

The private owners of these properties lost a takings lawsuit, largely because the overlay districts allowed agriculture, thereby permitting economic use of the land. Santa Cruz activists then worked hard for the passage of Proposition 70, a statewide initiative adopted in 1988. In return, Proposition 70 earmarked $15 million for the preservation of Pogonip, a beloved 640-acre property that now forms a portion of the city's northern greenbelt (Press 2002).

In 1994, the city adopted its Greenbelt Master Plan and used general fund money to buy Arana Gulch, which constitutes a key segment of the city's eastern greenbelt (Press 2002). In 1998, the voters approved a park and open space bond measure that funded acquisition of Moore Creek Preserve, a 246-acre greenbelt parcel that now forms much of the western boundary of the city (Santa Cruz 2009). In addition, the city and the state have succeeded in protecting many of the beaches and bluffs of the Pacific coastline, which serves as the city's southern edge, including Natural Bridges State Beach and Lighthouse Field State Beach.

The State of California has been a major ally in the war against sprawl in Santa Cruz County. In 1969, plans were unveiled to build a 10,000-dwelling unit development on Wilder Ranch, a project that would have doubled the population of the city of Santa Cruz. This proposal sparked a heated controversy that ended in 1973 when the state approved the purchase of the ranch. The city's 1990 general plan later called for preservation of nearby Gray Whale Ranch and adjacent agricultural lands (Santa Cruz 1992). In 1996, the Save the Redwoods League bought Gray Whale Ranch and donated it to the state to enlarge Wilder Ranch State Park, which is now 7,000 acres in size (*Santa Cruz Sentinel* 2007).

Big Basin Redwoods State Park also effectively forms a permanently preserved 18,000-acre green buffer between Santa Cruz County and San Mateo County to the north. California created Big Basin Redwoods State Park in 1902, shortly after photographer Andrew Hill and a group of educators, writers, and women's club members explored the redwood-studded Santa Cruz Mountains and were inspired to form the Sempervirens Club. In addition to sparking the protection of Big Basin Redwoods, California's first state park, this nonprofit conservancy, now named the Sempervirens Fund, has been instrumental in the preservation of more than 25,000 acres throughout the Santa Cruz Mountains, including Castle Rock State Park, which largely preserves the northeastern corner of Santa Cruz County at its junction with San Mateo and Santa Clara counties (Sempervirens Fund 2011).

California now manages five state parks, seven state beaches, and two other open space preserves in Santa Cruz County, with a total of roughly 43,000 acres (Circuit Rider Productions and NOAA 2004). The U.S. Fish and Wildlife Service preserves 298 acres at the Ellicott Slough National Wildlife Refuge, home of the Santa Cruz long-toed salamander and other endangered species (U.S. Fish and Wildlife Service 2008). In addition to transferring land to state and local park systems, some private nonprofit conservancies in Santa Cruz County retain and manage their own preserves. For example, the Land Trust of Santa Cruz County, formed in 1978, has partnered with other organizations in the protection of more than 9,000 acres and also owns, manages, or maintains conservation easements on more than 1,500 acres of land in Santa Cruz County (Land Trust of Santa Cruz County 2009).

As a good example of teamwork, Santa Cruz County Proposition 70 funds preserved the spectacular Coast Dairies property in 1998, in cooperation with the Trust for Public Land, the David and Lucile Packard Foundation, the California Coastal Conservancy, the Save the Redwoods League, the William and Flora Hewlett Foundation, and anonymous donations(Trust for Public Land 2007).

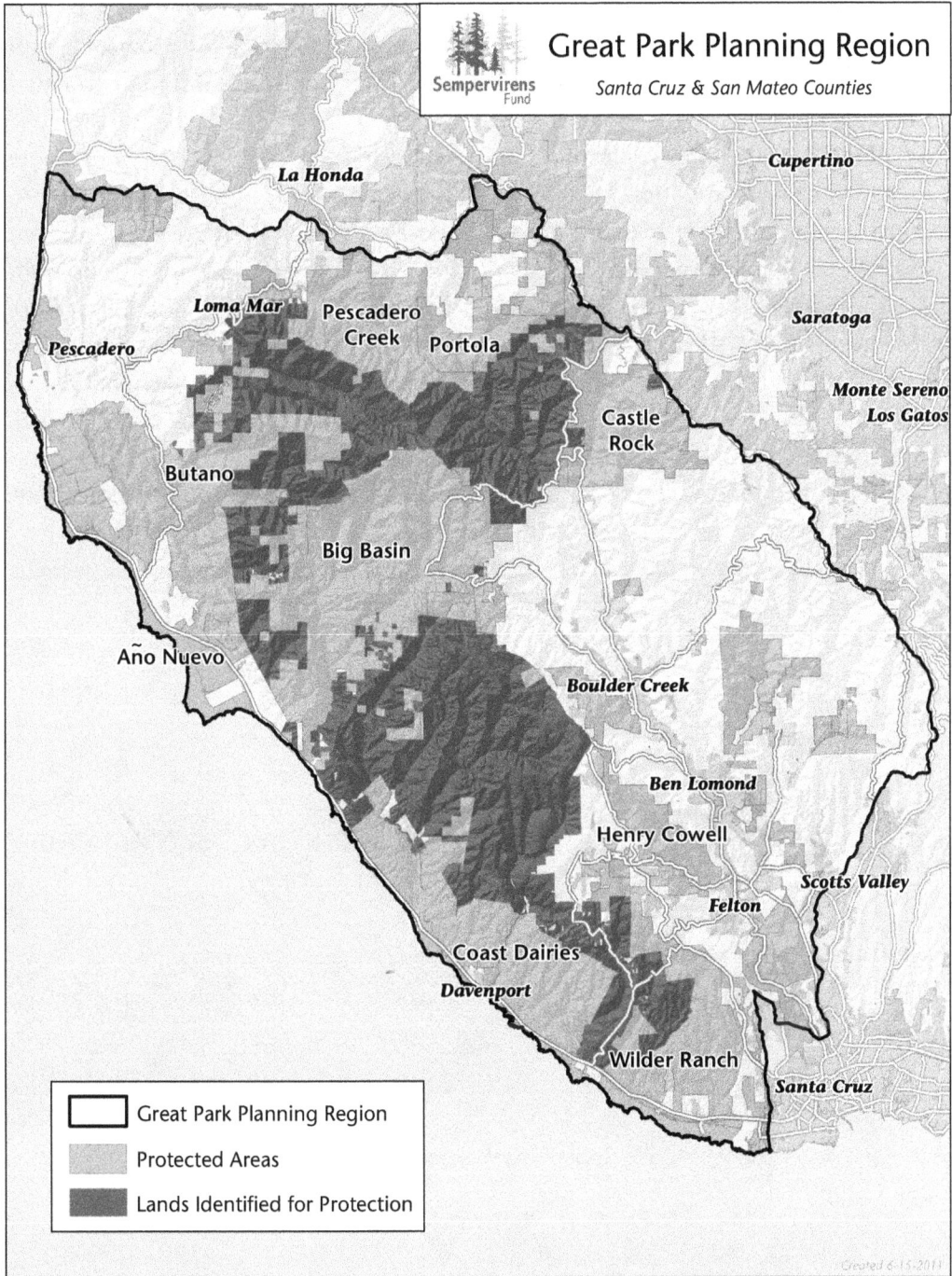

Figure 21-3. The Great Park Plan envisioned by the Sempervirens Fund
[Source: Sempervirens Fund]

Together with the adjacent Sand Hill Bluff property, the 7,000-acre Coast Dairies site creates a chain of preserved coastal land stretching from the City of Santa Cruz to Año Nuevo State Reserve, in San Mateo County. This acquisition also fills in a critical link in the California Coastal Trail, the ocean-side hiking path that will eventually allow the trekking of California's entire 1,300-mile coastline (Hailey 2007).

Since it gave birth to California's first state park, Santa Cruz County has been a leader in the preservation of greenbelts and parks that curb sprawl while protecting watersheds, farmland, habitat, forests, outdoor recreational land, and other critical natural resources. Looking to the future, the Sempervirens Fund is building support for a concept it calls the Great Park. To form the Great Park, the fund proposes the acquisition of additional land linking parks in Santa Cruz County with preserved open space in San Mateo County and Santa Clara County. This goal surely complies with Daniel Burnham's famous advice to "make no little plans." But given the tradition of teamwork between Santa Cruz County, other governmental agencies, and nonprofit organizations, this Great Park vision seems quite attainable.

22

SANTA FE COUNTY, NEW MEXICO

Until the 1990s, open space preservation was not the highest priority for Santa Fe County, possibly because one-third of the land area there is owned by federal and state agencies. But inevitably, an increasing number of people were drawn to Santa Fe's spectacular scenery, diverse culture, and year-around recreational opportunities. The county's population, which now stands at 150,000, rose more than 30 percent during the 1990s alone. As developments sprang up, people began losing access to lands and trails that had traditionally been available for public use. County voters responded by overwhelmingly approving a $12 million bond. Guided by its Open Land and Trails Plan, adopted in 2000, Santa Fe County began a program that protects cultural and historic sites as well as critical natural areas. Even though the program is relatively new, it has already won national recognition, including a County Leadership in Conservation Award from the Trust for Public Land and the National Association of Counties.

Santa Fe County's Open Land and Trails Plan emphasizes the need to protect the connections between the natural landscape and the centuries of past civilizations that both shaped and were shaped by their environment.

> Cultural landscapes result from the interaction of people (culture) and nature on the land over time. Throughout New Mexico's history, how people live their lives, earn a living, and make decisions about land, water and community help define the many landscape layers that transform physical spaces into meaningful places. How the many different and culturally diverse communities in Santa Fe County have acted out those decisions have defined their heritage, their traditions, and themselves, and have shaped the unique flavor of the County. (Santa Fe County 2000, 17)

Santa Fe County immediately began implementing the 2000 Open Land and Trails Plan using funding from the original open space bond as well as an $8 million conservation bond approved in 2000, another $3.5 million parks bond approved in 2008, and an increase in gross receipts tax that generates an extra $1.2 million in annual revenue for the program (Trust for Public Land 2006).

In keeping with its multiple objectives, the county quickly bought the land that is now Cerrillos Hills State Park, a 1,100-acre property that combines historic, cultural, natural, and recreational resources. The park's pygmy forest habitat shelters bobcats and bats, while its trail system accommodates hikers, mountain bikers, and equestrians. Those with an interest in history can follow in the steps of the Rio Grande Pueblo potters who dug for turquoise in the 1300s and the miners who flocked there in the late 1800s, staking more than 1,000 mining claims and turning the adjacent village of Cerrillos into a short-lived boomtown (Cerrillos Hills Park Coalition 2009).

The 1,904-acre Thornton Ranch Open Space also fits this profile, with a world-class collection of petroglyphs and lots of room for hiking, biking, and horse trails. This open space preserve sits at the center of the Galisteo Basin Archaeological Sites and has been eyed as a likely site for interpretive facilities that are expected to be built as a result of the planning process called for in the Gallisteo Basin Archaeological Sites Preservation Act, which is discussed below (Santa Fe County 2010).

Santa Fe County's 2010 Sustainable Growth Management Plan builds on the 2000 plan and emphasizes that land preservation and trail development are essential to ecotourism, the fastest growing segment of the tourism industry. Ecotourism is a natural economic development strategy here, given the 2010 plan's vision statement: "Santa Fe County is a place of natural beauty, diverse cultures and enduring sustainable communities." As of 2010, the Open Space and Trails Program had preserved 16 sites containing almost 5,600 acres and nine trail segments, including the nationally recognized Santa Fe Rail Trail (Santa Fe County 2010).

The 2010 Sustainable Growth Management Plan also stresses the need for strategic open space acquisitions as a way of curbing sprawl as well as protecting natural, cultural, and agricultural resources. The plan identifies key open space projects, including a greenway along the Santa Fe River, as well as extensive trail development and the preservation of farms and ranchlands. The county is particularly interested in preserving the small farms historically irrigated by an extensive system of ditches called acequias. By protecting this traditional style of farming, Santa Fe County also implements its related goals of securing a reliable local source of sustainably grown food (Santa Fe County 2010).

The 2010 plan observes that Santa Fe County partners with more than 75 federal, state, and local agencies and private conservation organizations in its open

Santa Fe County Sustainable
Growth Management Plan

Future Land Use Map
(2010 - 2030)

Legend

┌┄┐
┆┆ Santa Fe County
└┄┘

Parcels

Regional Centers

Community Centers

[Opportunity Centers

┌┄┐
┆┄┘ Adopted or Proposed Community Plans

Municipalities

City of Santa Fe Annexation Area

Tribal Lands

Federal and State Public Lands

Future Land Use

Conservation

Ag / Ranch

Rural

Rural Fringe

Residential Fringe

Residential Estate

Traditional Community

Mixed-Use Residential

Mixed-Use Non-Residential

Any land or water which is subject to Santa Fe County's planning or
zoning jurisdiction, but is not depicted on this map within a County
future land use category, shall be construed by default to be
located in the Ag / Ranch future land use category, unless otherwise specifically provided for in the Santa Fe County Sustainable
Land Development Plan or Santa Fe County Land Development Code.

5   2.5   0   5 Miles

Santa Fe County
Growth Management
Department
Planning Division

Nov. 1, 2010
sgmp_future_land_
use_map_11_1_10_web_map.mxd

®

Figure 22-1.   Santa Fe County's Sustainable Growth Management Plan uses open
space preservation to curb sprawl while protecting natural, cultural,
and agricultural resources. [Source: Santa Fe County]

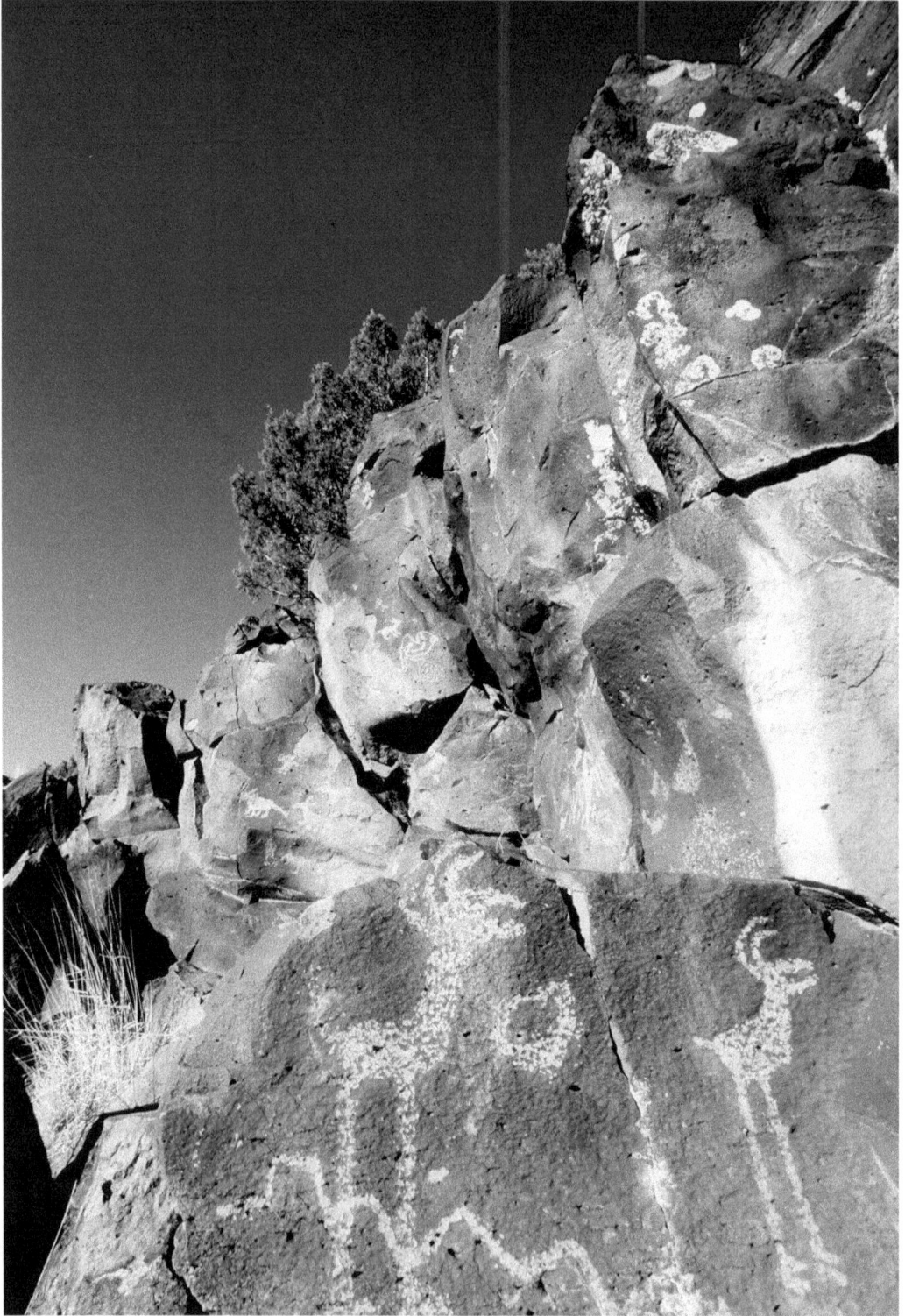

Figure 22-2. The Santa Fe County Open Space and Trails Program aims to preserve land with historic and cultural as well as environmental significance, such as this petroglyph-covered mesa.

space preservation efforts. Among its biggest allies is the U.S. Forest Service, which protects more than 241,000 acres of the Santa Fe National Forest within Santa Fe County. In the far northeastern corner of the county, the U.S. Forest Service manages a portion of the Pecos Wilderness, home to elk, bighorn sheep, and Rio Grande cutthroat trout (Santa Fe County 2010; U.S. Forest Service 2009).

Private conservation organizations have preserved 11,527 acres in Santa Fe County (Santa Fe County 2010). The Nature Conservancy owns and manages the 525-acre Santa Fe Canyon Preserve, where industrious beavers are helping restore a stretch of the Santa Fe River (Nature Conservancy 2011). The National Audubon Society manages the Randall Davey Audubon Center on 135 acres of land near Santa Fe, which provides habitat for 130 bird species (Audubon New Mexico 2011).

The federal Bureau of Land Management (BLM) controls another 62,390 acres in Santa Fe County, including the 4,500-acre La Cienega Area of Critical Environmental Concern (ACEC), which includes rock art from the 14th century and a portion of the historic El Camino Real as well as springs and wetlands within the Santa Fe River canyon. In 2007, the Trust for Public Land (TPL) facilitated the expansion of the ACEC as part of a plan to ultimately link public open space in this historically and environmentally rich area (Trust for Public Land 2007).

Figure 22-3.   The Santa Fe County Open Space and Trails Program protected the setting of El Santuario de Chimayo, completed in 1816 and listed in the National Register of Historic Places.

In another demonstration of public-private cooperation, the TPL and Santa Fe County teamed up to preserve a pasture that serves as the backdrop for El Santuario de Chimayo, 25 miles north of the City of Santa Fe. This small adobe chapel was built between 1813 and 1816 and is now listed in the National Register of Historic Places. Visited by 300,000 people a year, it is famously known as the "Lourdes of America" for the pilgrimages undertaken by those who believe in the healing power of dirt from the chapel's *el pocito*, or "little well." The owners of the pasture were tempted to sell this prominent scenic site to developers. But ultimately, they sold the property to TPL and Santa Fe County for preservation as grazing land, as a historic setting for the Santuario, and as a segment in the county's future trail system (Mahler 2002).

The BLM is also cooperating with Santa Fe County, the state of New Mexico, and affected Native American pueblos in the development of a management plan for archaeological sites in Santa Fe County's Galisteo Basin. The largest ruins of Pueblo Indian settlements in the nation lie within the Galisteo Basin, as well as the remains of settlements from the Spanish colonial era and extraordinary displays of Native American rock art. Even today, Native American Pueblos gather plants in the Galisteo Basin and use it for cultural and religious ceremonies. These archaeological treasures were gradually being destroyed by development and vandalism as well as natural causes until enactment of the Galisteo Basin Archaeological Sites Protection Act of 2004, which calls for the protection of 4,591 acres of land within 24 sites (Santa Fe County 2010; U.S. Congress 2004).

Santa Fe County is also part of a three-county region containing additional archaeological sites and eight Native American pueblos. In 2006, Congress designated this region as the Northern Rio Grande National Heritage Area to recognize a nationally distinctive landscape formed by human activity as well as natural forces. Santa Fe County is participating in the development of a cultural resource management plan for this region (Santa Fe County 2010).

The National Park Service has added 1,068 acres of open space to Santa Fe County, in the Tsankawi section of Bandelier National Monument. There, visitors can climb ladders to view petroglyphs, ancient cave dwellings, and ruins of the ancestral Pueblo village of Tsankawi (National Park Service 2010). Private development projects have preserved another 16,253 acres, and the park systems of Santa Fe County and the City of Santa Fe contribute additional open space, most famously historic Santa Fe Plaza, the heart of the community, surrounded by landmark buildings dating from the early 1600s (City of Santa Fe 2011; Santa Fe County 2010).

The combined work of public and private agencies has preserved 278,210 acres of land, or more than 25 percent of the land area subject to Santa Fe County's land-use and zoning authority (Santa Fe County 2010). In addition to the natural resources typically preserved by jurisdictions, Santa Fe County's open space inventory includes historic mining areas, trail corridors that date back to the 1300s, and archaeological sites from the civilizations that shaped and were shaped by this environment over the past seven centuries. In keeping with the vision stated in its first Open Land and Trails Plan, Santa Fe County is succeeding in linking human history with natural landscapes and transforming physical spaces into meaningful places.

23

SONOMA COUNTY, CALIFORNIA

Sonoma County, with shores on the northern end of San Francisco Bay as well as the Pacific Ocean, saw its population almost double between 1970 and 1990. The 1989 general plan warned that growth threatened to replace the county's famous vineyards, forests, foothills, and dairy farms with uninterrupted sprawl. In response, the plan recommended the formation of the Sonoma County Agricultural Preservation and Open Space District. One year later, the voters voiced their agreement by approving funding for the district with a dedicated open space sales tax. With the continuation of strong public support and the help of numerous public and private partners, Sonoma County has become one of the nation's conservation superstars, winning the 2007 County Leadership in Conservation Award from the Trust for Public Land and the National Association of Counties.

During its first 10 years, the district primarily acquired easements from farmers and ranchers. Of the 32,500 acres protected by the district as of 2000, only 3,800 acres were accessible to the public. This contrasted sharply with the accessibility of land preserved by the East Bay Regional Park District and the Midpeninsula Regional Open Space District, also in the San Francisco Bay region. There were concerns that this emphasis on farmland preservation could jeopardize voter reauthorization of the Sonoma County Agricultural Preservation and Open Space District. In response, the Sonoma County Board of Supervisors approved a new acquisition plan in 2000 that ensured balanced funding of greenbelts, natural resources, and recreational land, as well as farmland (Wells 2000).

By 2006, the county had leveraged the $212 million generated by the district's quarter-cent sales tax with an additional $26 million in other local, state, and private funds. At this point, the district had preserved more than 70,000 acres, with much of the preservation in keeping with the acquisition plan's goals for improved balance between parks, greenbelts, natural areas, and agricultural

Figure 23-1.   Trails crisscross the Kruse Rhododendron State Natural Reserve, in northern Sonoma County.

lands. The voters were so pleased with this performance that they extended the sales tax through 2031 by a 75 percent margin (Trust for Public Land 2007).

The current general plan, adopted in 2008, maintains the county's commitment to open space preservation. In addition to conserving habitat, rural character, farmland, and forests, the plan designates eight specific community separators as well as 15 scenic landscapes and corridors. The plan implements these ambitious goals through a combination of regulations and preservation, including the acquisition and administration of open space using the Agricultural Preservation and Open Space District, which receives roughly $18 million per year of funding from the quarter-cent open space sales tax (Sonoma County 2008).

As of 2010, the district had preserved 83,000 acres of land, including 30 farms and ranches, 31 parks, 27 natural areas, and 35 greenbelts. Many of these properties achieve multiple general plan goals. Windsor Oaks, for example, is a 711-acre greenbelt between Healdsburg and Santa Rosa that preserves fields and ponds for wildlife and protects a vineyard and winery, in support of Sonoma County's tourism as well as agricultural industries (Sonoma County Agricultural Preservation and Open Space District 2011). With 43,128 acres of preserved farmland, Sonoma County now ranks number 12 in the nation for locally operated farmland preservation programs (*Farmland Preservation Report* 2010).

Figure 23-2.   Bicyclists can pedal through one of Sonoma County's famous wine regions on the West County Trail.

Sonoma County acknowledges that its success in open space preservation is greatly helped by the work of other public agencies and private conservation organizations. In partnership with the Agricultural Preservation and Open Space District, the nonprofit organization LandPaths aims to "foster a love of the land in Sonoma County" by creating ways for people to "experience the beauty, understand the value and assist in healing the land in their local communities." LandPaths guides outings to some of the farms and ranches preserved by the district as well as offering a full schedule of hiking, biking, and equestrian trips throughout the county. In a program called In Our Own Backyard, LandPaths takes kids from local schools on theme-based field trips that progressively deepen their attachment to the land, culminating in a stewardship project. LandPaths also organizes events in which volunteers remove nonnative vegetation and plant trees to help restore watersheds and habitat (LandPaths 2011).

The district works closely with the Sonoma Land Trust, a private nonprofit organization that has preserved more than 25,000 acres of land by using land donations and private funding to extend and leverage public dollars. The trust retains ownership of key holdings, called anchor preserves, such as Baylands–Sears Point, a 2,327-acre preserve that combines agricultural preservation with tidal wetlands restoration, habitat protection, and outdoor recreation, including a segment of the 500-mile San Francisco Bay Trail (Sonoma Land Trust 2009).

The district is also helped by several other private nonprofit conservation organizations. The Save the Redwoods League has funded various open space acquisitions there, most recently an addition to the Lake Sonoma National Recreation Area (Save the Redwoods 2010). The organization Audubon Canyon Ranch adds 535 acres of preserved land to Sonoma County's open space inventory through the Bouverie Preserve, in the Valley of the Moon (Audubon Canyon Ranch 2010). Sonoma State University owns the 411-acre Osborn Preserve, which was originally donated to the Nature Conservancy by the family of Fairfield Osborn Jr., author of the influential 1948 book *Our Plundered Planet* (Sonoma State University 2008).

Supplementing district lands, Sonoma County Parks offers 44 additional parks, trails, and points of coastal access. Hood Mountain Regional Park alone protects 1,750 acres of wilderness, with trails to places such as Gunsight Rock, where hikers are rewarded with views of the Sonoma Valley and the Golden Gate Bridge. Bicyclists can peddle the Joe Rodota and West County trails, which follow abandoned railroad rights-of-way through the vineyards surrounding the rural town of Sebastopol, in the heart of one of Sonoma County's most famous wine regions (Sonoma County 2011).

The California State Parks system protects more than 31,000 acres in Sonoma County. Three state parks alone preserve more than 12,000 acres on the coast, including Fort Ross, which features a reconstruction of the Russian-American

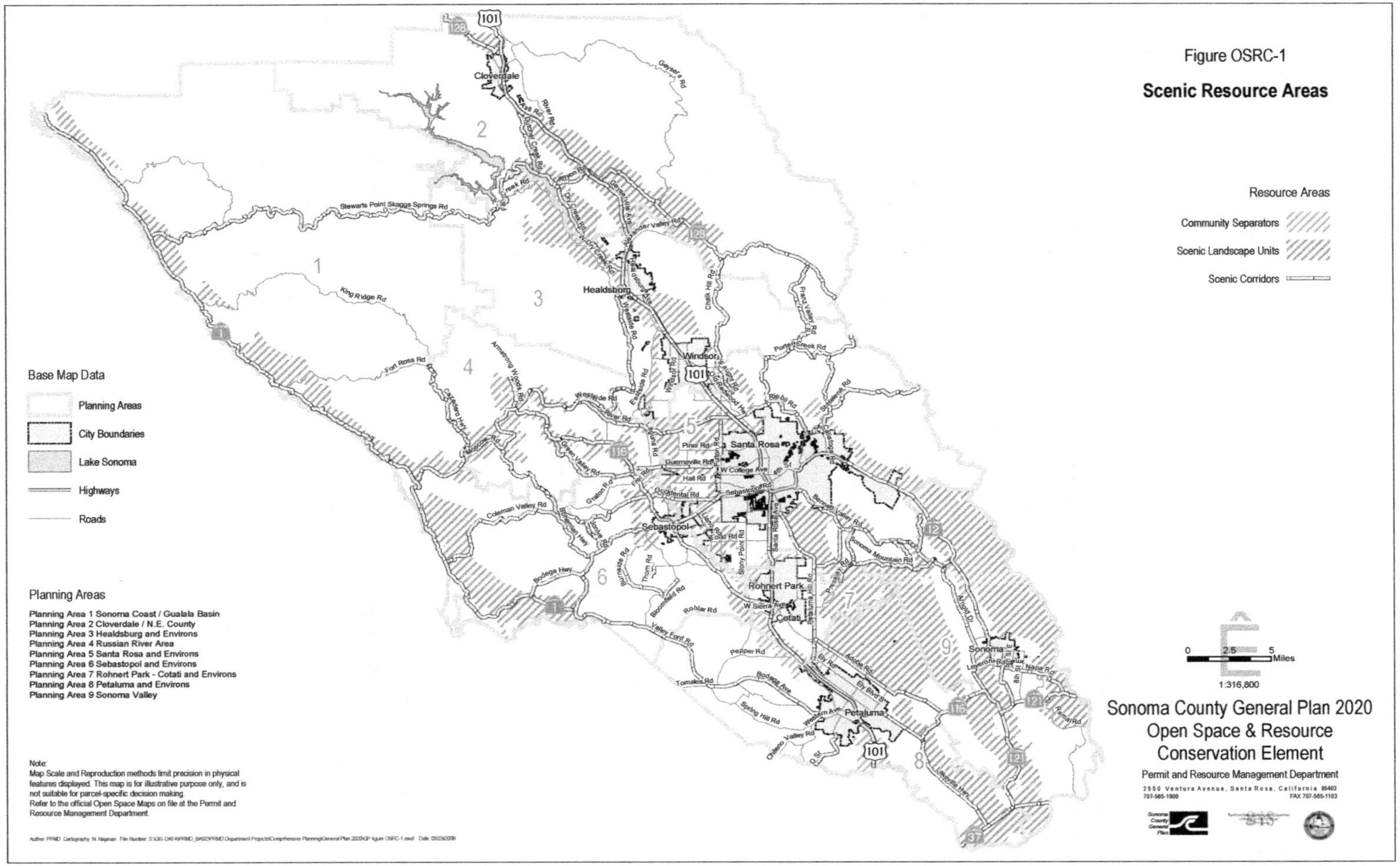
Figure OSRC-1
Scenic Resource Areas
Resource Areas
Community Separators
Scenic Landscape Units
Scenic Corridors
Base Map Data
Planning Areas
City Boundaries
Lake Sonoma
Highways
Roads
Planning Areas
Planning Area 1 Sonoma Coast / Gualala Basin
Planning Area 2 Cloverdale / N.E. County
Planning Area 3 Healdsburg and Environs
Planning Area 4 Russian River Area
Planning Area 5 Santa Rosa and Environs
Planning Area 6 Sebastopol and Environs
Planning Area 7 Rohnert Park - Cotati and Environs
Planning Area 8 Petaluma and Environs
Planning Area 9 Sonoma Valley
Note:
Map Scale and Reproduction methods limit precision in physical features displayed. This map is for illustrative purpose only, and is not suitable for parcel-specific decision making.
Refer to the official Open Space Maps on file at the Permit and Resource Management Department.
0
2.5
5
Miles
1:316,800
Sonoma County General Plan 2020
Open Space & Resource
Conservation Element
Permit and Resource Management Department
2550 Ventura Avenue, Santa Rosa, California 95403
707-565-1900
FAX 707-565-1103
Cloverdale
Healdsburg
Windsor
Santa Rosa
Sebastopol
Rohnert Park
Cotati
Petaluma
Sonoma
Stewarts Point Skaggs Springs Rd
King Ridge Rd
Fort Ross Rd
Armstrong Woods Rd
Chalk Hill Rd
Franz Valley Rd
Porter Creek Rd
River Rd
Westside Rd
Green Valley Rd
Coleman Valley Rd
Bodega Hwy
Bohemian Hwy
Graton Rd
Occidental Rd
Hall Rd
Guerneville Rd
Piner Rd
W College Ave
Sebastopol Rd
Stony Point Rd
Santa Rosa Ave
Bennett Valley Rd
Sonoma Mountain Rd
Petaluma Hill Rd
W Sierra Ave
Roblar Rd
Bloomfield Rd
Valley Ford Rd
Pepper Rd
Tomales Rd
Bodega Ave
Spring Hill Rd
Western Ave
Chileno Valley Rd
Adobe Rd
Ely Blvd S
Lakeville Hwy
Arnold Dr
Leveroni Rd
8th St E
Napa Rd
Ramal Rd
101
128
116
12
121
37
1
2
3
4
5
6
7
8
9

Figure 23-3. **In addition to conserving habitat, rural character, farmland, and forests, the Sonoma County General Plan 2020 designates eight specific community separators as well as 15 scenic landscapes and corridors.** *[Source: Sonoma County]*

Company settlement that thrived there between 1812 and 1841. The Armstrong Redwoods State Natural Reserve preserves an old growth grove of coast redwoods, including one that towers 300 feet above the forest floor and another estimated to be more than 1,400 years old. The Kruse Rhododendron State Natural Reserve protects a forest of second growth redwoods and firs featuring an understory of rhododendrons and other flowers, which create a spectacular display of color every spring (California State Parks 2009).

Several other public agencies contribute to Sonoma County's open space inventory. The California Department of Fish and Game protects the 539-acre Laguna Wildlife Area, the second-largest remaining freshwater wetland in northern California. The U.S. Fish and Wildlife Service's San Pablo Bay National Wildlife Refuge preserves what remains of the once vast tidal lands on Sonoma County's wedge of San Francisco Bay (California Department of Fish and Game 2011; U.S. Fish and Wildlife Service 2010). The U.S. Army Corps of Engineers safeguards 17,615 acres of land surrounding Lake Sonoma. Together with Sonoma County Parks and California State Parks, these agencies protect a total of more than 52,000 acres in Sonoma County (Sonoma County 2003).

With more than 138,000 acres permanently protected to date, open space preservation continues to succeed largely through strong public support and cooperation between various public agencies and private organizations. As a recent case in point, the Jenner Headlands was acquired in 2009 by the Sonoma Land Trust using a combination of funding and bridge loans from the Sonoma County Agricultural Preservation and Open Space District, two federal agencies, the California Coastal Conservancy, the California Wildlife Conservation Board, two philanthropic foundations, the Save the Redwoods League, and the Wildlands Conservancy. At 5,630 acres in size and at a cost of $36 million, the Jenner Headlands purchase represents the largest single conservation acquisition in Sonoma County history. In addition to protecting habitat and allowing for the creation of an improved corridor for the California Coastal Trail, preservation of the Jenner Headlands saves a spectacular scenic landscape, described as follows by Ralph Benson, executive director of the Sonoma Land Trust: "There is a 19th Century etching of the Jenner Headlands showing the Russian River flowing into the Pacific, and it's a wonder to know that the old Rule Ranch will look as open, beautiful and wild in the 21st Century as it did through time immemorial" (Benson 2009, 1).

24

SUFFOLK COUNTY, NEW YORK

The people of Suffolk County saw the development sprawling out of nearby New York City in the early 1960s and realized that their countryside would soon be unrecognizable unless they took action. The county's planning department responded in 1964 by preparing *Planning for Open Space in Suffolk County*, the first of many plans that have guided Suffolk County's highly successful preservation efforts. Following that plan, Suffolk County adopted the first farmland purchase of development rights (PDR) program in the nation in 1974. Today, the county has no fewer than 10 preservation programs and has spent more than $1 billion on open space and farmland protection, reportedly more than any other community in the nation (American Farmland Trust 2009). As a result, Suffolk County has preserved more than 55,000 acres of farmland, habitat, wetlands, and other environmentally significant land, a remarkable accomplishment considering that the county lies only 50 miles east of Manhattan.

Suffolk County occupies the easternmost two-thirds of Long Island, which begins at the Brooklyn Bridge and extends east. Given its location, it is not too surprising to learn that Suffolk County's population expanded more than fivefold in slightly more than five decades, growing from 276,000 in 1950 to more than 1,495,000 in 2006. During the 1950s and early 1960s, Suffolk County only had to look at the suburbanization of its western neighbor, Nassau County, to see its own future unless it adopted and implemented a preservation plan. In 1964, Suffolk County took a decisive step with its pioneering report *Planning for Open Space in Suffolk County*, followed shortly after by the Nassau-Suffolk Comprehensive Plan.

In 1974, Suffolk County began implementing those plans by creating the first farmland preservation program in the United States using PDR. In a PDR program, private property owners continue to own their land subject to an easement that allows acceptable activities, such as farming, but prohibits some or all future nonagricultural development. The first two phases of the PDR program were funded by issuance of $31 million in bonds (Reilly 2000). To assist the county's efforts, similar farmland PDR programs were established by the townships of Southampton, East Hampton, and Southold.

In 1986, Suffolk County supplemented its Farmland Preservation Program with the Open Space Preservation Program, funded by general obligations bonds. As of 2006, the Open Space Preservation Program had spent more than $82 million for the acquisition of 4,914 acres of wetlands, woodlands, and watershed lands. In 1987, the voters of Suffolk County approved the Drinking Water Protection Program to fund open space acquisitions using a 0.25 percent sales tax. This became Suffolk County's largest open space preservation program to date, generating $216 million in revenue and preserving 13,943 acres (Suffolk County 2007).

In the early 1990s, a large portion of Suffolk County known as the Central Pine Barrens became the site of one of the most innovative regional preservation plans in the nation. The Central Pine Barrens consists of 102,500 acres of forests, ponds, and marshes that provide habitat for numerous threatened species and shelter one of the nation's last remnants of the pine barrens ecosystem (Central Pine Barrens Commission 2010). The Central Pine Barrens also provides recharge areas for aquifers that supply drinking water to 1.8 million people. In 1989, the Long Island Pine Barrens Society filed a lawsuit to halt development within the Central Pine Barrens until the environmental impacts could be determined (Long Island Pine Barrens Society 2010). To resolve the uncertainty produced by this litigation, the state adopted the Long Island Pine Barrens Protection Act in 1993, which led to passage of the Central Pine Barrens Comprehensive Land Use Plan (the Central Pine Barrens Plan) in 1995.

The Central Pine Barrens Plan prohibits development in a 55,000-acre core preservation area, limits development in a 47,500-acre buffer zone, and calls for land preservation through tax-funded acquisition. In addition, the Central Pine Barrens Commission manages a transfer of development rights (TDR) program that allows development potential to be transferred from sending sites that deserve preservation to receiving sites that can accommodate growth. The receiving sites are located in communities outside the planning area as well as within the towns of Southampton, Brookhaven, and Riverhead, which surround the Central Pine Barrens.

By 1996, implementation of the Central Pine Barrens Plan had begun, and Suffolk County had three other substantial preservation programs in place: the Farmland Preservation and Open Space Preservation programs and the so-called Old Drinking Water Protection Act. The Farmland Preservation Program alone had spent roughly $40 million by that year and preserved almost 7,000 acres through PDR (Suffolk County 1996).

Despite this effort, farmland preservation was being outpaced by growth, with Suffolk County losing more than 18,000 acres of agricultural land between 1968 and 1996 (Suffolk County 1996). A growing number of people realized that farmland and open space in general were in a sudden-death showdown with development. In *Preservation: Now or Never*, Robert Yaro, president of the Regional Plan Association, penned the following candid summary:

> The question today is whether the Island [Long Island] can build on this innovative open space legacy to protect its remaining open spaces. We are truly in an "end game" in which the Island is approaching build out. You no longer need to be a visionary to see that we're approaching the end of the road—literally—in Montauk and Orient. Our actions in the next few years will determine whether the Island's remaining open spaces, natural areas and countryside are permanently protected or irrevocably destroyed. (Yaro 2007, iii)

Suffolk County was committed to being a strong contestant in the race for the last remaining farms. The Suffolk County Department of Planning followed the 1964 report, *Planning for Open Space*, with the 1996 Agricultural and Farmland Protection Plan (the 1996 Plan). The 1996 Plan emphasized the significance of agriculture to the local economy, pointing out that Suffolk County farms surpassed those of all other counties in the state in crop sales, producing 8,000 jobs and generating more than $250 million in farm revenue (Suffolk County 1996). In addition to acknowledging the importance of farm sales, the 1996 Plan recognized farmland as a scenic resource and one of the reasons why Suffolk County has been a popular tourist destination, with an estimated 35,000 vacation homes in 1990 (Suffolk County 1996). The 1996 Plan forecast that if the charm of the rural countryside disappeared, there would be a decline in tourism and vacation homes, which are considered fiscal assets since they typically don't generate school-age children (Suffolk County 1996).

In Suffolk County, towns and villages control land-use regulations and decisions (Suffolk County 2007). Many Suffolk County townships adopted zoning allowing residential development at a density of up to one dwelling unit per acre, even in rural areas. The 1996 Plan found that this density failed to discourage development and resulted in an extremely inefficient use of the county's rapidly dwindling stock of vacant land. The plan discussed the merits of agricultural zoning as a way of maintaining parcels that are large enough to support farming. But the plan did not hold out much hope that townships would be able to change the current rural zoning given the fierce opposition to previous downzoning proposals. Consequently, the plan advocated that Suffolk County and its partners reinvigorate the 1974 Farmland Preservation Program, which offered compensation to landowners who voluntarily preserve farmland in perpetuity.

The 1996 Plan proposed 20,000 acres of permanently preserved farmland as the critical mass needed to ensure the long-term viability of agriculture in Suffolk County. Although PDR had gotten farmland preservation started, the 1996 Plan conceded that the original farmland preservation program was costly and slow moving. At the mid-1990s funding rate of $1.5 million per year, the county would not be able to save the necessary 13,000 additional acres, because farmland preservation would be outpaced by farmland conversion. To meet the 20,000-acre

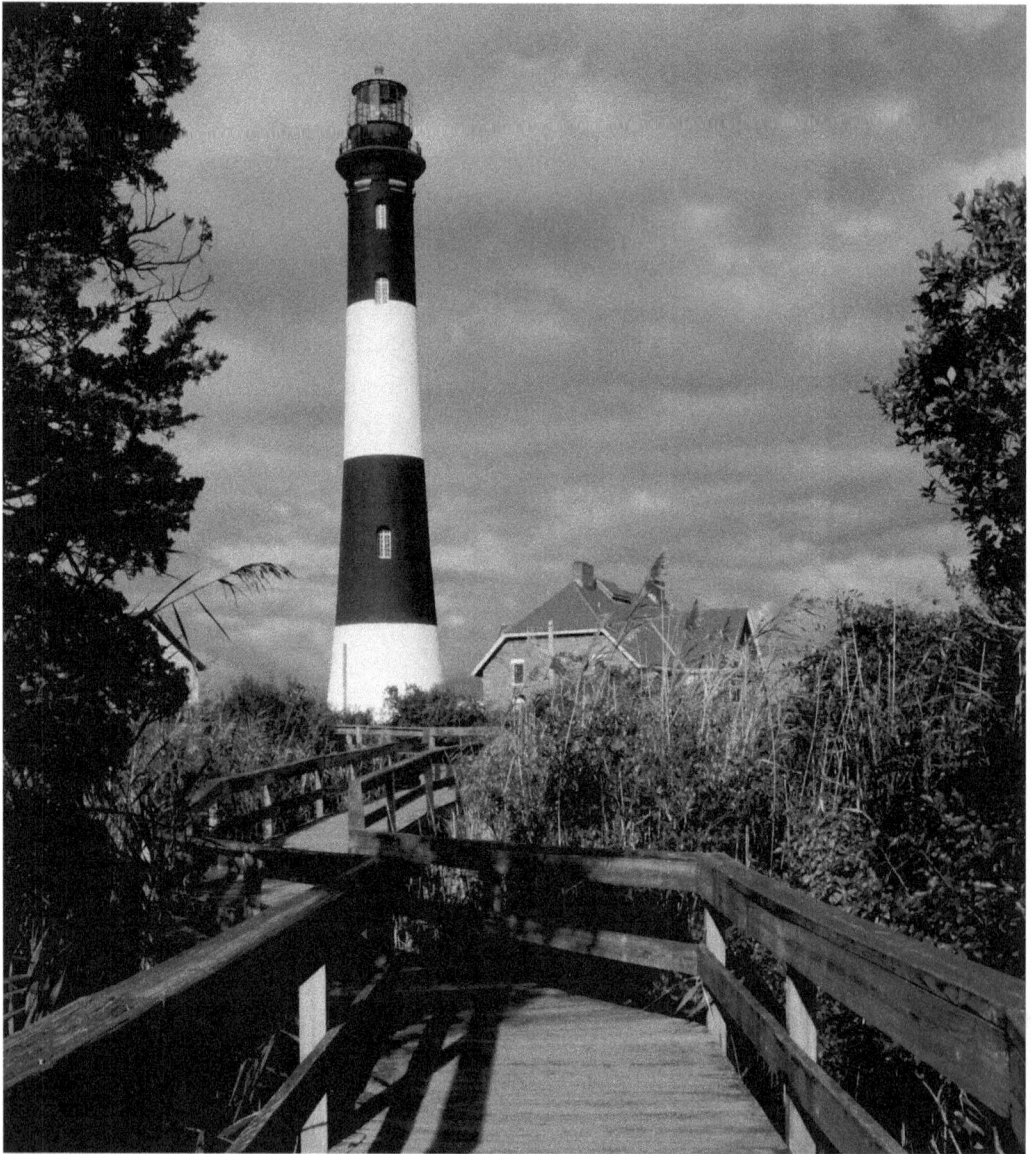

Figure 24-1.   As recommended by the Regional Plan Association's 1960 plan, the Fire Island National Seashore was added to the National Park System in 1964, creating 19,579 acres of federally owned open space in Suffolk County.

goal, the plan recommended a tenfold increase in funding, from $1.5 million to $15 million per year. The plan advocated a referendum on extending the sales tax to fund multiple open space preservation objectives. It also recommended that preservation partners, such as the Peconic Land Trust and the Nature Conservancy, accelerate their efforts in this race against the clock, particularly because these private entities can often act faster than public agencies.

In addition to suggesting that the PDR program be put on steroids, the 1996 Plan recommended exploration of all potential funding strategies, since the land preservation window of opportunity was about to close. Transfer of development rights was high on the plan's list of potential tools, because it funds preservation though private development rather than tax dollars. In addition, TDR was not a new concept, since Suffolk County and three townships had already adopted this mechanism as a primary means of implementing the Central Pine Barrens Plan.

The 1996 Plan succeeded in sounding the alarm and generating action. In 1997, Suffolk County started its Land Preservation Partnership Program, in which the county provides 50-50 matching funds when towns and villages preserve open space. In 1998, Suffolk County also started its Community Greenways Fund for the acquisition of active recreational open space, which included a 70 percent county–30 percent local cost-sharing formula (Suffolk County 2007).

In 1998, New York state adopted legislation that allowed all five townships in eastern Suffolk County to preserve land by creating community preservation funds financed by a 2 percent tax on all real estate transfers (Reilly 2000). In 10 years, these community preservation funds have raised $500 million for farmland and open space preservation (American Farmland Trust 2009). As of 2008, the Town of Southold's Community Preservation Fund had been used to preserve almost 1,000 acres, which constituted roughly one-fifth of the 4,900 acres preserved in Southold using all of its preservation tools (Southold 2009).

Following the 1996 Plan, land preservation programs tended to apply to a wider range of objectives. As advocated by the plan, revenue from the 1999 voter-approved extension of the 0.25 percent sales tax could be used to preserve farmland as well as wetlands, watersheds, coastal zones, and groundwater, even though it was called the New Drinking Water Protection Program (Suffolk County 2007). The Multifaceted Land Preservation Program, adopted in 2002, can be used, as the name suggests, for preserving anything from farmland and watershed protection to sensitive environmental areas and parkland. The Save Open Space Program, approved by the voters in 2004, provides $75 million in serial bonds for acquisition of open space, parklands, and farmland development rights. In 2007, Suffolk County launched its Environmental Legacy Fund, through which public and private partners plan to generate $100 million in funding for open space, farmland, parkland, and historic properties (Suffolk County 2007).

CENTRAL PINE BARRENS AREA

CENTRAL PINE BARRENS
JOINT PLANNING AND POLICY COMMISSION

Peter A. Scully, Chair
Mark Lesko, Member
Steve A. Levy, Member
Anna E. Throne-Holst, Member
Sean M. Walter, Member

Legend:
- Central Pine Barrens Area
- Core Preservation Area
- Compatible Growth Area
- Water Bodies
- Township Boundary
- Road, Highway
- Railroad

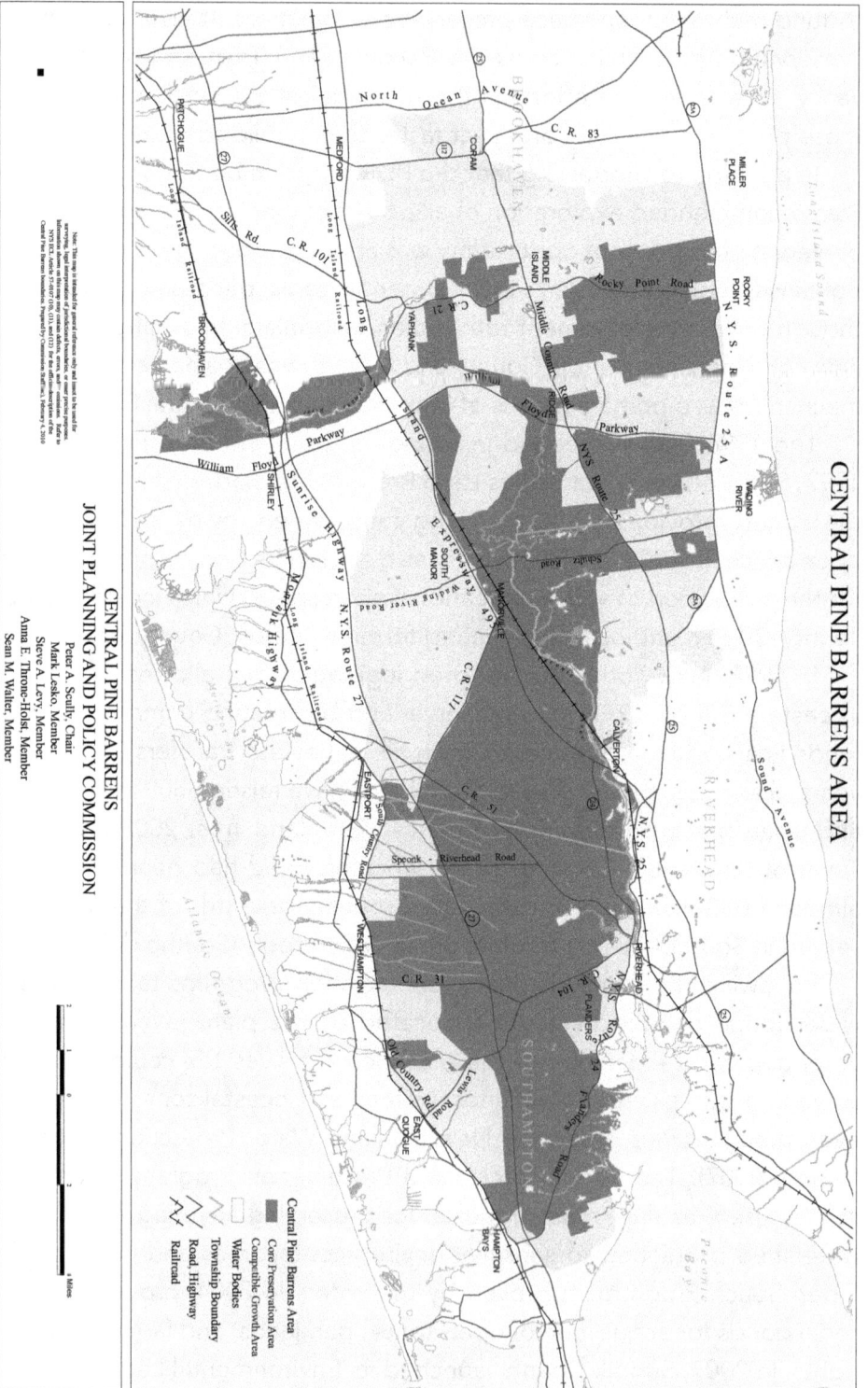

Figure 24-2. The Central Pine Barrens Plan preserves land in its 102,000-acre planning area through tax-funded acquisitions and TDR. [Source: Central Pine Barrens Commission]

Figure 24-3.   While preserving sensitive habitat, parkland, and scenic places, the
                Central Pine Barrens Plan protects recharge areas that supply drinking
                water to 1.8 million people.

As recommended in the 1996 Plan, several Suffolk County townships also started or expanded their own agricultural preservation programs. As mentioned above, the towns of Brookhaven, Riverhead, and Southampton adopted TDR mechanisms to implement the Central Pine Barrens Plan. Between 2001 and 2005, these three jurisdictions also adopted their own separate TDR programs to supplement the Central Pine Barrens effort as well as their other preservation strategies. Similarly, other Suffolk County jurisdictions, including the Town of Huntington in 2008 and the Town of Southold in 2009, tailored TDR mechanisms to meet local preservation needs.

The state and federal governments have been essential to the preservation of the environmentally significant land in Suffolk County. As recommended by the Regional Plan Association's 1960 plan, *The Race for Open Space*, the Fire Island National Seashore, a 30-mile-long barrier island, was added to the National Park System in 1964, creating 19,579 acres of federally owned open space in Suffolk County. The state operates 20 parks in Suffolk County, with a combined total of 15,339 acres. Suffolk County itself manages more than 8,000 additional acres of parkland plus more than 10,000 acres in nature preserves, which primarily protect significant resources while offering limited passive recreation (*Newsday* 2006).

As urged by the 1996 Plan, private conservation organizations have responded to the open space end game in Suffolk County. In 2006, the Nature Conservancy formed a coalition of more than 100 businesses, environmental groups, governments, and individuals in a campaign called "Long Island's Last Stand." This effort aims to raise $5.1 billion to preserve an additional 25,000 acres of open space and 10,000 acres of farmland before final build out, projected to occur by 2015. The effort was hampered by the meltdown of the global economy that started in 2008. However, according to a 2007 report card, the campaign produced impressive results in its first two years, gaining commitments for $2.8 billion in funding and preserving roughly 2,700 acres of open space and 1,500 acres of farmland. Most significantly, in 2007, Suffolk County voters extended the 0.25 percent sales tax and approved a new version of the Drinking Water Protection Program, which will be in effect until 2030 and is capable of generating $600 million for the preservation of coastal wetlands and other vital environmental resources (Nature Conservancy 2007).

In 2008, the National Association of Counties and the Trust for Public Land honored Suffolk County with their County Leadership in Conservation Award for the county's pioneering farmland PDR program and its commitment to open space preservation. In the past five decades, Suffolk County spent more than $1 billion on open space preservation, protecting more than 55,000 acres of farmland, parkland, wetlands, habitat, and lands critical to drinking-water supplies (Suffolk County 2007). That feat is particularly impressive considering that Suffolk County is just an hour's drive from the heart of the largest city in the nation.

25

TRAVIS COUNTY AND AUSTIN, TEXAS

When Austin, Texas, created its first preserve in 1934, the city had a population of roughly 80,000 people and was principally known as the state capital and home of the University of Texas. But between 1950 and 1980, the population of Travis County, which now tops one million, more than doubled. In response, Austin adopted a comprehensive plan aimed largely at managing growth while protecting environmental resources. Since the adoption of that plan in 1979, Austin, Travis County, and its public and private partners have had remarkable success at preserving open space, endangered species, and the region's precious but vulnerable springs.

The Austin Tomorrow Comprehensive Plan, adopted in 1979, balanced reasonable growth with environmental protection, including the preservation of critical habitat and watersheds (Austin 2008). One year after the adoption of that plan, the city conducted a survey of important biological and geological sites in Travis County and found that many of these important environmental resources were at risk. In 1982, a bond package was prepared with input from the Sierra Club, the Travis Audubon Society, and Wildlife Rescue and Rehabilitation, which resulted in voter approval of a $5.7 million bond for open space acquisition. Today, the Austin Parks and Recreation Department manages 15 preserves as part of a 19,000-acre system of parks, greenbelts, and other open space (Austin Parks and Recreation Department 2011). Travis County protects another 10,922 acres in its system of 32 parks and four nature preserves (Travis County 2006).

In 1987, the black-capped vireo, a tiny songbird found in Travis County, was listed as endangered. One year later, work began on a regional habitat conservation plan designed to protect enough land to ensure the survival of the species while allowing other habitat to be converted to development in accordance with the plan. By 1990, the golden-cheeked warbler had also been listed, along with six invertebrates that make their home in Travis County's caves. In 1992, Austin

Figure 25-1.   A cactus at the Lady Bird Johnson Wildflower Center, in Austin, offers a subtle reminder that Travis County would be a thirsty place without its precious aquifers and springs.

voters approved $22 million in bonds for the acquisition of land to protect water quality, conserve endangered species, and provide open space for passive recreation. In addition, Austin voters approved an extra $22 million in 1992 to acquire Barton Creek Wilderness Park, which is dedicated as part of the Balcones Canyonlands Preserve and also serves as parkland (Conrad 2011). In 1996, after an eight-year planning and approval process, the Balcones Canyonlands Conservation Plan (BCCP) was officially approved by the U.S. Fish and Wildlife Service to protect 27 species of concern as well as the eight endangered species mentioned above. The BCCP requires Austin, Travis County, and several other partners to complete the Balcones Canyonlands Preserve by 2016 by preserving at least 30,428 acres of land and 62 caves (Austin 2011; Farmer 2011).

By 2009, the Balcones Canyonlands Preserve had grown to 28,513 acres, with the City of Austin and Travis County accounting for 19,030 acres. The Nature Conservancy of Texas adds 4,244 acres, including more than 4,000 acres in its Barton Creek Habitat Preserve, which protects the water quality as well as habitat of the Barton Springs segment of the Edwards Aquifer. The Lower Colorado

Figure 25-2.   Austin protects its most prized resource—water—with extensive watershed regulations.

River Authority, a multipurpose public service provider, adds another 2,707 acres in five separate properties. The remainder is preserved by 19 separate owners, including the Travis Audubon Society, which contributes its Baker Sanctuary, 680 acres of juniper-woodland habitat beloved by the golden-cheeked warbler (Austin 2010; Nature Conservancy 2011; Lower Colorado River Authority 2011; Travis Audubon Society 2011). As of 2011, 98 percent of the 30,428-acre minimum requirement had been acquired, and some protection has been achieved for 45 of the 62 caves that must also ultimately be preserved (Farmer 2011).

In addition to the Balcones Canyonlands Preserve, there is the similarly named Balcones Canyonlands National Wildlife Refuge, formed by the U.S. Fish and Wildlife Service to provide supplemental habitat for the endangered and listed species covered by the BCCP. The refuge currently protects 23,815 acres and is planned to grow to 46,000 acres, primarily through federal funding from the Land and Water Conservation Fund (Friends of Balcones Canyonlands National Wildlife Refuge 2011; Unbehaun 2011).

Due to the vulnerability of water there, Austin also embarked on a third land preservation strategy known as the Water Quality Protection Land program. The limestone bedrock underneath Austin and Travis County has eroded into an underground terrain known as karst, which is characterized by sinkholes, caves, underground streams, and springs. Karst can store vast quantities of water, but it is also susceptible to disruption and contamination from activities on the surface, including development. In 1998, Austin voters approved Proposition 2, which authorized $65 million in bonds to buy 15,000 acres of land for water-quality protection in the Barton Springs segment of the Edwards Aquifer (Austin 2011). The voters authorized additional land purchases by approving subsequent bond measures in 1998, 2002, and 2006 (Austin 2011). Between 1992 and 2006, Austin voters approved eight water-quality, open space, and park bonds totaling $235 million, while Travis County voters passed three separate bond measures worth $84 million in total for watershed, park, and open space preservation (Trust for Public Land 2009). The Water Quality Protection Land program now manages 23,577 acres, with 9,050 acres owned in fee and the remaining 14,527 acres protected by conservation easement (Austin 2011).

In 2002, Austin created the Wildland Conservation Division to protect and manage land in the Balcones Canyonlands Preserve, primarily for habitat conservation, and land in the Water Quality Protection Land primarily to optimize the quantity and quality of water recharging the Barton Springs segment of the Edwards Aquifer. Public access for passive recreation is allowed on some portions of the wildland sometimes under strict limitations (Austin 2011).

In addition to undertaking traditional land preservation with public funding, Austin acquires land using a combination of regulations and a form of transfer of development rights (TDR) in which land coverage as well as development

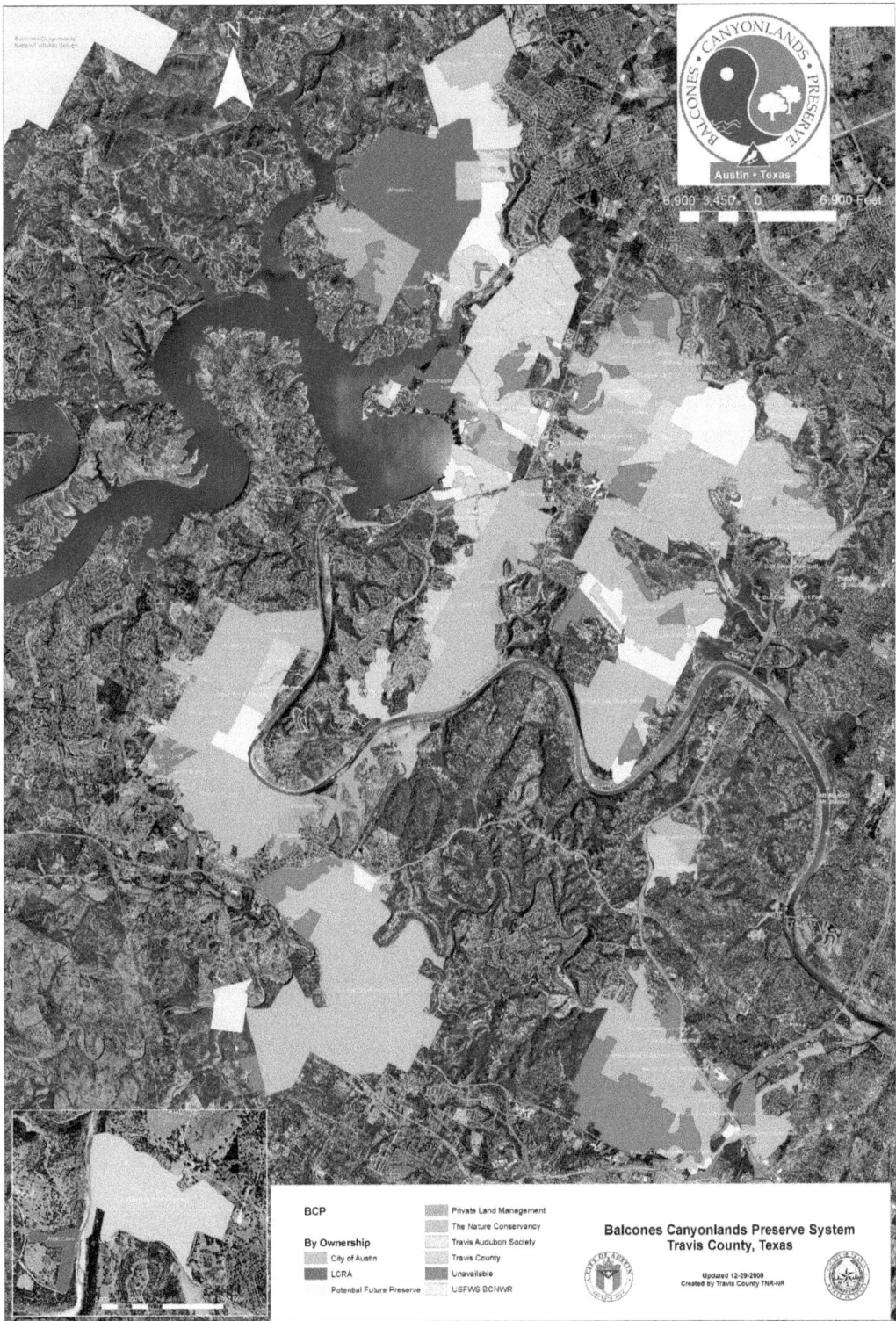

Figure 25-3. Austin, Travis County, and their partners have protected more than 98 percent of the planned 30,428-acre Balcones Canyonlands Preserve.

[Source: Travis County – Unpublished Work © 2011 Travis County, Texas]

potential can be transferred from critical water-quality zones to upland zones. Under the Austin City Code, development in critical water-quality zones is limited to parks, golf courses, open space, and water-related uses such as docks and marinas. Landowners can also take advantage of various TDR options. Under one variation, each acre of land in a critical water-quality zone that is dedicated to the city in fee entitles the owner to transfer either one single-family residential housing unit or 6,000 square feet of impervious coverage to an upland zone.

In 2005, Austin and Travis County joined a coalition of six cities, three counties, three groundwater conservation districts, and a village in adopting the Regional Water Quality Protection Plan for the Barton Springs Segment of the Edwards Aquifer and its Contributing Zone. This regional plan recommended preserving natural cover on an additional 20,000 acres of land just to offset the effects of existing development in excess of the plan's land-coverage limitations. Preserving 20,000 acres would be an expensive proposition using only traditional public funding tools. But the plan calls for the full range of implementation tools including intra-jurisdictional TDR ordinances similar to the one already adopted in Austin (Naismith Engineering 2005).

One of Austin's most unique treasures is Barton Springs Pool, a 900-foot-long spring-fed swimming hole that annually cools an estimated 300,000 people. In addition to being a famous landmark, Barton Springs Pool is a barometer of local environmental health. Austinites are justifiably concerned when the pool suffers from low flow, flooding, or water contamination. Advocates estimate that an additional 50,000 acres of land must be preserved in order to permanently save Barton Springs (Save Our Springs Alliance 2005). This would be a daunting task. But Austin and Travis County have repeatedly demonstrated their ability to achieve ambitious preservation goals in the past by careful planning, innovation, cooperation, and of course, citizens who are willing to pay for the defense of their beloved springs.

GLOSSARY

Comprehensive plan: A blueprint adopted by a community that establishes goals and policies for land use and typically transportation, housing, conservation, and other resources, as well as the tools needed to implement those goals and policies.

Conservation easement: A document recorded with the deed to a property that permanently restricts the future development of the property and may also limit the future uses of the property.

Density: The level of development in an area, measured as the number of residential dwelling units on a specified amount of land, usually per acre of land.

Endangered Species Act: The federal law created in 1973 and administered by the U.S. Fish and Wildlife Service to identify wildlife species threatened with extinction and regulate their protection through permit procedures and habitat conservation plans.

Floodplain: An area subject to periodic flooding as determined by the Federal Emergency Management Agency (FEMA).

Green infrastructure: Natural areas, farms, and rural open space that provide services to communities, such as floodwater retention, watershed protection, habitat preservation, and the provision of outdoor recreation opportunities.

Greenways: Linear open spaces that often preserve watercourses while serving multiple purposes, including watershed protection, floodwater retention, habitat preservation, and the provision of wildlife corridors and trails as well as other outdoor recreation opportunities.

Habitat conservation plan (HCP): A plan that allows a limited amount of development to occur on the sensitive habitat of threatened or endangered wildlife species as long as that development complies with planning requirements designed to ensure the survival of those species, including the establishment and maintenance of preserves for those species.

Infrastructure: Support systems for development, including roads, sewers, water mains, schools, and parks.

Land Evaluation and Site Assessment (LESA): A means of measuring the suitability of land for agriculture using productivity ratings and economic, social, and geographic factors that estimate development pressure and farm viability.

Land trust: A private nonprofit land conservation organization with an Internal Revenue Service designation of 501c(3) capable of accepting donations of cash, land, and conservation easements and able to buy land and conservation easements.

National Register of Historic Places: A list of historic places approved by the U.S. Department of the Interior.

Purchase of development rights (PDR): A preservation tool in which the owners of farmland and other important rural lands sell some or all of their development potential but retain title to the land and continue to use it for nondevelopment purposes as allowed by an easement recorded on the property. In PDR, the development rights removed from the preserved property are permanently retired rather than sold to private-sector developers to allow bonus development, as in TDR.

Smart growth: Planning and design principles, regulations, and development that promote compact communities, preserve rural areas, and curb sprawl.

Transfer of development rights (TDR): A plan implementation tool that works within a community's land-use regulations to encourage the voluntary redirection of growth away from places where a community wants less or no development, called sending areas, to places where additional growth is planned, called receiving areas. Transfer of development rights (TDR) can be thought of as a form of dual zoning in which developers in receiving areas are allowed to exceed a threshold of development potential, called baseline, only by participating in the preservation of sending areas. To achieve this bonus development potential, receiving area developers must typically acquire transferable development rights (TDRs), which are generated by sending-area property owners when they preserve their properties. When TDR works, sending-area property owners are compensated for voluntarily preserving their land; receiving-area developers achieve greater development potential and therefore greater profits, despite the addition cost of TDRs; and communities are able to reach the preservation as well as the development goals of their plans without reliance on taxes. (The acronym TDR refers to the transferable development rights technique, while the acronym TDRs refers to the transferable development rights that are used as currency in this technique.)

Urban growth boundary: A line around a city or other urbanized area within which urban development is confined unless and until the boundary is relocated.

Zoning: Land-use regulations adopted by local governments controlling allowable land uses and various characteristics of development, including residential density, parking, and building height, bulk, and setbacks.

REFERENCES

Chapter 1: Introduction: Planning Preservation

Ahrens, Pete. 2006. "A Park for the People: Origins of the East Bay Regional Park District." Unpublished ms. Available at www.nexialquest.com/Park%20for%20the%20People.pdf.

Albuquerque, City of. 2010. "Albuquerque Open Space Program." Available at www.cabq.gov/openspace.

American Farmland Trust. 2009. "On the Road to Planning a Future for Farms." Available at www.farmland.org/programs/states/ny/focus_tour.asp.

American Planning Association (APA). 1999. "Policy Guide on Agricultural Land Preservation." Available at www.planning.org/policy/guides/adopted/agricultural.htm.

———. 2000. "Policy Guide on Planning for Sustainability." Available at www.planning.org/policy/guides/adopted/sustainability.htm.

———. 2011. "APA Mission and Vision." Available at www.planning.org/apaataglance/mission.htm.

Berks County. 2007. *Berks County Greenway, Park and Recreation Plan*. Reading, Pa.: Berks County Planning Commission and Berks County Parks and Recreation Department.

Blue Ribbon Commission for Agriculture in Lancaster County, Pennsylvania. 2005. *Keep Lancaster County Farming*. Lancaster, Pa.: Lancaster County Board of Commissioners.

Boulder, City of. 2009. "Boulder's Open Space & Mountain Parks: A History." Available at http://joomla.ci.boulder.co.us/index.php?option=com_content&view=article&id=1167&Itemid=1085.

Boulder County. 2008. "Open Space Lands." Available at www.bouldercounty.org/openspace/about_us/acquisitions.htm.

Brandywine Conservancy. 2010. "Brandywine Conservancy." Available at www.brandywineconservancy.org/conservancy.html.

Buckland, Jeffrey. 1987. "The History and Use of Purchase of Development Rights in the United States." *Landscape and Urban Planning* 14:237–52.

Burlington County. 2008. *Burlington County Comprehensive Farmland Preservation Plan (2009–2018)*. Pemberton, N.J.: Burlington County Agricultural Development Board.

Chester County. 2002. *Linking Landscapes: A Plan for the Protected Open Space Network in Chester County, PA*. West Chester, Pa.: Chester County Board of Commissioners.

———. 2008. "Preservation Partnership Program Manual." Available at http://dsf.chesco.org/openspace/lib/openspace/manuals/PPPmanual.pdf.

Collier County. 2010. "Annual Update and Inventory Report." Available at www.colliergov.net/Index.aspx?page=1581.

Dane County. 2007. *Dane County Comprehensive Plan* (September 11, draft). Madison, Wis.: Dane County Board of Supervisors.

Daniels, Tom. 2011. Interviewed by author, April 1.

DeLong, Jennifer. 2010. In discussion with the author, April 30.

East Bay Regional Park District. 2010. "Welcome." Available at www.ebparks.org.

Farmland Preservation Report. 2010. "Nation's Top 12 Locally Operated Farmland Preservation Programs." Available at www.farmlandpreservationreport.com/2010/09/14/september-2010.

Greenbelt Alliance. 2003. "Contra Costa County: Smart Growth or Sprawl?" Available at www .greenbelt.org/downloads/resources/report_CCLUA.pdf.

Lancaster County. 2005. *Strategic Tourism Development Element—Envision Lancaster County: The Comprehensive Plan for Lancaster County, Pennsylvania.* Lancaster, Pa.: Lancaster County Board of Commissioners.

———. 2006. *Balance—Growth Management Element: The Comprehensive Plan for Lancaster County, Pennsylvania.* Lancaster, Pa.: Lancaster County Board of Commissioners.

Lexington–Fayette County. 1999. *Rural Service Area Management Plan: Our Rural Heritage in the Next Century, Adopted April 8, 1999.* Lexington, Ky.: Lexington–Fayette Urban County Government.

———. 2011. "PDR Program." Available at www.lexingtonky.gov/index.aspx?page=497.

Marin County. 2008. *Marin County Parks and Open Space Strategic Plan—Appendices.* San Rafael, Calif.: Marin County Board of Supervisors.

Maryland–National Capital Park and Planning Commission. 1980. *Functional Master Plan for the Preservation of Agriculture and Rural Open Space in Montgomery County.* Silver Spring, Md.: Maryland–National Capital Park and Planning Commission.

McCreery, Laura. 2010. *Living Landscape: The Extraordinary Rise of the East Bay Regional Park District and How It Preserved 100,000 Acres.* Berkeley, Calif.: Wilderness Press.

Midpeninsula Regional Open Space District (MROSD). 2010. "About the District." Available at www.openspace.org/about_us.

Muir, John. 1911. *My First Summer in the Sierras.* Boston: Houghton Mifflin.

Nature Conservancy. 2007. "Long Island's Last Stand—Status Report 2007." Available at www.nature .org/wherewework/northamerica/states/newyork/files/last_stand_status_2007.pdf.

Palm Beach County. 2005. *2004–2005 TDR Annual Report.* West Palm Beach, Fla.: Palm Beach County.

———. 2010. "NENA." Available at www.pbcgov.com/erm/nena.

Phoenix, City of. 1972. *An Open Space Plan for the Phoenix Mountains.* Phoenix, Ariz.: City of Phoenix, Arizona.

Pima County. 1998. *Sonoran Desert Conservation Plan: Concept.* Tucson, Ariz.: Pima County Board of Supervisors.

Press, Robert. 2002. *Saving Open Space: The Politics of Local Preservation in California.* Berkeley, Calif.: University of California Press.

Pruetz, Rick. 2010. "TDR Program Profiles." Available at www.beyondtakingsandgivings.com/updates.htm.

Roberts, Marc. 2010. "Use of TDRs and TDCs in Livermore." Presentation at American Planning Association National Conference, New Orleans. April 12.

Roise, Charlene. 2000. *Making the City Itself a Work of Art: An Historical Context for the Grand Rounds, Minneapolis.* Minneapolis: Minneapolis Park and Recreation Board.

Santa Clara County. 1994. *Santa Clara County General Plan 1995–2010.* San Jose, Calif.: Santa Clara County.

Santa Cruz County. 1994. *1994 General Plan and Local Coastal Program.* Santa Cruz, Calif.: Santa Cruz County.

Santa Fe County. 2000. *Open Land and Trails Plan: For the Wildlife, Mountains, Trails and Historic Places Program.* Santa Fe, N.M.: Santa Fe County.

Smart Growth Network. 2011. "Smart Growth Principles." Available at www.smartgrowth.org/engine/index.php/principles/open_space.

Suffolk County. 1996. *Agricultural and Farmland Protection Plan*. Hauppauge, N.Y.: Suffolk County Planning Department.

———. 2007. *Open Space Acquisition Policy for Suffolk County*. Hauppaugue, N. Y.: Suffolk County Planning Department.

Trust for Public Land. 2007. "2007 Conservation Awards." Available at www.tpl.org/news/press-releases/third-annual-county-land-conservation.html.

U.S. Fish and Wildlife Service. 2005. *Florida Panther National Wildlife Refuge*. Naples, Fla.: U.S. Fish and Wildlife Service.

———. 2010. "Ten Thousand Islands National Wildlife Refuge." Available at www.fws.gov/refuges/profiles/index.cfm?id=41555.

Wells, Janet. 2000. "Greenbelt Gaining Ground in Sonoma County." *San Francisco Chronicle*. September 28.

Zawitoski, John. 2011. TDR Program Presentation. March 28. Derwood, Md.: Agriculture Services Division, Montgomery County Department of Economic Development.

Chapter 2: Alameda County, California

Ahrens, Pete. 2006. "A Park for the People: Origins of the East Bay Regional Park District." Available at www.nexialquest.com/Park%20for%20the%20People.pdf.

California State Parks. 2010. "Find a Park." Available at www.parks.ca.gov/parkindex.

East Bay Regional Park District. 1997. *Master Plan 1997*. Oakland, Calif.: East Bay Regional Park District.

———. 2010a. "Crab Cove Visitor Center." Available at www.ebparks.org/parks/vc/crab_cove.

———. 2010b. "Measure WW: Regional Open Space, Wildlife, Shoreline and Parks Bond Extension." Available at www.ebparks.org/node/1011.

———. 2010c. "Welcome." Available at www.ebparks.org.

Kent, Jerry. 2009. "A Brief History of the East Bay Regional Park District." Available at www.ebparks.org/75/timeline.

McCreery, Laura. 2010. *Living Landscape: The Extraordinary Rise of the East Bay Regional Park District and How It Preserved 100,000 Acres*. Berkeley, Calif.: Wilderness Press.

Oakland, City of. 2010. "Wildlife Sanctuary." Available at www.oaklandnet.com/parks/parks/lakemerritt_wildlifesanctuary.asp.

Olmsted Brothers and Ansel Hall. 1930. *Report on Proposed Park Reservations for East Bay Cities (California)*. Berkeley, Calif.: Bureau of Public Administration, University of California. Quoted in Ahrens 2006.

Roberts, Marc. 2010. "Use of TDRs and TDCs in Livermore." Presentation at American Planning Association National Planning Conference, New Orleans. April 12.

U.S. Fish and Wildlife Service. 2010. "Don Edwards San Francisco Bay National Wildlife Refuge." Available at www.fws.gov/desfbay.

Chapter 3: Albuquerque and Bernalillo County, New Mexico

Albuquerque, City of. 2010a. "Albuquerque Open Space Program—History." Available at www.cabq.gov/openspace/history.html.

———. 2010b. "Albuquerque Open Space Lands." Available at www.cabq.gov/openspace/lands.html.

———. 2010c. "33.1 ABQ Open Space Acres & Total City Land Area" Available at www.cabq.gov/progress/environmental-protection-enhancement/dcc-33/indicator-33-1.

Albuquerque/Bernalillo County. 2003. *Albuquerque/Bernalillo County Comprehensive Plan*. Albuquerque, N.M.: Albuquerque Planning Department/Bernalillo County Zoning, Building and Planning Department.

Bernalillo County. 2003. *Bernalillo County Parks, Open Space & Trails Master Plan*. Albuquerque, N.M.: Bernalillo County Parks and Recreation Department.

———. 2010. "Open Space: Properties." Available at www.bernco.gov/open-space-properties-3948.

Friends of Albuquerque's Environmental Story. 2010. *Albuquerque's Environmental Story*. Available at www.abqenvironmentalstory.org.

Lamb, Susan. 1993. *Petroglyph National Monument*. Tucson, Ariz.: Southwest Parks and Monuments Association.

Wilderness.net. 2010. "Sandia Mountain Wilderness." Available at www.wilderness.net/index.cfm?fuse=NWPS&sec=wildView&wname=Sandia%20Mountain%20Wilderness.

Chapter 4: Berks County, Pennsylvania

Berks County. 2003. *Berks Vision 2020: A Comprehensive Plan for the County of Berks*. Reading, Pa.: Berks County Planning Commission.

———. 2007. *Berks County Greenway, Park and Recreation Plan*. Reading, Pa.: Berks County Planning Commission and Berks County Parks and Recreation Department.

———. 2008a. "Berks County Background." Available at www.co.berks.pa.us/Pages/BerksCounty Background.aspx.

———. 2008b. "Land Preservation—Program Statistics." Available at www.co.berks.pa.us/alp/cwp/view.asp?a=1333&Q=453995&alpNav=|.

———. 2008c. *Natural Land, Farmland and Open Space Conservation Program. August 2006—Amended December 18, 2008*. Reading, Pa.: Berks County Board of Commissioners.

———. 2009. "Joint Comprehensive Planning Program." Available at www.co.berks.pa.us/Dept/Planning/Pages/JointComprehensivePlanningProgram.aspx.

Berks County Agricultural Land Preservation Board. 2008. *Agriculture Is Everyone's Business!* Leesport, Pa.: Berks County Agricultural Land Preservation Board.

Berks County Conservancy. 2010. "About Us—Introduction." Available at www.berks-conservancy.org/Introduction/tabid/54/Default.aspx.

Bowers, Deborah. 2003. *A National View of Agricultural Easement Programs: Profiles and Maps—Report 1*. Northampton, Mass.: American Farmland Trust.

DeLong, Jennifer. 2010. In discussion with the author, April 30.

Farmland Preservation Report. 2010. "Nation's Top 12 Locally Operated Farmland Preservation Programs." Available at www.farmlandpreservationreport.com/2010/09/14/september-2010.

Hawk Mountain Sanctuary. 2007. "The Hawk Mountain Landscape." Available at www.hawkmountain.org/index.php?pr=The_Sanctuary.

Hildebrand, Tami. 2006. "2006: A Banner Year for Farmland Preservation." *Berks County Agricultural Land Preservation Board Quarterly Newsletter* 6(1): 1–2.

Oberholtzer, Lydia, and Dick Esseks. 2008. *Berks County, Pennsylvania. Case Study: Farm Viability in Urbanizing Areas*. Washington, D.C.: Cooperative State Research, Education and Extension Service, U.S. Department of Agriculture.

Pennsylvania, State of. 2008. *Review of the Agricultural Conservation Easement Purchase Program*. Harrisburg, Pa.: Legislative Budget and Finance Committee, a Joint Committee of the Pennsylvania General Assembly.

U.S. Department of Agriculture (USDA). 2007. *Berks County, Pennsylvania Profile: 2007 Census of Agriculture*. Washington, D.C.: USDA, National Agricultural Statistics Service.

Chapter 5: Boulder and Boulder County, Colorado

Boulder, City of. 2009. "Boulder's Open Space and Mountain Parks: A History." Available at http://joomla.ci.boulder.co.us/index.php?option=com_content&view=article&id=1167&Itemid=1085.

Boulder County. 2008. "Parks and Open Space." Available at www.bouldercounty.org/openspace/about_us/acquisitions.htm.

———. 2010a. *Boulder County Comprehensive Plan.* Adopted 1999 and amended and updated through 2010. Boulder, Colo.: Boulder County Land Use Department.

———. 2010b. "Boulder County Parks and Open Space." Available at www.bouldercounty.org/openspace/about_us/abt_index.htm.

Cushman, Carol, and Glenn Cushman. 2006. *Boulder Hiking Trails: Best of the Plains, Foothills and Mountains.* Boulder, Colo.: Pruett Publishing.

Hudson, Suzanne. 1990. *A History of Boulder's Parks and Recreation.* Boulder, Colo.: Boulder Parks and Recreation Department.

Olmsted, Frederick Law, Jr. 1910. *The Improvement of Boulder, Colorado; Report to the City Improvement Association.* Boulder, Colo.: Boulder City Improvement Association.

Plantico, Cailyn. 2008. "The Blue Line Amendment and the Enchanted Mesa Purchase: Setting the Stage for Boulder's Open Space Program." Available at www.bouldercolorado.gov/files/openspace/pdf_education/e_mesa_purchase.pdf.

Pruetz, Rick. 2003. *Beyond Takings and Givings: Saving Natural Areas, Farmland and Historic Landmarks with Transfer of Development Rights and Density Transfer Charges.* Marina Del Rey, Calif.: Arje Press.

Chapter 6: Burlington County, New Jersey

Burlington County. 2002. *Burlington County Parks and Open Space Master Plan 2002.* Pemberton, N.J.: Burlington County Department of Resource Conservation.

———. 2008. *Burlington County Comprehensive Farmland Preservation Plan (2009–2018).* Pemberton, N.J.: Burlington County Agricultural Development Board.

———. 2010. "Burlington County Farmland Preservation: Preserved Acreage Totals by Township" (June 16). Available at www.co.burlington.nj.us/upload/Farmland/Images/Preserved_Totals_By_Township.pdf.

Chesterfield, Township of. 2011. "Old York Village." Available at www.chesterfieldtwp.com/Smart%20Growth/smartgrowthpage.html.

Farmland Preservation Report. 2010. "Nation's Top 12 Locally Operated Farmland Preservation Programs." Available at www.farmlandpreservationreport.com/2010/09/14/september-2010.

New Jersey Pinelands Commission. 2010. "New Jersey Pinelands Development Credit Program." Fact Sheet, revised April. Available at www.state.nj.us/pinelands/infor/fact/PDCfacts.pdf.

New Jersey Department of Environmental Protection (NJDEP). 2010a. "Bass River State Forest." Available at www.state.nj.us/dep/parksandforests/parks/bass.html.

———. 2010b. "Brendan T. Byrne State Forest." Available at www.state.nj.us/dep/parksandforests/parks/byrne.html.

———. 2010c. "Rancocas State Park." Available at www.state.nj.us/dep/parksandforests/parks/rancocas.html.

———. 2010d. "Wharton State Forest." Available at www.state.nj.us/dep/parksandforests/parks/wharton.html.

Pruetz, Rick. 2003. *Beyond Takings and Givings: Saving Natural Areas, Farmland and Historic Landmarks with Transfer of Development Rights and Density Transfer Charges.* Marina Del Rey, Calif.: Arje Press.

Pruetz, Rick, and Noah Standridge. 2009. "What Makes Transfer of Development Rights Work? Success Factors from Research and Practice." *Journal of the American Planning Association* 75:78–87.

Trust for Public Land. 2005. County Leadership in Conservation Award—2005 Winner: Medium Category. Article not archived.

Walls, Margaret, and Virginia McConnell. 2007. *Transfer of Development Rights in U.S. Communities: Evaluating Program Design, Implementation, and Outcomes.* Washington, D.C.: Resources for the Future.

Chapter 7: Chester County, Pennsylvania

Agricultural Land Preservation Board. 2010. "Welcome to the Agricultural Land Preservation Board." Available at www.chesco.org/agriculture/site/default.asp?agricultureNav=|&agricultureNav=|.

Brandywine Conservancy. 2009. "Franklin Township: Land Preservation Success." *Currents: Newsletter of the Brandywine Conservancy's Environmental Management Center*, Summer.

———. 2010. "Brandywine Conservancy." Available at www.brandywineconservancy.org/conservancy.html.

———. 2011. "Conservancy Preserves: Laurels Preserve." Available at www.brandywineconservancy.org/laurelsPreserve.html.

Chester County. 2002. *Linking Landscapes: A Plan for the Protected Open Space Network in Chester County, PA.* West Chester, Pa.: Chester County Board of Commissioners.

———. 2008. "Round 22 Preservation Partnership Program Manual." Available at http://dsf.chesco.org/openspace/lib/openspace/manuals/PPPmanual.pdf.

———. 2009a. *Chester County Nature Preserve Guide.* West Chester, Pa.: Chester County Open Space Preservation Department.

———. 2009b. *Landscapes 2: Bringing Growth and Preservation Together for Chester County—Chester County Comprehensive Policy Plan.* West Chester, Pa.: Chester County Board of Commissioners.

———. 2010a. "Completed Preservation Partnership Program Grants as of August 2, 2010." Available at http://dsf.chesco.org/openspace/lib/openspace/pdfs/PPPWebChart.pdf.

———. 2010b. "Municipal Acquisition and Development Grants as of August 02, 2010." Available at http://dsf.chesco.org/openspace/lib/openspace/pdfs/MuniWebChart.pdf.

Delaware Valley Regional Planning Commission (DVRPC). 2008. "Year 2007 Delaware Valley Protected Open Space by Ownership." Available at www.dvrpc.org/OpenSpace/inventory.htm.

———. 2009. "Active Locally-Funded Open Space Programs as of 2009." Available at www.dvrpc.org/OpenSpace/local.htm.

East Bradford Township. 2009. *Open Space, Recreation & Environmental Resources Plan.* West Chester, Pa.: East Bradford Township Board of Supervisors.

Farmland Preservation Report. 2010. "Nation's Top 12 Locally Operated Farmland Preservation Programs." Available at www.farmlandpreservationreport.com/2010/09/14/september-2010.

French and Pickering Creeks Conservation Trust. 2010. "About French and Pickering Creeks Conservation Trust." Available at www.frenchandpickering.org/about.

Natural Lands Trust. 2010. "ChesLen Preserve." Available at www.natlands.org/preserves-to-visit/list-of-preserves/cheslen-preserve.

Tracy, Tara. 2010. Correspondence with author, May 13.

Trust for Public Land. 2008. "Fourth Annual County Land Conservation Awards Announced." Available at www.tpl.org/news/press-releases/fourth-annual-county-land-conservation.html.

Chapter 8: Collier County, Florida

Buchheister, Carl. 1967. "The Acquisition and Development of the Corkscrew Swamp Sanctuary, 1952–1967." Available at http://corkscrew.audubon.org/Information/Buchheister.html.

Butcher, Niki. 2010. "History of Big Cypress." Available at www.evergladesonline.com/history-big -cypress.htm.

Collier County. 2010a. *Collier County Growth Management Plan—Future Land Use Element.* Tampa, Fla.: Collier County Board of County Commissioners.

———. 2010b. "Overview: Conservation Collier." Available at www.colliergov.net/Index.aspx?page=528.

———. 2010c. "Update and Inventory Report." Available at www.colliergov.net/Index.aspx?page =1581.

———. 2011a. "Rural Land Stewardship Area (RLSA) Overlay Program." Available at www.colliergov .net/Index.aspx?page=1515.

———. 2011b. "TDR Program—Rural Fringe Mixed Use District." Available at www.colliergov.net/ Index.aspx?page=270.

Florida Department of Environmental Protection. 2009. "About the Rookery Bay Preserves." Available at www.dep.state.fl.us/coastal/sites/rookery.

———. 2010. "State Lands History." Available at www.dep.state.fl.us/lands/history_more.htm.

Florida Division of Forestry. 2010. "Picayune Strand State Forest." Available at www.fl-dof.com/state _forests/picayune_strand.html.

Florida State Parks. 2008. "Collier-Seminole State Park." Available at www.floridastateparks.org/ history/parkhistory.cfm?parkid=120&CFID=33967226&CFTOKEN=95779526.

Friends of Fakahatchee Strand State Preserve. 2005. "History." Available at www.friendsoffakahatchee .org/history.php.

Rookery Bay National Estuarine Research Reserve. 2010. "Rookery Bay Reserve Timeline." Available at www.rookerybay.org/about-us/timeline.

Spagna, Neno. 1979. "Transfer of Development Rights: The Collier County Experience." *Florida Environmental and Urban Issues,* January / February.

U.S. Fish and Wildlife Service (USFWS). 2005. *Florida Panther National Wildlife Refuge.* Naples, Fla.: USFWS.

———. 2010. "Ten Thousand Islands National Wildlife Refuge." Available at www.fws.gov/refuges/ profiles/index.cfm?id=41555.

Chapter 9: Contra Costa County, California

Ahrens, Pete. 2006. "A Park for the People: Origins of the East Bay Regional Park District." Available at www.nexialquest.com/Park%20for%20the%20People.pdf.

California Department of Fish and Game. 2010. "Wildlife Areas." Available at www.dfg.ca.gov/ lands/wa/region3/index.html.

California State Parks. 2000. "Mount Diablo State Park." Available at www.parks.ca.gov/ mediagallery/?page_id=517&viewtype=7.

———. 2010. "State Parks—Contra Costa County." Available at www.parks.ca.gov/parkindex/ results.asp?searchtype=4&county_id=7&searchtext=Contra+Costa.

Contra Costa County. 2005. *General Plan 2005–2020.* Martinez, Calif.: Contra Costa County Department of Conservation and Development.

East Bay Regional Park District. 2000. "Regional Economic Analysis." Available at www.ebparks .org/files/econalysis.pdf.

———. 2010a. "Parks." Available at www.ebparks.org/parks.

———. 2010b. "Welcome." Available at www.ebparks.org.

East Contra Costa County Habitat Conservancy. 2010. "Overview/History." Available at www.co .contra-costa.ca.us/depart/cd/water/HCP/overview.html.

East Contra Costa County Habitat Conservation Plan Association (HCPA). 2006. *East Contra Costa County HCP/NCCP. Volume 1.* Martinez, Calif.: East Contra Costa HCPA.

Greenbelt Alliance. 2003. "Contra Costa County: Smart Growth or Sprawl?" Available at www.green belt.org/downloads/resources/report_CCLUA.pdf.

Kent, Jerry. 2009. "A Brief History of the East Bay Regional Park District." Available at www.ebparks .org/75/timeline.

League of Women Voters. 2007. "Measure L: Urban Limit Line County of Contra Costa." Available at www.smartvoter.org/2006/11/07/ca/cc/meas/L.

McCreery, Laura. 2010. *Living Landscape: The Extraordinary Rise of the East Bay Regional Park District and How It Preserved 100,000 Acres.* Berkeley, Calif.: Wilderness Press.

National Park Service. 2010. "Parks." Available at www.nps.gov/findapark/index.htm.

Save Mount Diablo. 2010. "Save Mount Diablo's History: 1971–2010." Available at www.savemount diablo.org/History.htm.

Chapter 10: Dane County, Wisconsin

Capitol Water Trails. 2010. "About Capitol Water Trails." Available at www.capitolwatertrails.org/ about.php.

Dane County. 2006. *Dane County Parks and Open Space Plan: 2006–2011.* Madison, Wis.: Dane County Board of Supervisors.

———. 2007a. *Comprehensive Plan. Dane County* (September 11, draft). Madison, Wis.: Dane County Board of Supervisors.

———. 2007b. "Yahara Waterways: Water Trail Guide." Available at http://danedocs.countyofdane .com/webdocs/PDF/lwrd/lakes/yaharaTrailGuide.pdf.

———. 2009. "Nine Springs E-Way." Available at www.countyofdane.com/lwrd/parks/nine_springs .aspx.

Dane County Food Council. 2010. "Who We Are and What We Do." Available at www.countyofdane .com/foodcouncil.

Dunn, Town of. 2010. "Purchase of Development Rights (PDR) Program." Available at http://town .dunn.wi.us/townofdunn/pdr/default.asp.

Ice Age Trail Alliance. 2010. "About the Ice Age Trail." Available at www.iceagetrail.org/ frequently-asked-questions.

Leopold, Aldo. 1949. *A Sand County Almanac.* New York: Oxford University Press.

Lower Wisconsin State Riverway Board. 2005. "Riverway Project History." Available at http://lwr.state .wi.us/index.asp.

MRPHA Partnership. 2010. "About Military Ridge Prairie Heritage Area Partnership." Available at www.militaryridgeprairie.org/About%20us.html.

Natural Heritage Land Trust (NHLT). 2010. "Accomplishments." Available at www.nhlt.org/ accomplishments.asp.

Nature Conservancy. 2010. "Thomson Memorial Prairie." Available at www.nature.org/where wework/northamerica/states/wisconsin/preserves/art33.html.

U.S. Department of Agriculture (USDA). 2007. *Dane County, Wisconsin Profile: 2007 Census of Agriculture.* Washington, D.C.: USDA, National Agricultural Statistics Service.

Wisconsin Department of Natural Resources (DNR). 2005a. "Overview of the Wisconsin Land Legacy Report." Available at http://dnr.wi.gov/master_planning/land_legacy/overview.html#places.

———. 2005b. "Wisconsin Statewide Comprehensive Outdoor Recreation Plan: 2005–2010." Available at http://dnr.wi.gov/planning/scorp.

———. 2010. "Mazomanie Bottoms." Available at http://dnr.wi.gov/org/land/er/sna/index.asp?SNA=142.

Chapter 11: King County, Washington

Buckland, Jeffrey. 1987. "The History and Use of Purchase of Development Rights in the United States." *Landscape and Urban Planning* 14:237–52.

Cascade Land Conservancy (CLC). 2008. "Progress Report." Available at http://cascadeagenda .com/files/CLC_Book_COMPILED_FINAL_04.pdf.

———. 2010. "About Us." Available at www.cascadeland.org/about-clc.

King County. 2010a. "About the King County Greenprint Project." Available at www.kingcounty .gov/environment/stewardship/sustainable-building/greenprint/about.aspx.

———. 2010b. "Farmland Preservation Program." Available at www.kingcounty.gov/environment/wlr/ sections-programs/rural-regional-services-section/agriculture-program/farmland-preservation -program.aspx.

———. 2010c. "History of Comprehensive Planning in King County." Available at www.kingcounty .gov/council/issues/comprehensive_plan/history.aspx.

———. 2010d. *King County Open Space Plan 2010.* Seattle: Metropolitan King County Council.

———. 2010e. "King County Parks and Recreation." Available at www.kingcounty.gov/recreation/ parks.aspx.

———. 2010f. "Transfer of Development Rights Program." Available at www.kingcounty.gov/ environment/stewardship/sustainable-building/transfer-development-rights.aspx.

Pruetz, Rick, and Noah Standridge. 2009. "What Makes TDR Work? Success Factors from Research and Practice." *Journal of the American Planning Association* 75:78–87.

Trust for Public Land. 2005. *Greenprint for King County.* Seattle: King County Department of Natural Resources and Parks.

———. 2004. *King County, Washington Land Conservation Financing Study.* Seattle: King County Department of Natural Resources and Parks.

U.S. Forest Service. 2010. "Mt. Baker Snoqualmie National Forest Special Places—Alpine Lakes Wilderness." Available at www.fs.usda.gov/wps/portal/fsinternet/!ut/p/c4/04_SB8K8xLLM9MSSzPy 8xBz9CP0os3gjAwhwtDDw9_AI8zPyhQoY6BdkOyoCAGixyPg!/?ss=110605&navtype=BROWSE BYSUBJECT&cid=stelprdb5189214&navid=100000000000000&pnavid=null&position=Not%20 Yet%20Determined.Html&ttype=detail&pname=Mt.%20Baker-Snoqualmie%20National%20 Forest-%20Special%20Places.

Chapter 12: Lancaster County, Pennsylvania

Blue Ribbon Commission for Agriculture in Lancaster County, Pennsylvania. 2005. *Keep Lancaster County Farming.* Lancaster, Pa.: Lancaster County Board of Commissioners.

Brandywine Conservancy. 2008. *Lancaster County TDR Practitioner's Handbook—A How-To Guide for Conserving Land and Managing Growth Using Transfer of Development Rights.* Lancaster, Pa.: Lancaster County Board of Commissioners.

Daniels, Tom. 1991. "The Purchase of Development Rights: Preserving Agricultural Land and Open Space." *Journal of the American Planning Association* 57:421–31.

———. 2000. "Integrated Working Landscape Protection: The Case of Lancaster County, Pennsylvania." *Society and Natural Resources* 13:261–71.

———. 2011. Interviewed by author, April 1.

Daniels, Tom, and Deborah Bowers. 1997. *Holding Our Ground: Protecting America's Farms and Farmland.* Washington, D.C.: Island Press.

Farmland Preservation Report. 2010. "Nation's Top 12 Locally Operated Farmland Preservation Programs." Available at www.farmlandpreservationreport.com/2010/09/14/september-2010.

Jaffe, Rachel. 2005. "Stopping Sprawl in Lancaster County: Making the Case for Mandatory Urban Growth Boundaries." *Temple Journal of Science, Technology and Environmental Law* 24:143–85.

Lancaster County. 2005. *Strategic Tourism Development Element—Envision Lancaster County: The Comprehensive Plan for Lancaster County, Pennsylvania*. Lancaster County, Pa.: Lancaster County Board of Commissioners.

———. 2006. *Balance—Growth Management Element: The Comprehensive Plan for Lancaster County, Pennsylvania*. Lancaster, Pa.: Lancaster County Board of Commissioners.

———. 2009. "The Lancaster County TDR Practitoners Handbook." In the Lancaster County Smart Growth Toolbox, available at www.co.lancaster.pa.us/toolbox/cwp/view.asp?a=3&q=605937.

Lancaster Farmland Trust. 2009. *2008 Annual Report*. Strasburg, Pa.: Lancaster Farmland Trust.

Maynard, Leigh, Timothy Kelsey, Stanford Lembeck, and John Becker. 1998. "Early Experience with Pennsylvania's Agricultural Conservation Easement Program." *Journal of Soil and Water Conservation* 53:106–12.

U.S. Census Bureau. 1995. "Pennsylvania—Population of Counties by Decennial Census: 1900 to 1990." Available at www.census.gov/population/cencounts/pa190090.txt.

U.S. Department of Agriculture (USDA). 2007. *Lancaster County, Pennsylvania—2007 Census of Agriculture: County Profile*. Washington, D.C.: USDA, National Agricultural Statistics Service.

Warwick Township. 2010. "Preserved Farms." Available at www.warwicktownship.org/warwick/cwp/view.asp?a=3&q=565099.

World Monuments Fund. 2010. "Watch Sites Since 1996." Available at www.wmf.org/watch/watch-sites-1996.

Chapter 13: Lexington–Fayette County, Kentucky

Bluegrass Conservancy. 2010. Bluegrass Conservancy Conservation Easement Portfolio. Available at www.uky.edu/Trustees/minutes/full/200809/aacr3.pdf.

Boone County. 2001. *A Study of PDR and TDR for Boone County, Kentucky*. Burlington, Ky.: Boone County Kentucky Planning Commission.

Eblen, Tom. 2010. "PDR Still a Great Deal for Taxpayers." *Lexington-Herald Leader*. February 28.

Fayette Alliance. 2011. "Our Farmland." Available at http://fayettealliance.com/category/farm-facts.

Fulton, William, Rolf Pendall, Mai Nguyen, and Alicia Harrison. 2001. *Who Sprawls Most? How Growth Patterns Differ Across the U.S.* Washington, D.C.: Brookings Institution.

Lexington–Fayette County. 1999. *Rural Service Area Management Plan*. Lexington, Ky.: Lexington–Fayette Urban County Government.

———. 2005. "Lexington–Fayette County Purchase of Development Rights Program." PowerPoint presentation. Available at www.lexingtonky.gov/Modules/ShowDocument.aspx?documentid=601#373,33,Slide 33.

———. 2009. *Destination 2040: Choosing Lexington's Future*. Lexington, Ky.: Lexington–Fayette Urban County Government.

———. 2011. "PDR Program." Available at www.lexingtonky.gov/index.aspx?page=497.

Schneider, Krista. 2003. *The Paris-Lexington Road: Community-Based Planning and Context-Sensitive Highway Design*. Washington, D.C.: Island Press.

Slayman, Andrew. 2007. "A Race Against Time for Kentucky's Bluegrass Country." *ICON* (World Monuments Fund newsletter), Spring.

U.S. Department of Agriculture (USDA). 2008. "Farm & Ranch Land Protection Program Helps Entity Reach Milestone." Available at www.ky.nrcs.usda.gov/news/FRPP_LFUCG.html.

———. 2010. "State Fact Sheets: Kentucky." Available at www.ers.usda.gov/StateFacts/KY.HTM.

Chapter 14: Maricopa County, Arizona

American Planning Association (APA). 2007. "Phoenix Open Space Wins APA Landmark Award." News release, December 18.

Bureau of Land Management. 2010a. "Big Horn Mountains Wilderness Area." Available at www.blm.gov/az/st/en/prog/blm_special_areas/wildareas/bighorn.html.

———. 2010b. "Sonoran Desert National Monument." Available at www.blm.gov/az/st/en/prog/blm_special_areas/natmon/son_des.html.

Corbett, Peter. 2010. "Scottsdale Likely to Bid on State Land Trust Land for Preserve." *The Arizona Republic*. September 3. Available at www.azcentral.com/arizonarepublic/local/articles/2010/09/03/20100903scottsdale-state-land-preserve-bid.html.

Gilbert, Dorothy. 1981. "Phoenix Mountains Preservation Council History." Available at www.phoenixmountains.org/history_by_dottie_gilbert.html.

Maricopa Association of Governments (MAG). 1995. *Desert Spaces: An Open Space Plan for the Maricopa Association of Governments*. Phoenix, Ariz.: MAG.

Maricopa County. 1997. *Eye to the Future: Maricopa County Comprehensive Plan 2020—Open Space Element*. Phoenix, Ariz.: Maricopa County Board of Supervisors.

———. 2004. *Maricopa County Regional Trail System Plan*. Phoenix, Ariz.: Maricopa County Board of Supervisors.

———. 2010. "History of Park System." Available at www.maricopa.gov/parks/history.aspx.

Phoenix, City of. 1972. *An Open Space Plan for the Phoenix Mountains*. Phoenix, Ariz.: City of Phoenix, Arizona.

———. 1998. *Sonoran Preserve Master Plan: An Open Space Plan for the Phoenix Sonoran Desert*. Phoenix, Ariz.: City of Phoenix, Arizona.

———. 2002a. "Phoenix Parks and Preserve Initiative." Available at http://phoenix.gov/PRL/pppi.html.

———. 2009a. "History of the Phoenix Park System." Available at http://phxcms.phoenix.gov/PRL/ataglance.html.

———. 2009b. "South Mountain: Trails and Desert Preserves." Available at http://phoenix.gov/recreation/rec/parks/preserves/locations/south/index.html.

Scottsdale, City of. 2010. "Scottsdale's McDowell Sonoran Preserve History." Available at www.scottsdaleaz.gov/preserve/history.asp.

Chapter 15: Marin County, California

California State Parks. 2007. "Mount Tamalpais State Park." Brochure available at www.parks.ca.gov/mediagallery/?page_id=471&viewtype=7.

Dyble, Louise. 2007. "Revolt Against Sprawl: Transportation and the Origins of the Marin County Growth-Control Regime." *Journal of Urban History* 34:38–66.

Faber, Phyllis. 1999. "MALT: The Land Trust Experience in Marin County." Pp. 125–40 in *California Farmland and Urban Pressures: Statewide and Regional Perspectives*, ed. Albert Medvitz, Alvin Sokolow, and Cathy Lemp. Oakland: University of California Agricultural Issues Center.

Farmland Preservation Report. 2010. "Nation's Top 12 Locally Operated Farmland Preservation Programs." Available at www.farmlandpreservationreport.com/2010/09/14/september-2010.

Hattam, Jennifer. 2002. "Where the Cows Come Home." *Sierra* 87:18–23.

Marin Conservation League. 2010a. "Marin County's Green Pioneers." Available at www.marinconservationleague.org/about-us/history.html.

Marin County. 2007. *Marin Countywide Plan*. San Rafael, Calif.: Marin County Board of Supervisors.

———. 2008. *Marin County Parks and Open Space Strategic Plan—Appendices.* San Rafael, Calif.: Marin County Board of Supervisors.

National Park Service (NPS). 2008. *Muir Woods.* Washington, D.C.: NPS.

———. 2009. "Creation of Golden Gate National Recreation Area." Available at www.nps.gov/goga/historyculture/creation-of-golden-gate-national-recreation-area.htm.

___. 2010. "Point Reyes—Exotic/Invasive Plants." Available at www.nps.gov/pore/naturescience/nonnativespecies_plants.htm.

Raives, James. Marin County Department of Parks and Open Space. 2010. Correspondence with author, May 10.

United Nations Educational, Scientific and Cultural Organization (UNESCO). 2002. "Golden Gate—Biosphere Information." Available at www.unesco.org/mabdb/br/brdir/directory/biores .asp?mode=all&code=USA+42.

U.S. Department of Agriculture (USDA). 2007. *Marin County, California Profile: 2007 Census of Agriculture.* Washington, D.C.: USDA, National Agricultural Statistics Service.

Vink, Erik. 1998. "Land Trusts Conserve California Farmland." *California Agriculture* 52:27–31.

Chapter 16: Minneapolis and the Twin Cities Region, Minnesota

Cleveland, Horace. 1883. Quoted in "About the Grand Rounds." Minneapolis Park and Recreation Board. Available at www.minneapolisparks.org/grandrounds/inf_about.htm.

———. 1888. From "The Aesthetic Development of the United Cities of St. Paul and Minneapolis" (Minneapolis: A. C. Bausman), as quoted in Daniel J. Nadenicek (1993), "Nature in the City: Horace Cleveland's Aesthetic," *Landscape and Urban Planning* 26:5–15.

———. 1890. Letter to William W. Folwell, October 22. Quoted in Roise 2000.

Duerksen, Christopher, and Cara Snyder. 2005. *Nature-Friendly Communities: Habitat Protection and Land Use Planning.* Washington, D.C.: Island Press.

Garvin, Alexander. 2002. *The American City: What Works, What Doesn't.* New York: McGraw-Hill.

Metropolitan Council. 2005. *2030 Regional Parks Policy Plan.* St. Paul, Minn.: Metropolitan Council.

———. 2006. *Metropolitan Urban Service Area.* St. Paul, Minn.: Metropolitan Council.

Minnesota Department of Natural Resources (DNR). 1997. *Metro Greenprint: Planning for Nature in the Face of Urban Growth.* St. Paul: Minnesota DNR.

Minneapolis Park and Recreation Board (MPRB). 2006. "About MPRB." Available at www .minneapolisparks.org/default.asp?PageID=70.

———. 2010. "Grand Rounds Missing Link." Available at www.minneapolisparks.org/default .asp?PageID=996.

Minnesota State Lottery. 2009. Trust Fund Projects—Anoka County: Metro Greenways. Available at www.lottery.state.mn.us/etf/anoka.html.

National Scenic Byways. 2010. "Grand Rounds Scenic Byway." Available at www.byways.org/explore/byways/2243.

Roise, Charlene. 2000. *Making the City Itself a Work of Art: An Historical Context for the Grand Rounds, Minneapolis.* Minneapolis: MPRB.

Three Rivers Park District. "Grimm Farm Historic Site." Available at www.threeriversparks.org/parks/carver-park/grimm-historical-farm.aspx.

Chapter 17: Montgomery County, Maryland

Benfield, F. Kaid, Jutka Terris, and Nancy Vorsanger. 2001. *Solving Sprawl: Models of Smart Growth in Communities across America.* New York: Natural Resources Defense Council.

Farmland Preservation Report. 2010. "Nation's Top 12 Locally Operated Farmland Preservation Programs." Available at www.farmlandpreservationreport.com/2010/09/14/september-2010.

Hanson, Royce. 2004. "Protecting Montgomery's Agricultural Reserve for the Next Generation." Available at http://maryland.sierraclub.org/montgomery/ProtAgRes.htm.

Maryland–National Capital Park and Planning Commission (M–NCPPC). 1980. *Functional Master Plan for the Preservation of Agriculture and Rural Open Space in Montgomery County.* Silver Spring, Md.: M–NCPPC.

Montgomery Countryside Alliance. 2010. "History of the Ag Reserve." Available at http://moco alliance.org/ag-reserve/history-of-the-ag-reserve.

Montgomery County Department of Economic Development, Agricultural Services Division. 2009. "Farmland Protected by Easements as of June 30, 2009." Available at www.montgomery countymd.gov/content/ded/agservices/pdffiles/protect09_piechart.pdf.

———. 2010. "Agricultural Facts." Available at www.montgomerycountymd.gov/agstmpl.asp?url =/Content/DED/AgServices/agfacts.asp.

Montgomery County Department of Parks. 2010. "Wild Montgomery." Available at http://montgomery parks.org/wildmontgomery/facts.shtm.

Pruetz, Rick, and Noah Standridge. 2009. "What Makes Transfer of Development Rights Work? Success Factors from Research and Practice." *Journal of the American Planning Association* 75:78–87.

Zawitoski, John. 2011. Untitled presentation on Montgomery County's TDR program, Derwood, Maryland, March 28.

Chapter 18: Palm Beach County, Florida

Comprehensive Everglades Restoration Plan (CERP). 2010a. "Everglades: A Brief History." Available at www.evergladesplan.org/about/learn_everglades.aspx.

———. 2010b. "Construction Starts Near Loxahatchee National Wildlife Refuge." Available at www .evergladesplan.org/news/features/102910_site1_groundbreaking_post.aspx.

Florida Department of Environmental Protection. 2005. "About the Loxahatchee River–Lake Worth Creek Aquatic Preserve." Available at www.dep.state.fl.us/coastal/sites/loxahatchee/info.htm.

Florida Fish and Wildlife Conservation Commission. 2010a. "J. W. Corbett Wildlife Management Area." Available at http://myfwc.com/viewing/recreation/wmas/lead/jw-corbett.

———. 2010b. "Holey Land Wildlife Management Area." Available at http://myfwc.com/viewing/ recreation/wmas/lead/holey-land.

———. 2010c. "Rotenberger Wildlife Management Area." Available at http://myfwc.com/viewing/ recreation/wmas/lead/rotenberger.

———. 2010d. "John C. and Mariana Jones/Hungryland Wildlife and Environmental Area." Available at http://myfwc.com/viewing/recreation/wmas/lead/jones-hungryland.

Florida State Parks. 2011. "John D. MacArthur Beach State Park." Available at www.floridastateparks .org/history/parkhistory.cfm?parkid=150.

Palm Beach County. 1989. *Comprehensive Plan: 1989* (rev. through November 19, 2009). West Palm Beach, Fla.: Board of Palm Beach County Commissioners.

———. 2005. *2004–2005 TDR Annual Report.* West Palm Beach, Fla: Palm Beach County.

———. 2010a. "PBC Lands History." Available at www.pbcgov.com/erm/nena/land-history.htm.

———. 2010b. "Natural Areas." Available at www.pbcgov.com/erm/natural.

———. 2010c. "NENA (Northeast Everglades Natural Area)." Available at Lasting_Value_ms_HOT .docxwww.pbcgov.com/erm/nena.

U.S. Fish and Wildlife Service. 2002. "Arthur R. Marshall Loxahatchee National Wildlife Refuge." Available at www.fws.gov/loxahatchee/Loxahatchee_brochure.pdf.

West Palm Beach. 2008. "Grassy Waters Master Plan." Available at http://wpb.org/park/grassy -waters-preserve.

Chapter 19: Pima County, Arizona

Bureau of Land Management. 2000. "Las Cienegas National Conservation Area Fact Sheet." Available at www.empireranchfoundation.org/BLMfacts.htm.

Clinton, William. 2000. "Ironwood Forest National Monument Proclamation." Available at www.blm.gov/pgdata/etc/medialib/blm/az/images/ironwood.Par.96263.File.dat/ironwood_proc.pdf.

Huckelberry, Chuck. 1999. "The Origins of the Sonoran Desert Conservation Plan." Paper presented to the Sonoran Desert Conservation Plan Steering Committee, May 22.

National Park Service. 2010. "Those Who Came Before—Prehistory at Sagauro National Park." Available at www.nps.gov/sagu/planyourvisit/upload/Those%20Who%20Came%20Before.pdf.

Pima County. 1998. *Sonoran Desert Conservation Plan: Concept.* Tucson, Ariz.: Pima County Board of Supervisors.

———. 2000a. *Draft Preliminary Sonoran Desert Conservation Plan.* Tucson, Ariz.: Pima County Board of Supervisors.

———. 2000b. *Land Stewardship in Pima County—Draft.* Tucson, Ariz.: Pima County Board of Supervisors.

———. 2004. "Bar V Ranch Acquisition." Available at www.pima.gov/cmo/sdcp/reports/d29/BarV Report.pdf.

———. 2007. *Canoa Ranch Master Plan: Final Report.* Tucson, Ariz.: Pima County Board of Supervisors.

———. 2009a. "A Vision for Mountain Parks and Natural Preserves." Available at www.pima.gov/cmo/sdcp/Parks.html.

———. 2009b. "A Vision for Cultural Resources." Available at www.pima.gov/cmo/sdcp/Cultural.html.

———. 2009c. "A Vision for Ranch Conservation." Available at www.pima.gov/cmo/sdcp/Ranch.html.

———. 2009d. "A Vision for Riparian Protection." Available at www.pima.gov/cmo/sdcp/Riparian.html.

———. 2009e. "A Vision for Biological Corridors and Critical Habitat." Available at www.pima.gov/cmo/sdcp/habitat.html.

———. 2009f. "An Overview of the Sonoran Desert Conservation Plan." Available at www.pima.gov/CMO/SDCP/intro.html.

———. 2010. *Multiple Species Conservation Plan.* Tucson, Ariz.: Pima County Board of Supervisors.

———. 2011. *Protecting Our Land, Water and Heritage: Pima County's Voter-Supported Conservation Efforts.* Tucson, Ariz.: Pima County Board of Supervisors.

U.S. Department of Agriculture and U.S. Forest Service. 2010. "Sky Islands—Coronado National Forest." Available at www.fs.fed.us/r3/coronado/index.shtml.

Chapter 20: Santa Clara County, California

California Department of Fish and Game. 2005. "Cañada de los Osos Ecological Reserve Management Plan." Available at www.dfg.ca.gov/lands/mgmtplans/cdloer/docs/cdloer_plan.pdf.

California State Parks. 2010. "Park Index." Available at www.parks.ca.gov/parkindex.

Committee for Green Foothills. 2006. "The Founding of CGF." Available at www.greenfoothills.org/about/founders.html.

Midpeninsula Regional Open Space District (MROSD). 2010a. "About the Midpeninsula Regional Open Space District." Available at www.openspace.org/about_us.

———. 2010b. "Open Space Preserves." Available at www.openspace.org/preserves.

Santa Clara County Open Space Authority (OSA). 2010a. "History." Available at www.openspaceauthority.org/about/history.html.

———. 2010b. "Protected Lands." Available at www.openspaceauthority.org/preservation/protected.html.

Palo Alto. 2010. "The Baylands." Available at www.cityofpaloalto.org/depts/csd/parks_and_open
_space/preserves_and_open_spaces/the_baylands.asp.

Press, Robert. 2002. *Saving Open Space: The Politics of Local Preservation in California*. Berkeley,
Calif.: University of California Press.

Santa Clara County. 1994. *Santa Clara County General Plan 1995–2010*. San Jose, Calif.: Santa
Clara County.

———. 2003. *Strategic Plan: Santa Clara County Parks and Recreation System*. San Jose, Calif.:
Santa Clara County.

———. 2007. *Almaden Quicksilver*. San Jose, Calif.: Santa Clara County.

———. 2010a. "About County Parks." Available at www.parkhere.org/portal/site/parks/parksarticle
?path=%252Fv7%252FParks%2520and%2520Recreation%252C%2520Department%2520of%
2520%2528DEP%2529&contentId=9ac3fc22be5bd110VgnVCM10000048dc4a92____.

———. 2010b. "Santa Clara Valley Habitat Plan: A Conservation Legacy—Frequently Asked Ques-
tions." Available at www.scv-habitatplan.org/www/site/alias__default/304/frequently_asked
_questions.aspx.

Stegner, Wallace. 1960. "Wilderness Letter." Available at www.wilderness.org/OurIssues/Wilderness/
wildernessletter.cfm.

U.S. Fish and Wildlife Service. 2010. "Don Edwards San Francisco Bay National Wildlife Refuge."
Available at www.fws.gov/desfbay.

Weintraub, David. 2004. *Peninsula Tales and Trails: Commemorating the Thirtieth Anniversary of
the Midpeninsula Regional Open Space District*. Portland, Ore.: Graphics Arts Books.

Chapter 21: Santa Cruz and Santa Cruz County, California

Circuit Rider Productions and the National Oceanic and Atmospheric Administration (NOAA).
2004. "Salmonid Habitat Restoration Planning Resource." Available at www.cfses.org/salmonid/
html/people/own.htm.

Hailey, Arin. 2007. "A Celebration of the Coast Dairies Protection." Available at www.tpl.org/
what-we-do/where-we-work/california/san-francisco-bay-area/a-celebration-of-the-coast.html.

Land Trust of Santa Cruz County. 2009. "Protected Lands." Available at www.landtrustsantacruz
.org/protectedlands.htm.

Press, Daniel. 2002. *Saving Open Space: The Politics of Local Preservation in California*. Berkeley,
Calif.: University of California Press.

Santa Cruz, City of. 1992. *City of Santa Cruz General Plan and Local Coastal Program 1990–2005*
(adopted 1992; last amended 2003). Santa Cruz, Calif.: City of Santa Cruz.

———. 2009. "Moore Creek." Available at www.cityofsantacruz.com/index.aspx?page=618.

Santa Cruz County. 1994. *1994 General Plan and Local Coastal Program*. Santa Cruz, Calif.: Santa
Cruz County.

Santa Cruz Sentinel. 1999. *Santa Cruz County—A Century*. Santa Cruz, Calif.: Santa Cruz Sentinel.

Sempervirens Fund. 2011. "Our History and Legacy." Available at www.sempervirens.org/history.php.

Trust for Public Land. 2007. "Protection of Five Miles of Coastline Celebrated (CA)." Available at
http://www.tpl.org/news/press-releases/protection-of-five-miles-of-coastline.html.

U.S. Fish and Wildlife Service. 2008. "Ellicott Slough National Wildlife Refuge." Available at www.fws
.gov/cno/refuges/ellicott/ellicott2_6-12-08.pdf.

Chapter 22: Santa Fe County, New Mexico

Audubon New Mexico. 2011. "Randall Davey Audubon Center." Available at http://nm.audubon
.org/center/index.html.

Cerrillos Hills Park Coalition. 2009. "Cerrillos Hills State Park: A Guide to the Park." Available at www .cerrilloshills.org/park_links.html.

Mahler, Richard. 2002. "Land as Healer: Preserving Sacred Soil and Tradition in Chimayo." *Land and People* 14:20–26.

National Park Service. 2010. "Bandelier: Tsankawi." Available at www.nps.gov/band/planyourvisit/ tsankawi.htm.

Nature Conservancy. 2011. "Santa Fe Canyon Preserve." Available at www.nature.org/ourinitiatives/ regions/northamerica/unitedstates/newmexico/placesweprotect/santa-fe-canyon-preserve-1 .xml.

Santa Fe, City of. 2011. "Historic Santa Fe Plaza." Available at www.santafenm.gov/index .aspx?NID=978.

Santa Fe County. 2000. *Open Land and Trails Plan: For the Wildlife, Mountains, Trails and Historic Places Program.* Santa Fe, N.M.: Santa Fe County.

———. 2010. *Sustainable Growth Management Plan.* Santa Fe, N.M.: Santa Fe County.

Trust for Public Land. 2006. "Conservation Awards Winners." Available at www.tpl.org/news/press -releases/2006-county-land-conservation.html.

———. 2007. "180 Acres Protected Southwest of Santa Fe." Available at www.tpl.org/news/ press-releases/180-acres-protected-southwest.html.

U.S. Congress. 2004. "Galisteo Basin Archaeological Sites Protection Act." Available at http:// galisteoarcheology.org/pdfs/Galisteo_Basin_Act.pdf.

U.S. Forest Service. 2009. "Santa Fe National Forest." Available at www.fs.fed.us/r3/sfe/about/ about_forest.html.

Chapter 23: Sonoma County, California

Audubon Canyon Ranch. 2010. "Bouverie Preserve." Available at www.egret.org/preserves_bouverie.

Benson, Ralph. 2009. "Jenner Headlands—protected forever!" Available at www.sonomalandtrust .org/protect/campaigns/jenner/jenner.html.

California Department of Fish and Game. 2011. "Laguna Wildlife Area—Sonoma County." Available at www.dfg.ca.gov/lands/wa/region3/laguna.html.

California State Parks. 2009. "State Parks—Sonoma County." Available at www.parks.ca.gov/ parkindex.

Farmland Preservation Report. 2010. "Nation's Top 12 Locally Operated Farmland Preservation Programs." Available at www.farmlandpreservationreport.com/2010/09/14/september-2010.

LandPaths. 2011. "About LandPaths." Available at www.landpaths.org/index.cfm/page/About-Land Paths.

Save the Redwoods League. 2010. "Donation of Forest Expands Lake Sonoma Recreation Area." Available at www.savetheredwoods.org/newsroom/news_detail.php?id=72.

Sonoma County. 2003. *Outdoor Recreation Plan.* Santa Rosa, Calif.: Sonoma County.

———. 2008. *General Plan 2020.* Santa Rosa, Calif.: Sonoma County.

———. 2011. "Parks." Available at www.sonoma-county.org/parks/table_text.htm.

Sonoma County Agricultural Preservation and Open Space District. 2011. "Profile." Available at www .sonomaopenspace.org/Content/10114/profile.html.

Sonoma Land Trust. 2009. "What We Do." Available at www.sonomalandtrust.org/discover/ what_we_do.html.

Sonoma State University. 2008. "About the Osborn Preserve." Available at www.sonoma.edu/ preserves/fop/aboutosborn.shtml.

Trust for Public Land. 2007. "2007 Conservation Awards." Available at www.tpl.org/news/ press-releases/third-annual-county-land-conservation.html.

U.S. Fish and Wildlife Service. 2010. "San Pablo Bay National Wildlife Refuge." Available at www.fws.gov/refuges/profiles/index.cfm?id=81644.

Wells, Janet. 2000. "Greenbelt Gaining Ground in Sonoma County." *San Francisco Chronicle*. September 28.

Chapter 24: Suffolk County, New York

American Farmland Trust. 2009. "On the Road . . . to Planning a Future for Farms." Available at www.farmland.org/programs/states/ny/focus_tour.asp.

Central Pine Barrens Commission. 2010. "Land Use Planning and Stewardship in the Central Pine Barrens—January 2010." Available at http://pb.state.ny.us/general/general_overview_extended.pdf.

Nature Conservancy. 2007. "Long Island's Last Stand—Status Report 2007." Available at www.nature.org/wherewework/northamerica/states/newyork/files/last_stand_status_2007.pdf.

Newsday. 2006. *Inside Long Island Parks*. Melville, N.Y.: Island Publications.

Reilly, Mark. 2000. "Evaluating Farmland Preservation through Suffolk County, New York's Purchase of Development Rights Program." *Pace Environmental Law Review* 18:197–220.

Southold, Town of. 2009. *Community Preservation Fund Management and Stewardship Plan*. Southold, N.Y.: Town of Southold.

Suffolk County. 1996. *Agricultural and Farmland Protection Plan*. Hauppauge, N.Y.: Suffolk County Planning Department.

———. 2007. *Open Space Acquisition Policy for Suffolk County*. Hauppauge, N.Y.: Suffolk County Planning Department.

Yaro, Robert. 2007. "Preservation Now or Never." In *On Course for Failure: A Call to Action on Open Space Preservation*. Riverhead, N.Y.: Long Island Pine Barrens Society.

Chapter 25: Travis County and Austin, Texas

Austin, City of. 2008. *Austin Tomorrow Comprehensive Plan Interim Update*. Austin, Tex.: City of Austin.

———. 2010. "Balcones Canyonlands Conservation Plan: Annual Report FY 2009." Available at www.ci.austin.tx.us/water/wildland/bccpannualreportfy09.htm.

———. 2011. "Wildland Conservation Division." Available at www.ci.austin.tx.us/water/wildland.

Austin Parks and Recreation Department. 2011. "Austin Parks and Recreation." Available at www.ci.austin.tx.us/parks/default.htm.

Conrad, William. 2011. Manager, City of Austin Wildland Conservation Division. Communication with author, June 29.

Farmer, Rose. 2011. Program Manager, Travis County Natural Resources and Environmental Quality Division. Conversation with author, June 23.

Friends of Balcones Canyonlands National Wildlife Refuge. 2011. "Help Complete the Refuge." Available at www.friendsofbalcones.org/help.

Lower Colorado River Authority. 2011. "Westcave Preserve." Available at www.lcra.org/parks/natural_resource/westcave.html.

Naismith Engineering. 2005. "Regional Water Quality Protection Plan for the Barton Springs Segment of the Edwards Aquifer and Its Contributing Zone." Available at www.waterqualityplan.org/index.php?BODY=finaldraft.

Nature Conservancy. 2011. "Barton Creek Habitat Preserve." Available at www.nature.org/ourinitiatives/regions/northamerica/unitedstates/texas/placesweprotect/barton-creek-habitat-preserve.xml.

Save Our Springs Alliance (SOSA). 2005. *Saving Barton Springs, Saving Austin, and Saving Tax Dollars.* Austin, Tex.: SOSA.

Travis Audubon Society. 2011. "Baker Sanctuary." Available at http://travisaudubon.org/?page_id=201.

Travis County. 2006. "Travis County Parks and Natural Areas Master Plan." Available at www.co.travis.tx.us/tnr/parks/press_releases/pos_plan_final.asp.

Trust for Public Land. 2009. "Land Vote Database." Available at www.quickbase.com/db/ba72nhu5n?a=q&qid=-1015655&dlta=pr%7E.

Unbehaun, Nancy. 2011. Senior Realty Specialist, U.S. Fish and Wildlife Service. Conversation with author, June 24.

INDEX

ABOUT THE AUTHOR

RICK PRUETZ, FAICP, is a planning consultant specializing in open space preservation strategies. He received his master's of urban planning degree in 1979 from the University of Wisconsin–Milwaukee and served as the city planner of Burbank, California, for more than 14 years before starting a consulting practice in 1999. Pruetz has written four books and coauthored two others on open space preservation planning. He maintains a website at www.SmartPreservation.net dedicated to open space preservation news.

For Product Safety Concerns and Information please contact our EU
representative GPSR@taylorandfrancis.com
Taylor & Francis Verlag GmbH, Kaufingerstraße 24, 80331 München, Germany

www.ingramcontent.com/pod-product-compliance
Lightning Source LLC
Chambersburg PA
CBHW080552270326
41929CB00019B/3282